THE PHILADELPHIA CAMPAIGN 1777

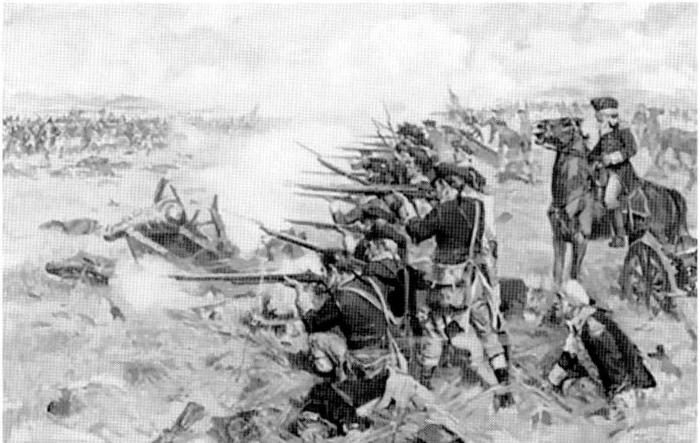

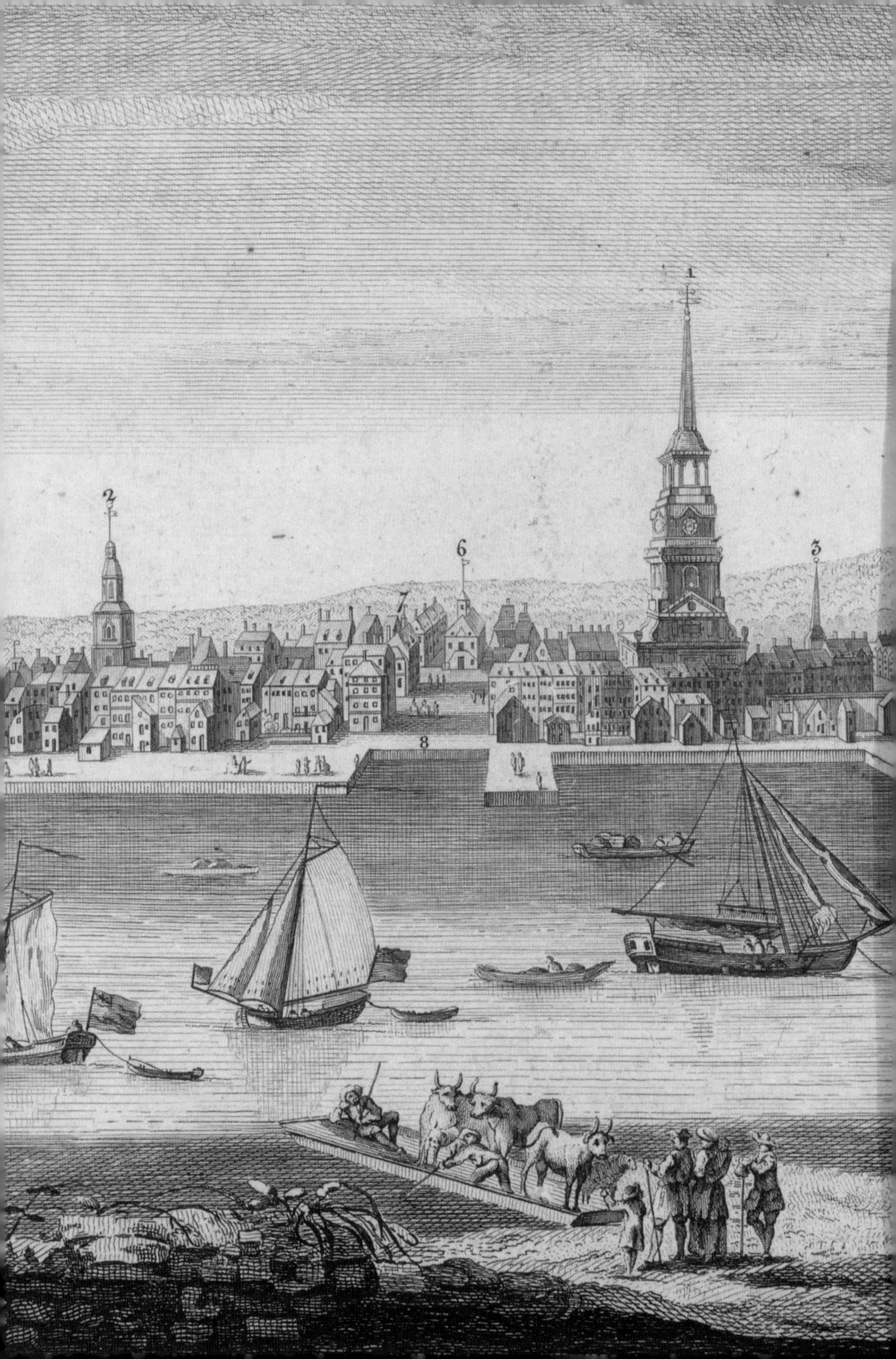
1
2
6
7
3
8

CASEMATE | ILLUSTRATED

THE PHILADELPHIA CAMPAIGN 1777

Michael C. Harris

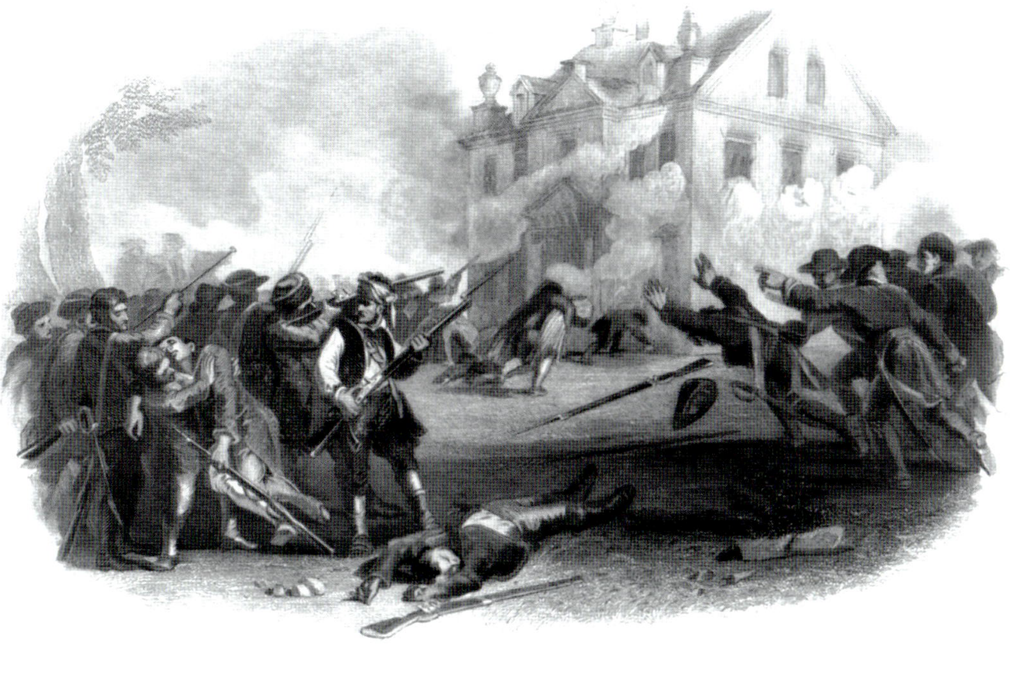

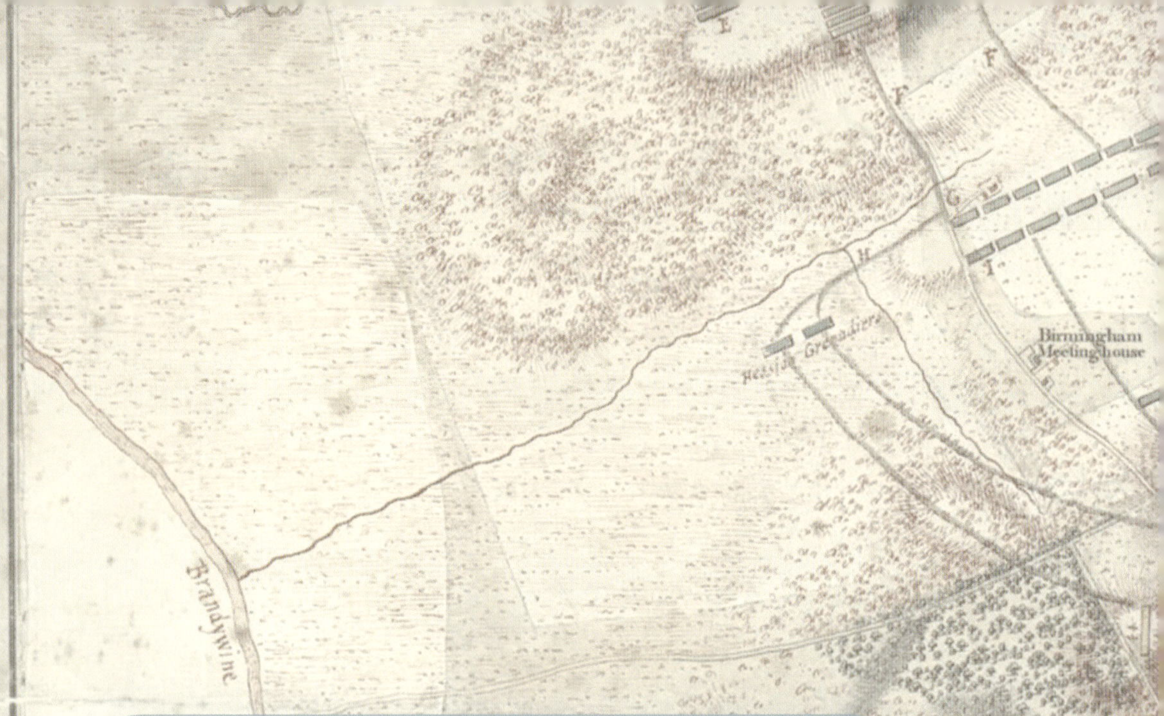

CIS0030
Published in 2023 by
CASEMATE PUBLISHERS
1950 Lawrence Road, Havertown, PA 19083, USA
and
The Old Music Hall, 106–108 Cowley Road, Oxford OX4 1JE, UK

Published in conjunction with Savas Beatie.

Paperback edition: ISBN 978-1-63624-264-4
Digital edition: ISBN 978-1-63624-265-1

A CIP record for this book is available from the British Library.

Maps by Hal Jesperson & Edward Alexander
Design by Myriam Bell
Printed and bound in the United Kingdom by Short Run Press, Exeter
For a complete list of Casemate titles, please contact:

CASEMATE PUBLISHERS (US)
Telephone (610) 853-9131
Fax (610) 853-9146
Email: casemate@casematepublishers.com
www.casematepublishers.com

CASEMATE PUBLISHERS (UK)
Telephone (0)1226 734350
Email: casemate-uk@casematepublishers.co.uk
www.casematepublishers.co.uk

Half-title page: Depiction of the Battle of Brandywine, by F. C. Yohn, 1898. (Library of Congress)
Title page: The Battle of Germantown (Chew's House). (Library of Congress)

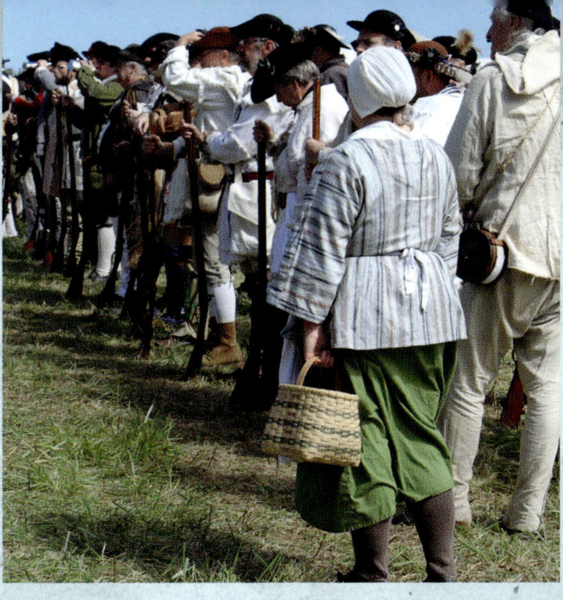

Contents

Timeline

The British Army in North American conducted two campaigns in 1777. John Burgoyne led one army south from Canada to seize control of the Lake Champlain–Hudson River corridor resulting in the Battle of Saratoga. Burgoyne's defeat led to that army's capture. Rather than assist Burgoyne's Campaign, William Howe led his army from New York City on the Philadelphia Campaign. Although Howe captured Philadelphia, the events of 1777 led to the French Alliance and ultimately American victory in the American Revolution.

May 28, 1777	Continental Army leaves Morristown
June 22	British evacuation of New Jersey
June 26	Battle of Short Hills, NJ
July 6	*Fort Ticonderoga captured*
July 7	*Battle of Hubbardton, VT*
July 23	William Howe departs New York Harbor
August 2	*Siege of Fort Stanwix, NY begins*
August 6	*Battle of Oriskany, NY*
August 16	*Battle of Bennington, VT*
August 22	Battle of Staten Island, NY; *siege of Fort Stanwix ends*
August 25	British landing on Elk River, MD
September 3	Battle of Cooch's Bridge, DE
September 11	Battle of Brandywine, PA
September 16	Battle of the Clouds, PA

September 19	*Battle of Freeman's Farm, NY*
September 21	Battle of Paoli, PA
September 26	British capture Philadelphia, PA
October 2	Battle of Billingsport, NJ
October 4	Battle of Germantown, PA
October 6	*Battles of Forts Clinton & Montgomery, NY*
October 7	*Battle of Saratoga*
October 17	*John Burgoyne surrenders his army at Saratoga, NY*
October 22	Battle of Fort Mercer, NJ
November 10	Siege of Fort Mifflin, PA begins
November 15	Articles of Confederation approved by the Continental Congress

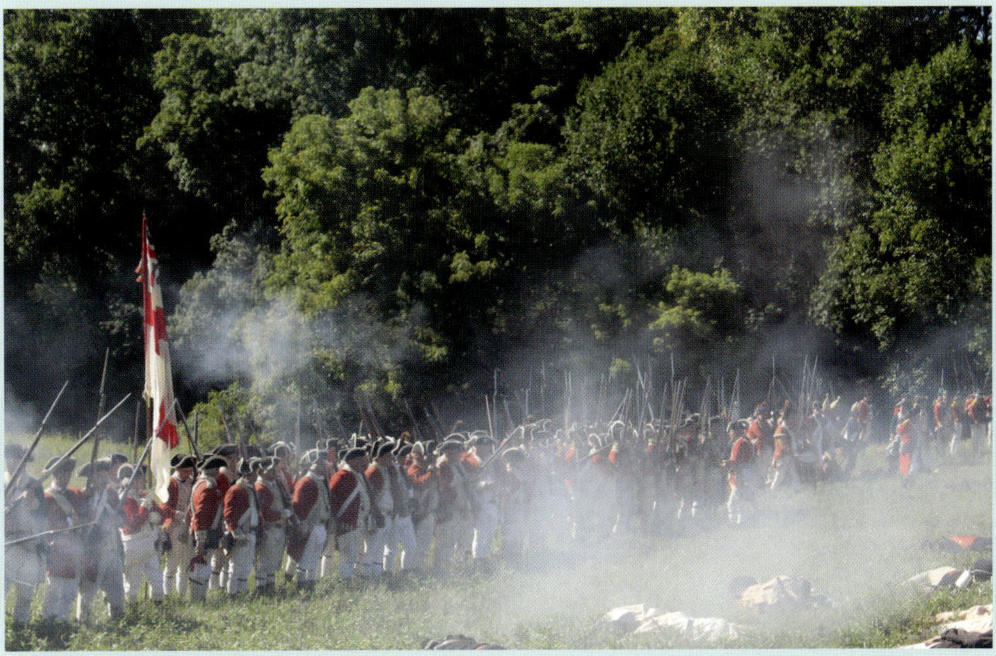

▶ In battle, the regular infantry formations proved the backbone of the British effort in 1777. (Author's collection)

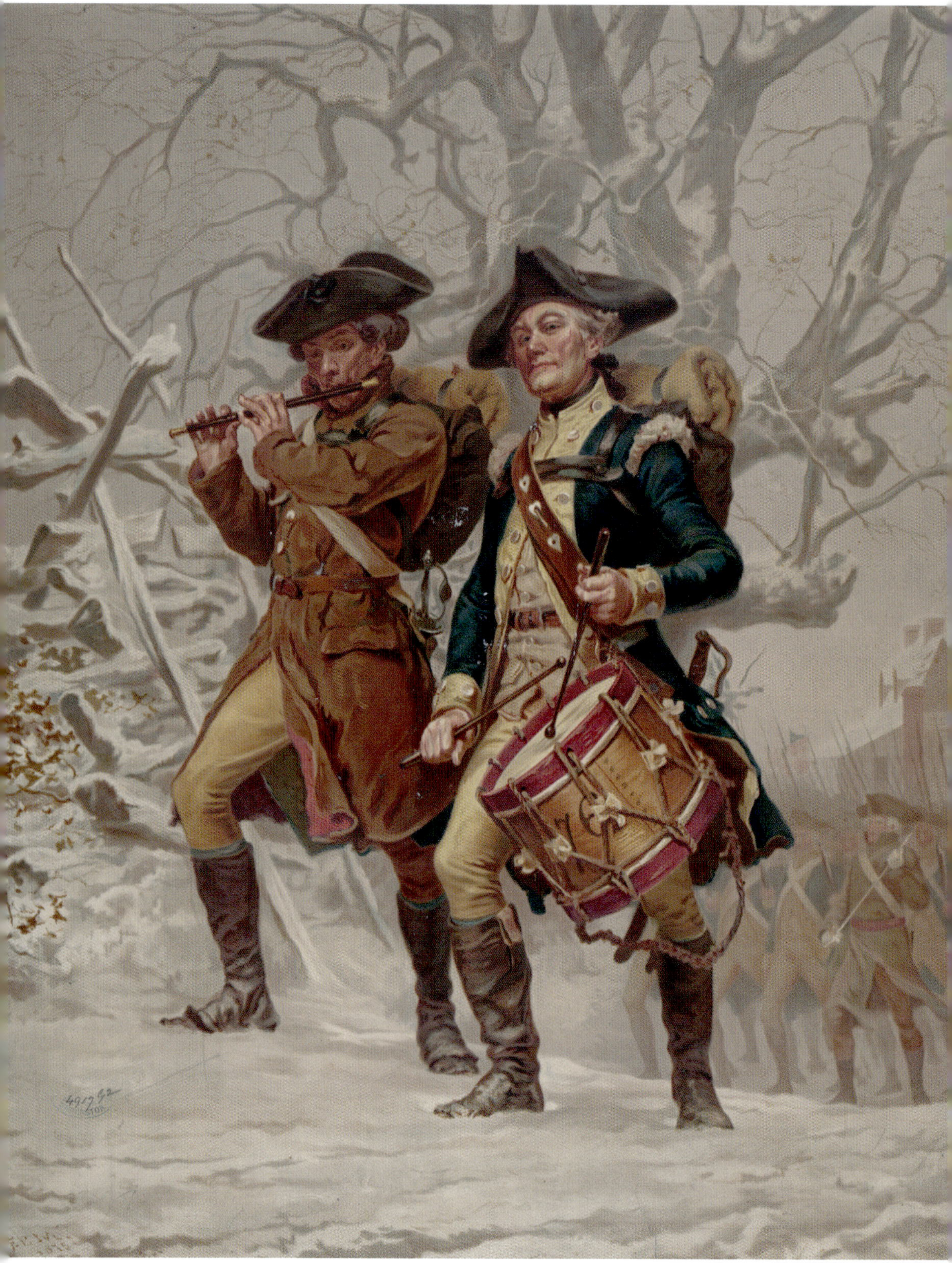

November 16	British occupation of Fort Mifflin, PA
November 25	Battle of Gloucester, NJ
December 5	Battle of Chestnut Hill, PA
December 7	Battle of Edge Hill, PA
December 11	Engagement at Matson's Ford, PA
December 19	George Washington's army marches into Valley Forge, PA

Events in italics relate to the simultaneous Saratoga campaign.

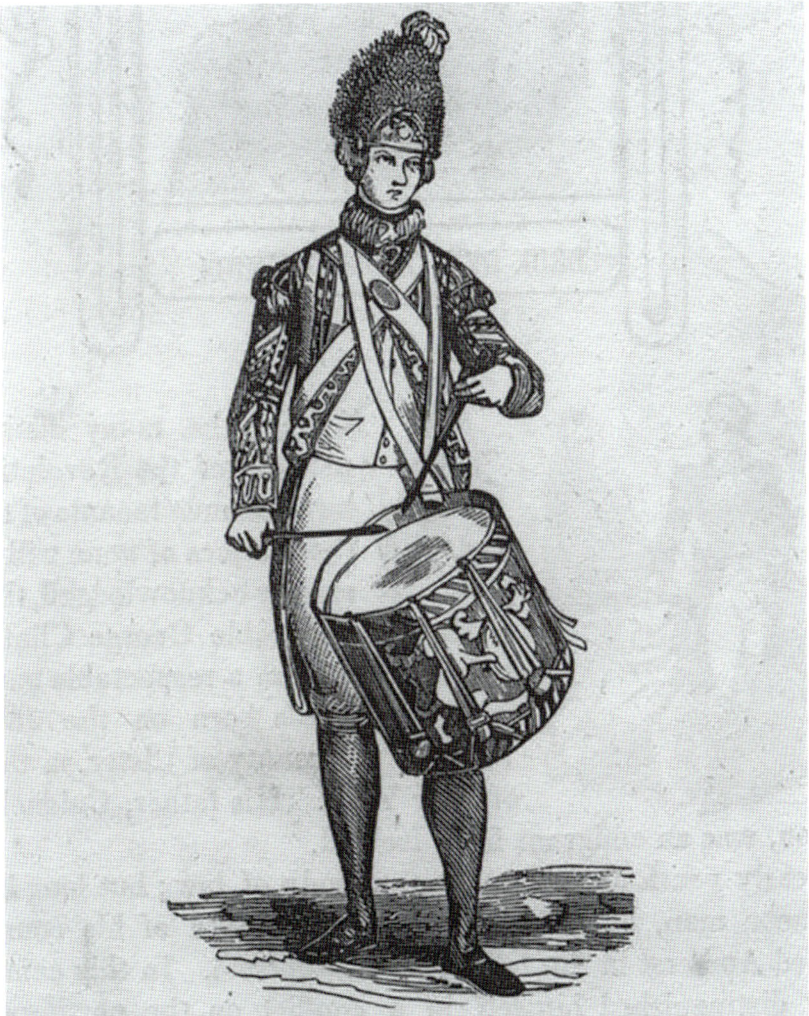

◀ The Continentals—two soldiers of the Continental Army color guard, playing fife and drum, marching in winter. (Library of Congress)

▶ British costume, 1777. (The New York Public Library)

British Costume, 1777.

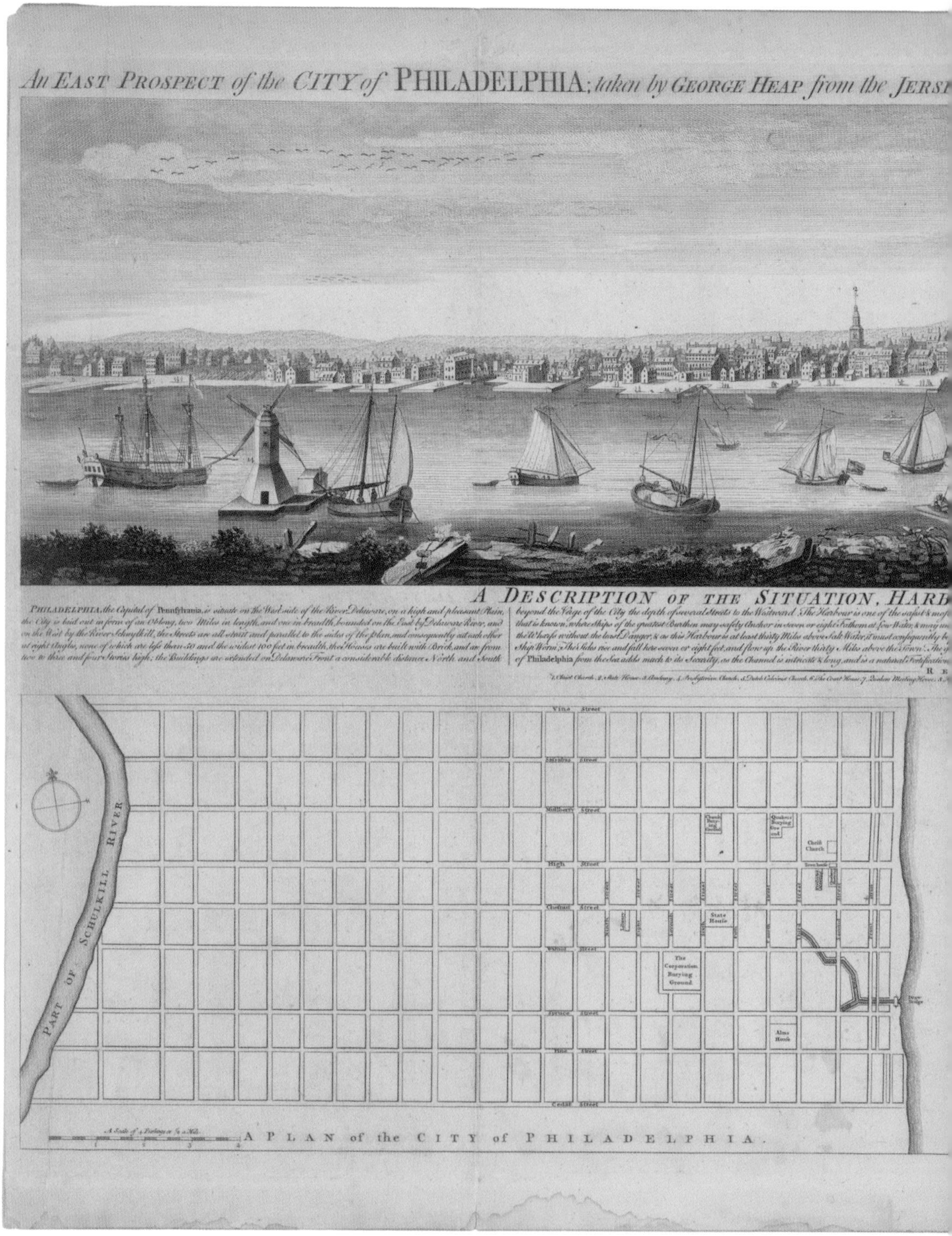

▲ An east prospect of the city of Philadelphia in 1768 taken by George Heap from the Jersey shore, under the direction of Nicholas Scull, surveyor general of the Province of Pennsylvania; engraved by T. Jefferys. (Library of Congress)

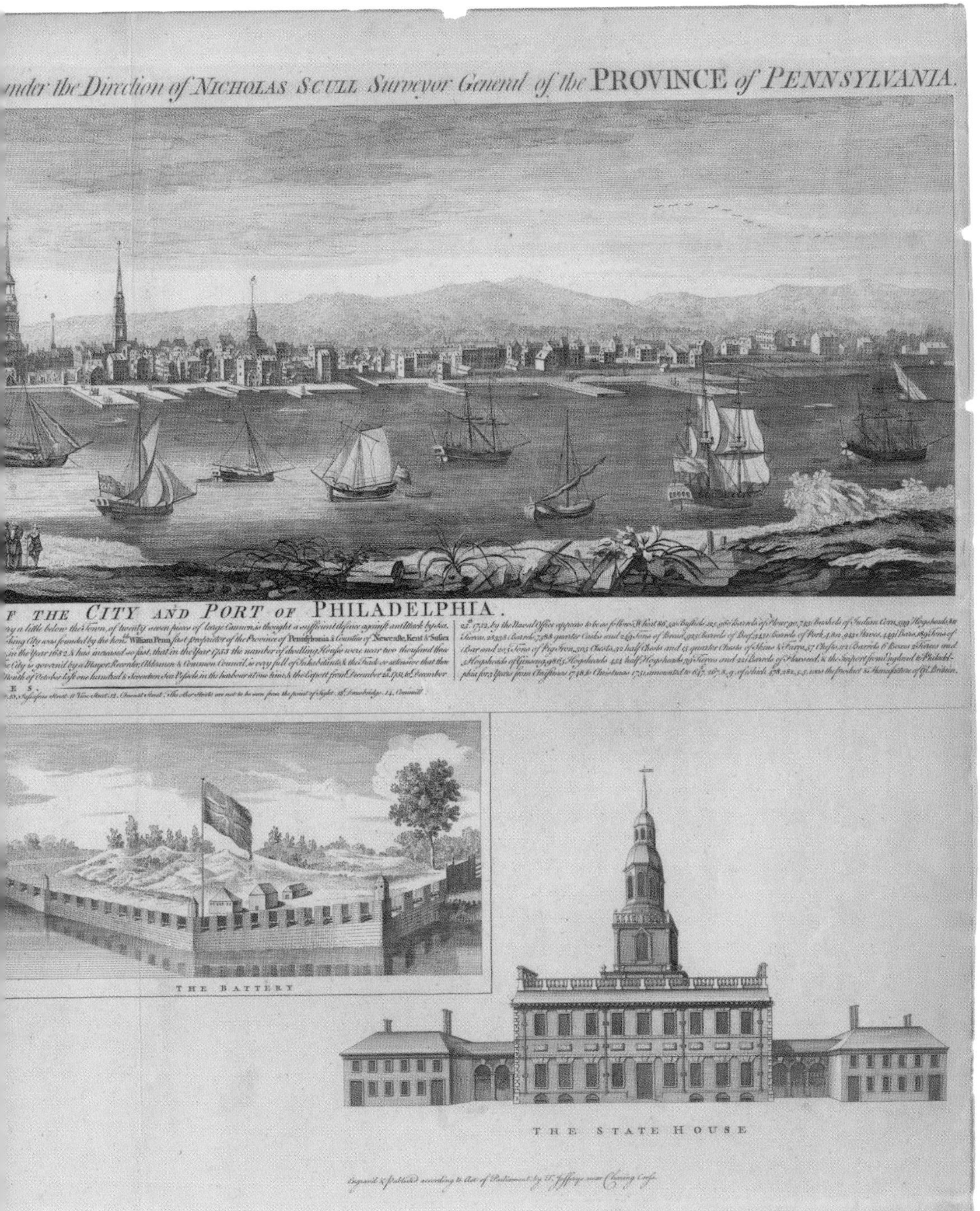
nder the Direction of NICHOLAS SCULL Surveyor General of the PROVINCE of PENNSYLVANIA.
F THE CITY AND PORT OF PHILADELPHIA.
THE BATTERY
THE STATE HOUSE
Engrav'd & Publish'd according to Act of Parliament by T. Jefferys near Charing Cross.

Introduction

The year 1777 was a major turning point in the American Revolution. While George Washington remained on the defensive, the British high command formulated plans to take the initiative. Two British armies in North America were available to carry out the King's strategy—one led by William Howe and the other by John Burgoyne. Although the latter's army would not be directly involved in the Philadelphia Campaign, his own campaign would have far-reaching repercussions on Howe's efforts, and Howe's on Burgoyne's.

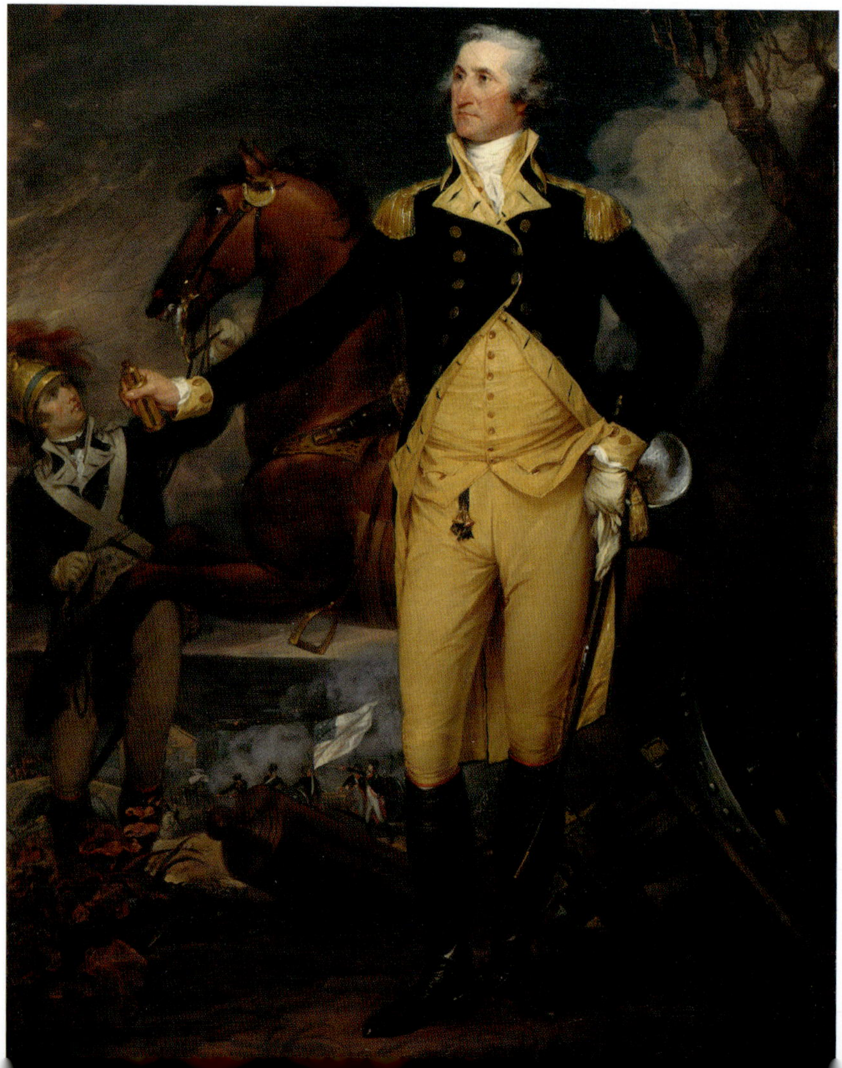

◄ George Washington before the battle of Trenton, by John Trumbull. After Lexington and Concord, Congress named Washington commander-in-chief of the Continental Army. He was 45 during the 1777 campaign. Modern perception imagines Washington as a gray-haired old man leading troops into battle. In fact, he pulled his dark reddish-brown hair (he never wore a wig) back into a queue and powdered it white during the Revolution. He was a formidable man, tall, strong and robust, but new to army command. His poor generalship nearly trapped the army on Long Island, but his bold unpredictable strikes at Trenton and Princeton demonstrated his ability in the field. He was in desperate need of a decisive battlefield victory in the 1777 campaign. (Metropolitan Museum of Art)

The British strategy for the opening years of the war had revolved around the New England colonies, targeting them as the core of the rebellion. The prevailing opinion was that New England should be isolated from the other colonies by seizing control of the Hudson River–Lake Champlain corridor. In the minds of the British leadership, dividing the colonies would mean victory.

Lieutenant General William Howe, 1729–1814

William Howe, Washington's chief antagonist for the 1777 Campaign, commanded the unimaginative assaults at Bunker (Breed's) Hill near Boston, and was elevated to overall command in North America that October. His 1776 New York Campaign nearly (and likely could have) destroyed the Continental Army and ended the war at that time.

(New York Public Library)

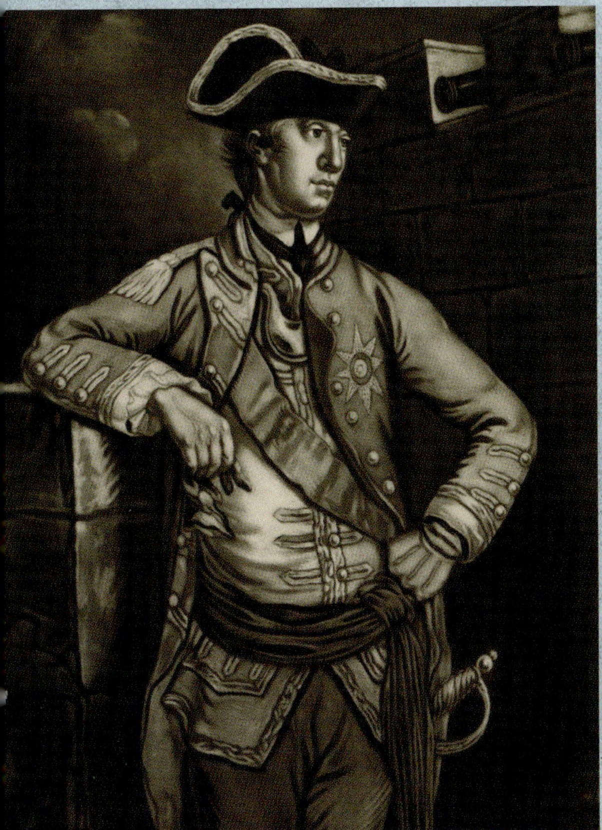

As far as Howe was concerned, the New England plan was no longer applicable due to changing strategic circumstances in North America by 1777. Thus, advancing up the Hudson River was no longer necessary, nor part of Howe's strategic thinking. Philadelphia became Howe's objective. As the largest American port and colonial seat of government, Philadelphia was an attractive objective. A threat to Philadelphia would force Washington to stand and fight a pitched battle, and Howe intended to beat him decisively in the field.

John Burgoyne received orders to lead the British army in Canada south along the Lake Champlain–Hudson River corridor to form a junction with William Howe's army near Albany. Burgoyne's proposals for the campaign were in line with the longstanding plan to split New England away from the other colonies. He would drive down the Lake Champlain corridor while a diversionary column operated in the Mohawk River Valley.

Howe decided that Philadelphia was more important than anything that might be happening on the northern front. Howe's decision to risk everything on taking Philadelphia played a large part in the disaster that would engulf Burgoyne in upstate New York.

Washington was unsure of Howe's intentions for the fighting season. From New York City, Howe could move north along the Hudson River to form a junction with the Canadian army, he could move directly overland toward the American capital at Philadelphia, or he could board a portion of his army onto ships to sail to any number of American ports. Washington was forced into a reactive strategy during the spring and summer months.

Opposing Forces

While George Washington constructed his Continental Army on European standards, William Howe led a professional European force in 1777. Washington's Continentals were supported by Congressionally approved dragoons and artillery as well as local state militias. The British Army likewise was supported by professional dragoons and artillery, but was also supplemented by Germanic soldiers and American loyalists recruited into provincial regiments.

George Washington's Continental Army

The army included Continentals and militia, and not just Americans but Canadians and Europeans as well. Like every army in history, even women and children marched with it. The army Washington gathered around him for the Philadelphia Campaign was a mixed bag of veterans and raw recruits. While many of the men and officers invaded Canada, fought in the battles around New York City, and had taken part in the fighting at Trenton and Princeton, just as many others had seen no action at all. Most of the first set of enlistments expired the previous year, and it took Washington the entire spring and much of the summer to rebuild

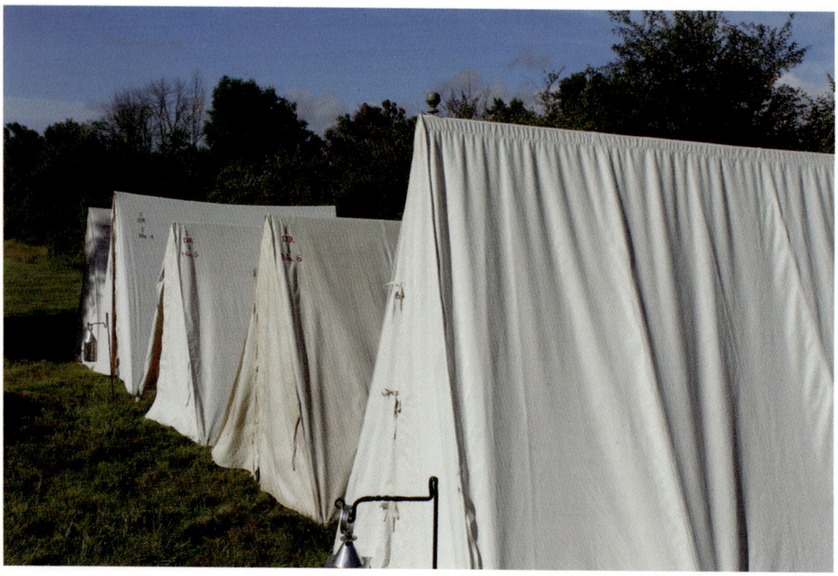

◀ Ideally, American soldiers lived in tents. However, throughout the campaign Washington's troops relied on brush huts or slept without any cover. (Author's collection)

his command. Many officers were new to their roles, and many of the regiments did not exist in their current form the previous year. The training and professional transformation through which all of these men would pass at Valley Forge during the approaching winter months was still in the future.

Desertion and the refusal to serve more than a single enlistment were constant

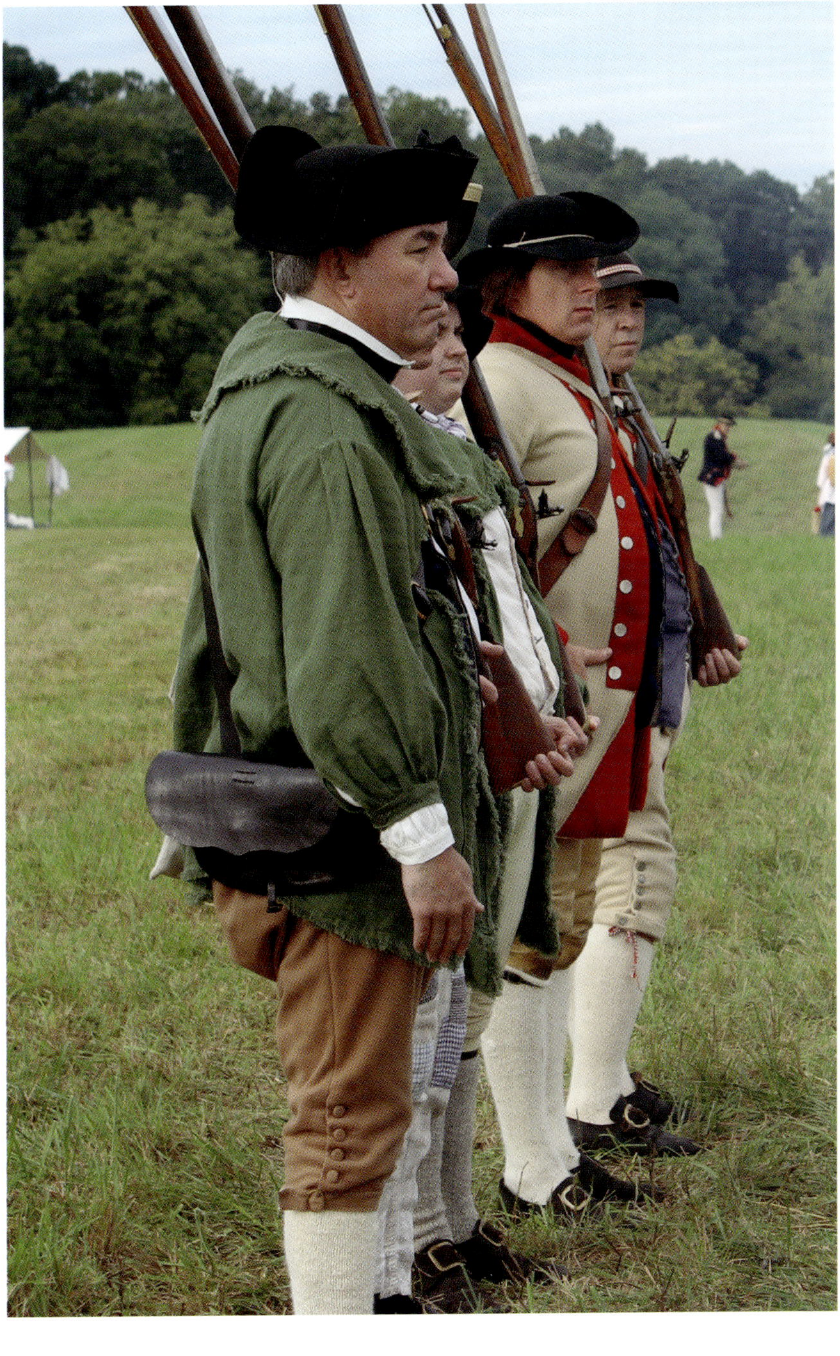

▶ Just like the British, line infantry proved to be Washington's main fighting force. (Author's collection)

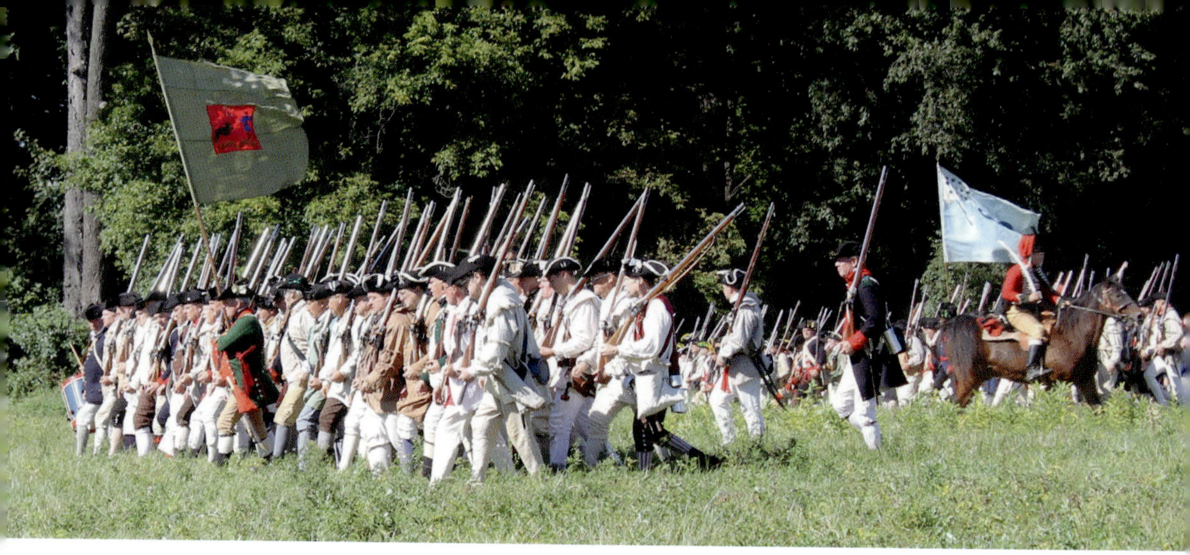

▲ The Continental Army went into battle in compact, shoulder-to-shoulder formations. (Author's collection)

problems for Washington and had been since the day he assumed command in 1775. The bulk of the men, enlisted or otherwise, left the ranks for what they believed were legitimate reasons. They had farms to run, businesses to keep out of debt, and wives and children who had been left alone for months on end. More day-to-day mundane concerns also drove them away. They were cold, hungry, lacked proper clothing, unpaid, and angry about missing promised bonuses. Others left because they refused to report to French officers. And as it was in any army, some men simply hated taking orders, and despised officers. Many feared contracting smallpox and other diseases common to the army. It was not uncommon for troops to desert after just a few weeks of service.

A well-trained and -seasoned army was needed if independence was going to be achieved. By the middle of May 1777, 43 regiments had been assembled averaging 200 men each. The Continentals modeled their regiments after British formations. The number of companies and the strength of regiments varied state to state throughout the long war.

Most recruits after 1776 were from the lowest rungs of society, including drifters,

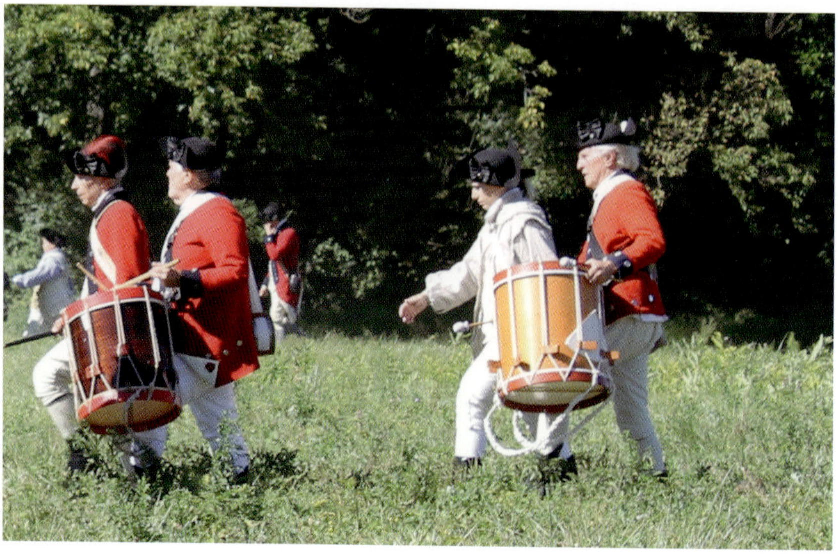

◀ Both armies relied on field music to relay commands during the confusion of battle. (Author's collection)

unemployed servants, and slaves. Few were independent farmers, merchants, or tradesmen. The latter class of people, if they served at all, usually chose the militia over Continental service so they spent less time away from home. Most recruits were in their late teens and early twenties, but some were under the age of fourteen. Few owned property. Many were unemployed laborers, recent immigrants to the colonies, and on occasion, criminals were allowed to avoid punishment by enlisting for service. Every northern state plus Maryland and Virginia allowed the enlistments of white indentured servants, free blacks, and slaves. Although forbidden by regulations, some number of British and Hessian deserters also found their way into American ranks.

Most companies included both a drummer and a fifer. These individuals often massed behind their regiments during battle to help signal orders rather than inspire morale. The sound of beating drums could carry for miles under good conditions, and when grouped could be heard above the chaos of battle. Musicians also administered corporal punishment, maintained regimental guard rooms, and assisted in the evacuation of casualties. As early as 1777, many also carried firearms.

Just as Washington's troops often lacked discipline, his officers often lacked maturity, which constituted a major discipline problem in its own way. Unfortunately for the commander in chief, he spent inordinate amounts of time

▼ Continental Army officers were often as naïve to military doctrine as those whom they led. (Author's collection)

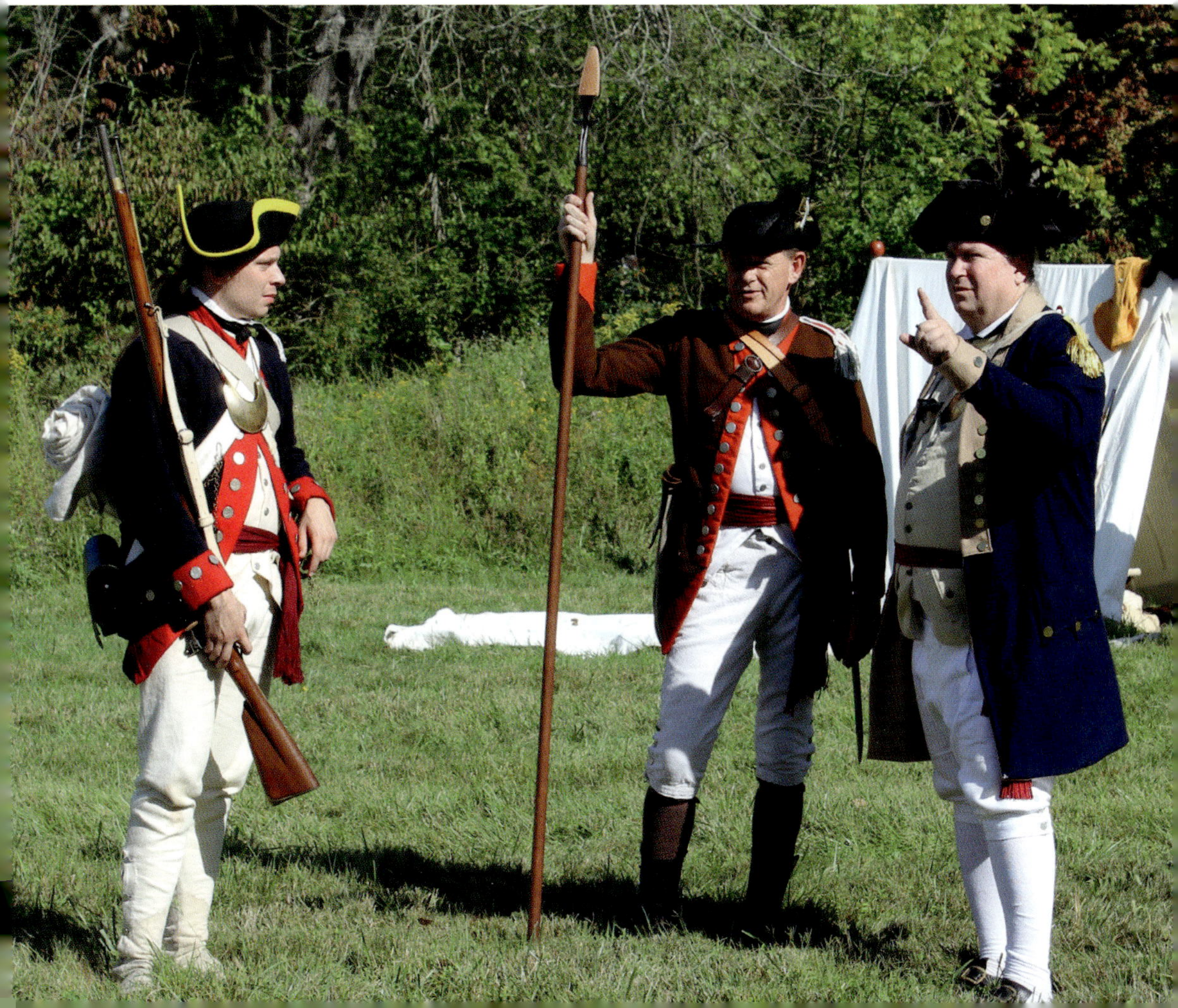

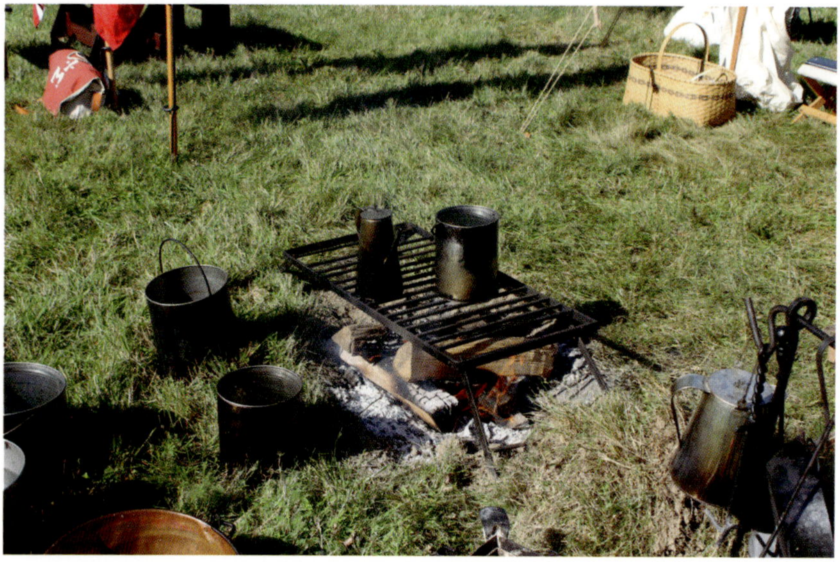

◀ Small groups of individual soldiers often cooked their own meals on open fires while on campaign. (Author's collection)

settling petty problems within the ranks of his officers. Disputes over rank were a typical and thorny issue. Aggrieved officers often submitted requests for permission to resign, which obligated the commander-in-chief to smooth hurt feelings to keep his men together. Many officers refused to lead by example, which added to the lack of discipline. Officers were guilty of the same offenses as the enlisted men, including desertion, gambling, drunkenness, and pillaging.

By regulation, the members of the army were entitled to a substantial daily ration of one pound of beef, ¾ pound of pork, or a pound of salted fish together with a pound of bread or flour. They were also to get three pints of peas or beans per week to supplement their meat and bread rations. A pint of milk each day was added, along with a half-pint of rice or a pint of Indian meal each week. A quart of spruce beer or cider to fight scurvy was also supposed to be issued each day. While the regulations read well on paper, reality was something else entirely. The men were rarely supplied in this manner, and especially during active campaigning. Through most of his enlistment, the standard Continental soldier subsisted on bread and meat alone, with the Commissary Department judged upon its ability to supply those two important staples.

A popular misperception has the army uniformly clothed in a blue and off-white uniform, something that was the exception rather than the rule. The predominant uniform colors throughout much of the war, however, were green and brown. In fact, blue was not adopted as the official color of the Continental Army's uniforms until early October 1779. It was a rare sight to see even a single regiment, let alone the entire army, uniformly clothed.

Another misconception is that the Continental Army that defeated the British was composed of Indian fighters and men who spent their lives wielding their deadly muskets or rifles. While it is certainly true that some of these men were sprinkled throughout the army, the majority of Washington's men—perhaps as many as nine out of 10—were recruited from the cities and villages east of the Appalachian Mountains and were at least one generation removed from the frontier of today's

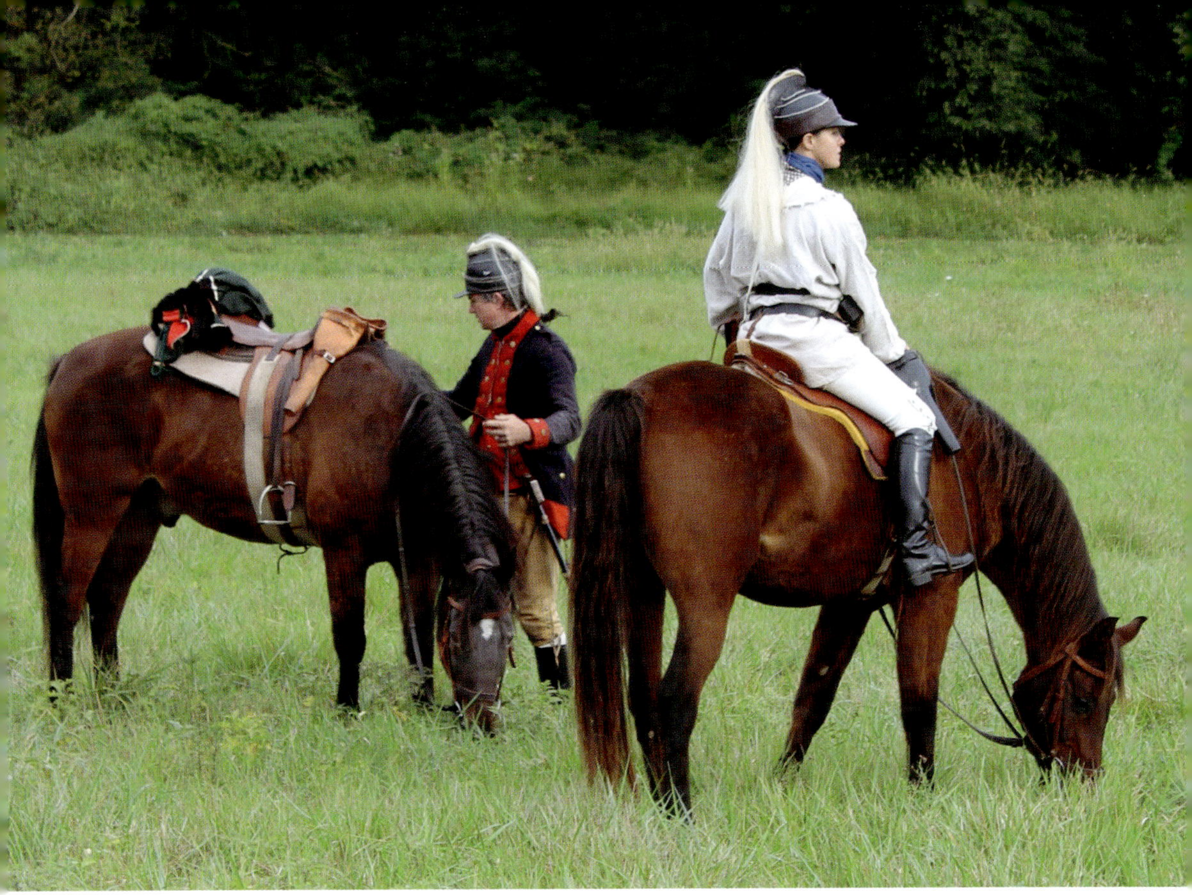

▲ Washington's army was supported by four regiments of mounted dragoons—used primarily for scouting and relaying messages for the army. (Author's collection)

imagination. Many in his army that fall had never seen an Indian nor fired a shot in anger until the Battle of Brandywine. Most, however, had some familiarity with firearms, had hunted game, or defended their livestock from predators, but that was a far cry from combat experience.

The Americans were armed with two basic types of muskets: the .75 caliber British Long Land pattern smoothbore flintlock

Brigadier General Henry Knox, 1750–1806

Henry Knox lost two fingers in a musket accident early in life. The native Bostonian opened a bookstore and became well-read on military issues in general, and ordnance in particular. During the winter of 1775–76 he orchestrated a daring removal of artillery from Fort Ticonderoga and oversaw its transfer to Boston—a bold success that earned him Washington's gratitude and a promotion to head the Continental artillery. Knox helped improve the defenses of Connecticut and Rhode Island, and was promoted after Trenton to brigadier general. During the winter of 1776–77, Washington commissioned Knox to raise a brigade of artillery. By 1777 he had been in command of the Continental artillery for more than a year.

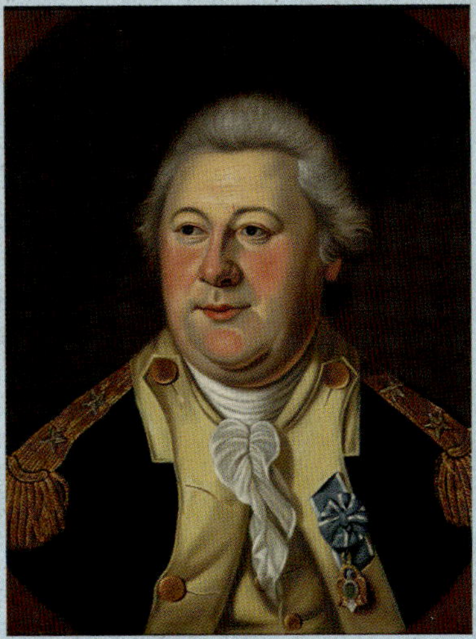

(National Portrait Gallery)

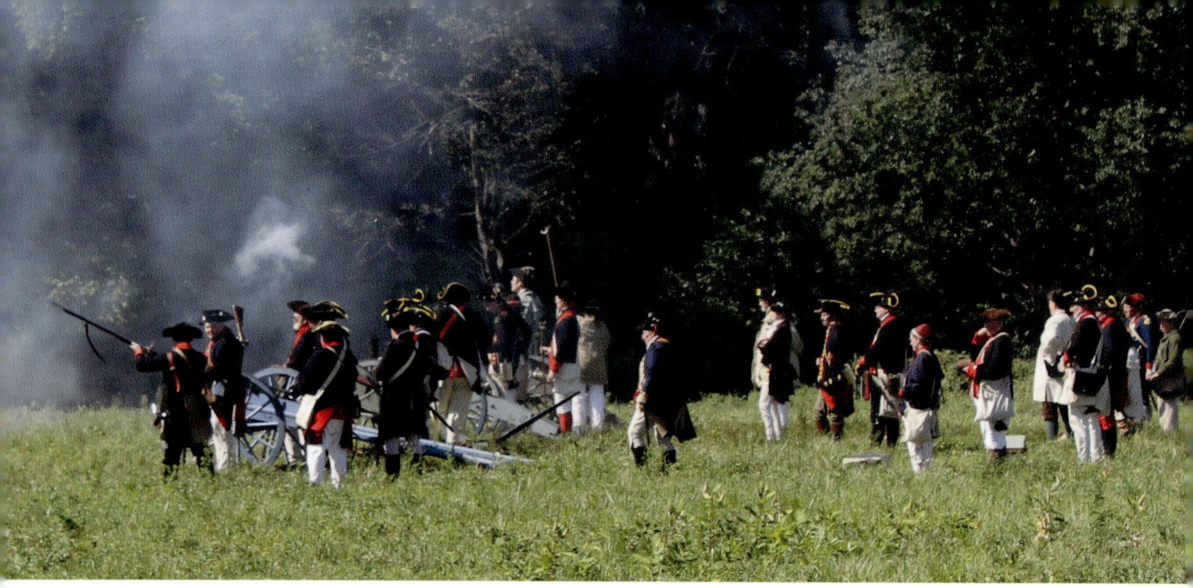

musket (more commonly called the Brown Bess), and the French Charleville .69 caliber smoothbore flintlock musket. American manufacturers produced muskets patterned on both types. The model 1763 French Charleville was the standard American weapon by 1777. The smoothbore fired a one-ounce lead ball, could be fitted with a 14-inch bayonet, and was more reliable and accurate than the British musket. Professional armies of this age no longer loaded loose ball and powder into muskets. Instead, the men were issued cartridges made of a paper or cloth filled with a single musket ball and gunpowder for one shot. The cartridges were held together with string and stored in cartridge boxes slung around a shoulder for combat. A soldier tore open one end of the cartridge with his teeth, dumped the gunpowder down the barrel, and then used a ramrod to seat the round lead ball.

Smoothbores were accurate up to 50 yards and took about 30 seconds to reload. Even when fired at a pointblank range of 25 or 30 yards hitting an enemy soldier was problematic. Effective firepower was generated by organizing men into disciplined ranks so volleys could be "concentrated and controlled" against similarly arranged enemy lines.

The questionable recruiting practices, the rawness of the recruits, and the diminishing patriotism did not mean these were poor

▲ A battery of American artillery such as this one was normally assigned to each infantry brigade. (Author's collection)

▼ Most American artillery pieces were of small caliber and primarily used as anti-personnel weapons. (Author's collection)

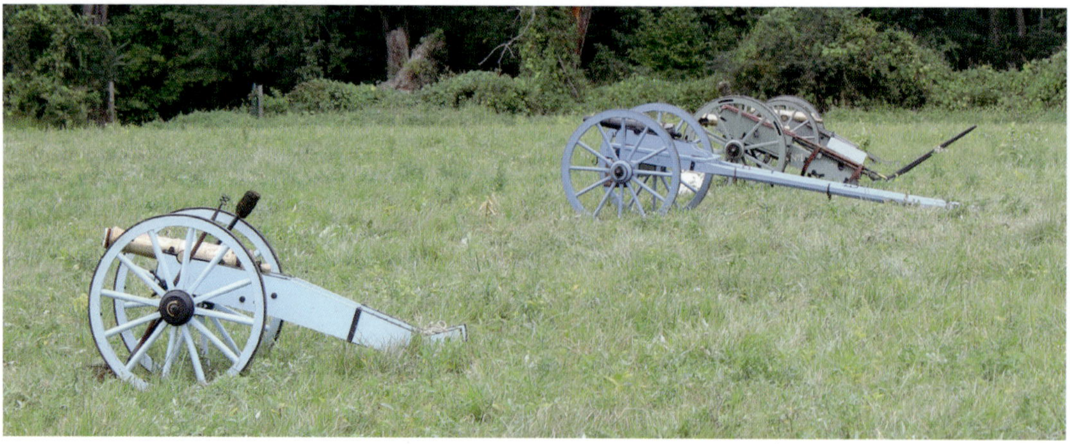

soldiers. Many proved themselves and became the backbone of the army that ultimately achieved victory at Yorktown. Some senior officers had fought in the French and Indian War, which made them familiar with British tactics and practices. Much of the organization and logistics that Washington attempted to instill were built upon British precedents. Many of the junior officers who were too young to serve in the latter war had read British publications and English translations of various French and German studies of military science and tactics. Although the end of enlistments had damaged the army it was not completely starting over from scratch, for many regular and noncommissioned officers had gained significant experience during the prior two years of service.

Camp followers attached themselves to every army in history, and the Continental Army was no exception. Hundreds of hangers-on gathered in the fields outside Philadelphia, including sutlers, women, wives, and children. Washington discouraged the practice and issued orders against their presence, but he realized these people helped hold his army together. They mostly traveled with the baggage train, received rations, and were expected to follow camp regulations just like the troops.

▼ Like the Americans, the British conducted the 1777 campaign without the benefit of tents and often used brush shelters known as wigwams. (Author's collection)

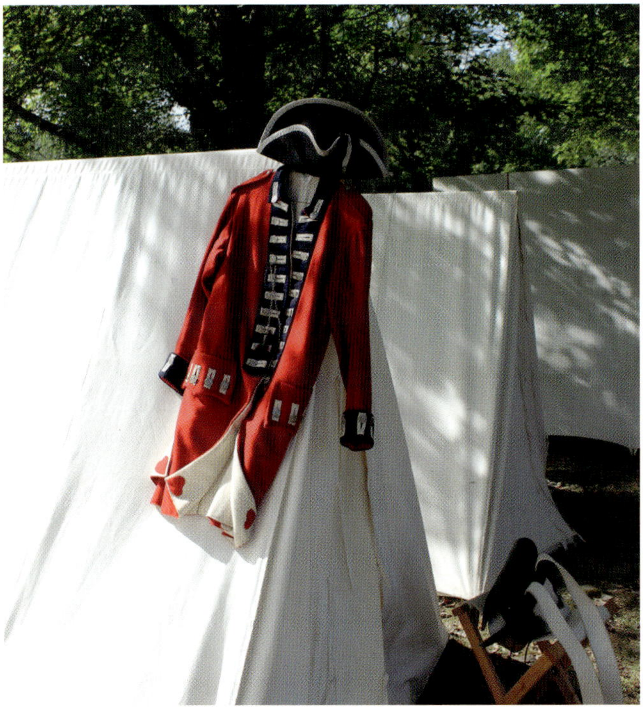

Continental Dragoons & Artillery

Congress did not authorize dragoon regiments until March 1, 1777. Due to supply shortages, expense, desertion, and occasional outright mutiny, these regiments rarely numbered more than 150 men. Filling the ranks was complicated by the need to procure enough horses, weapons, and special equipment. The men and the horses needed specialized training.

The Artillery Brigade, commanded by Brig. Gen. Henry Knox, consisted of about 600 men in three regiments. Each regiment consisted of between eight and a dozen companies. Knox attached portions of the brigade to each division. By 1777, it was common practice to assign an artillery company to each brigade of the army. Other companies served as part of a general reserve. The ideal armament for each brigade was two 6-pounders, although this caliber gun required the largest crew—12 to 15 men—of any field piece with the army.

The American Militia

Washington had long believed the fledgling country needed a professional army to win a war against Great Britain, and that relying on militia was a losing proposition. Congress believed otherwise, and many of its members argued that the maintenance of a standing army was one of the chief American complaints against England. Besides, a militia was cheaper and easier to maintain.

One major sticking point with militia was the system of rotation practiced by most states. A portion of eligible men left for the front at a given time, but rotated home after a few weeks or months and were replaced by others. What little discipline and training had been instilled within these men was lost when they rotated back home. Since most of them had never seen combat before joining the army, whatever experience they gained during a campaign or battle was lost when they left the front. It was a vexing cycle that taxed the patience of the commander in chief.

Their poor reputation preceded the arrival of Pennsylvania's militiamen. Due to the longstanding influence of Quakerism on the Pennsylvania Assembly, the colony had no official militia system prior to or during the early months of the Revolution. Militia was notoriously ill-trained and poorly disciplined, but the problems were compounded in Pennsylvania. The New Jersey militia was next to worthless, but the Pennsylvania militia was even worse.

The British Army

While there were similarities between William Howe's professional European army deployed around Philadelphia and Washington's American command, the differences were striking.

Great Britain had all the material advantages. The population of the 13 colonies hovered around 2.5 million in 1775, including 500,000 mostly enslaved African Americans. In contrast, the British home isles were home to eleven million souls, 48,000 of whom served in the standing army. The outbreak of war brought with it a massive recruiting campaign. The British military establishment was one of the first global bureaucracies. Separate departments existed for barracks, boatmen, commissaries, engineers, hospitals, ordnance, and quartermasters. Officers worked long hours filling out endless detailed reports.

Like their American counterparts, most British soldiers wanted to be in the army

▼ Each British regiment of foot served during the campaign with eight battalion companies such as this one. (Author's collection)

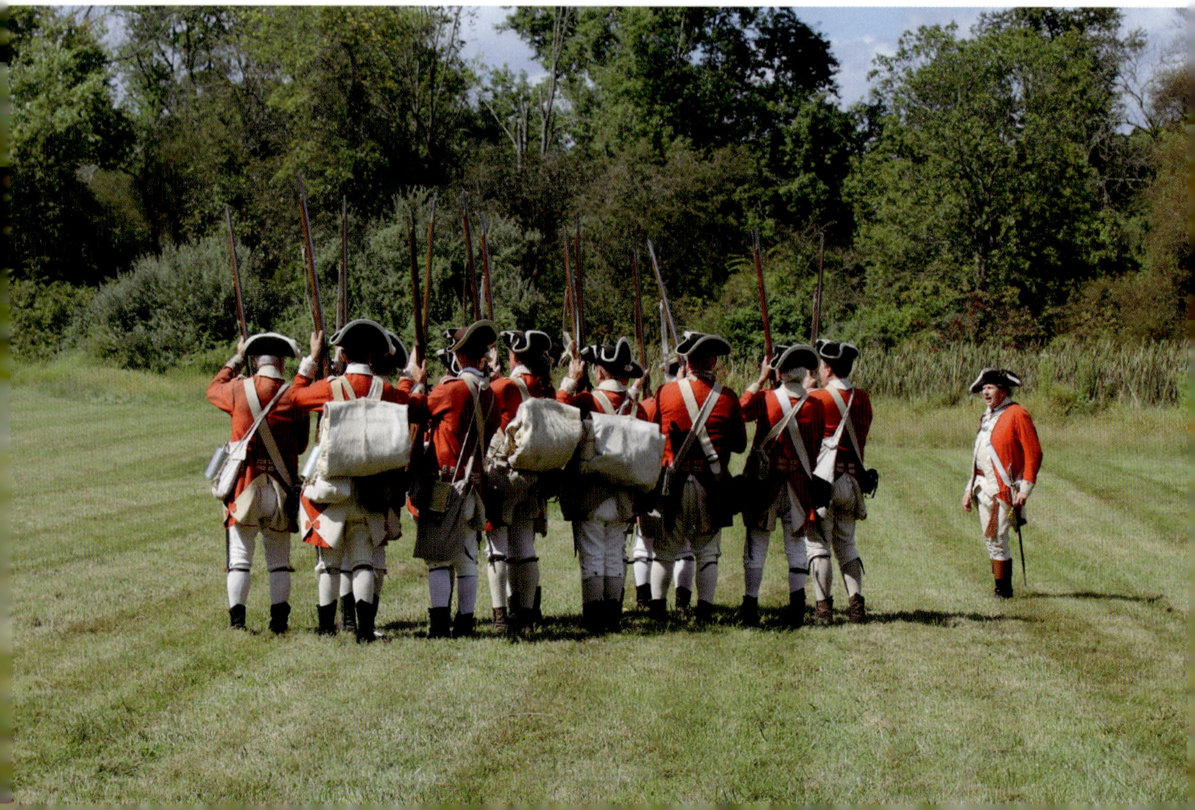

because of its promise of adventure and the supposed attractions that came with a military life. This was not an army of outcasts and criminals. Many were farmers, weavers, and laborers with clean records. Prior to 1775, soldiers enlisted for life, and most were veterans of long service in faraway places—every one of them fiercely proud of their regiments. Recruiting during wartime was often difficult, so the British offered three-year enlistments to fill the ranks. When the line regiments arrived in North America in 1776, recruiting parties left behind forwarded replacements throughout the war.

The regiment was the basic unit of the British Army. While "regiment" was the administrative term for British army units, in tactical terms the unit was called a "battalion." The terms are synonymous for purposes of discussing eighteenth-century operations since virtually every British regiment consisted of a single battalion. Because colonels often functioned as generals in field armies, they did not physically command their regiments on campaign. Normally this privilege was borne by the regiment's lieutenant colonel.

Prior to the Revolution, the British army was composed of 70 regiments of foot (infantry). With the onset of war, the army was expanded by creating new regiments and adding battalions to existing regiments. By the end of the war, 105 regiments were on the rolls.

Every British regiment was composed of eight battalion companies and two flank companies. One flank company was composed of grenadiers, and the other of light infantry. On paper each full-strength regiment consisted of a colonel, a lieutenant colonel, a major, nine captains, 14 lieutenants, 10 ensigns, one chaplain, an adjutant, a quartermaster, a surgeon and his mate, 36 sergeants, 36 corporals, 24 drummers, two fifers, and 672 privates, all for a grand total of 811 men. Every regiment was understrength because of attrition, illness, and other factors. Private soldiers wore black shoes with brass buckles, with heavy linen half or full gaiters over the top. Their breeches and waistcoats were of white linen or wool.

Howe's decisions were shaped by the need to preserve his army's fighting capacity. It was difficult to replace troops lost in battle, especially so far from the home country. The mechanism for replacements in Great Britain was archaic, and the 3,000-mile Atlantic voyage consumed both time and lives. The revulsion Howe experienced as a witness to the bloody frontal assaults against Breed's Hill explains his repeated use of flanking movements thereafter. The difficulty inherent in replacing veteran troops in the eighteenth century caused considerable concern amongst general officers, who strove to avoid unnecessarily losing troops through sickness and desertion, or by exposing them to short rations or inclement weather. This conservative mindset, in turn, limited field mobility, tying armies to magazines, bread ovens, and baggage trains.

British Battalion Companies

Privates in the battalion companies were armed with the 10-pound flintlock known as the Brown Bess. Most American and British soldiers carried this smoothbore musket, which fired a large .75 caliber lead ball and sported a 17-inch bayonet that made it a fearsome close-quarters weapon, but diminished its already limited accuracy. A dozen separate motions were required to fire the weapon. The soldier ripped away one end of a paper cartridge with his teeth, sprinkled a small amount of black powder into the priming pan, and used his ramrod to seat the cartridge and ball down the

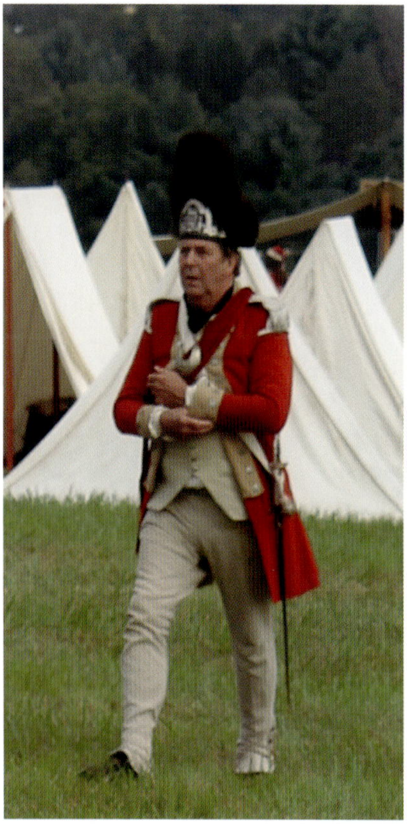

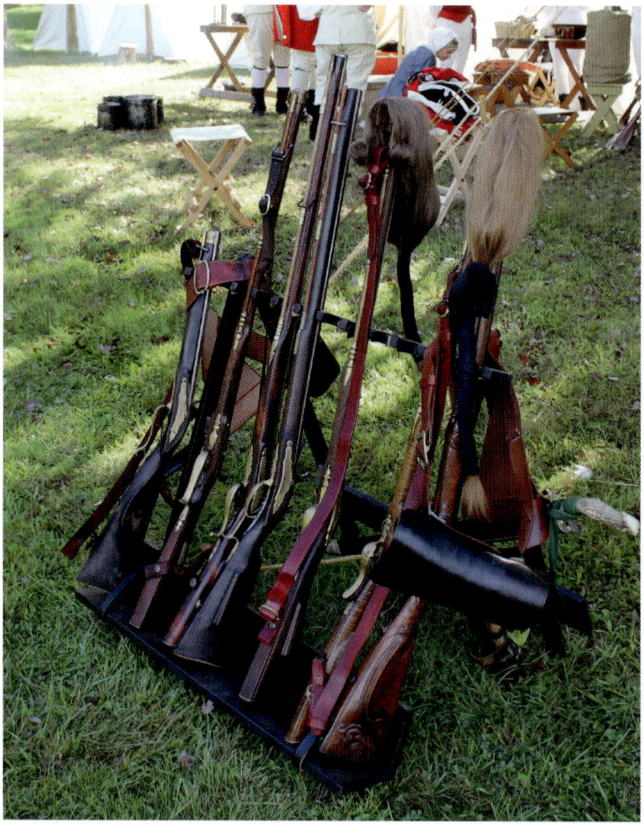

◄ British grenadiers were elite soldiers and served as shock troops for William Howe. (Author's collection)

▲ Hessian jaegers carried some of the limited rifled weapons for either army. These are reproduction jaeger rifles. (Author's collection)

muzzle. A well-trained soldier could get off at least two and as many as three shots a minute under combat conditions. A mounted bayonet made the loading process even more difficult, and many soldiers could only depend upon a single effective shot per minute. The inaccuracy of the musket made volleys a preferred method of fire delivery, and the difficulty in loading was one of the reasons the British made the bayonet charge their primary assault tactic.

There is a common misconception that the British army fought in rigid lines of battle, arrayed shoulder-to-shoulder. Each line of battle consisted of two ranks (with a small interval between each) with the men formed in open order about arm's-length apart. Even in open order, however, the men were not spread out to the extent they operated independently. They presented a solid mass (and thus a ready target) and delivered volleys at a similarly compact enemy formation, often at point-blank range. The first two ranks were responsible for delivering the battalion's firepower. Six paces behind them stood a rank of file closers ready to step up and fill gaps created by the wounded and the dead.

British soldiers rarely picked individual targets and fired at their own pace. Instead, the men loaded and fired on command at an enemy line. Smoothbore muskets were inaccurate beyond 50 yards and there was little interest in target practice, since the cost of lead and powder was not worth the expense and time.

The strict discipline and harsh living conditions that made life difficult for the average British soldier also molded him into a well-trained and formidable

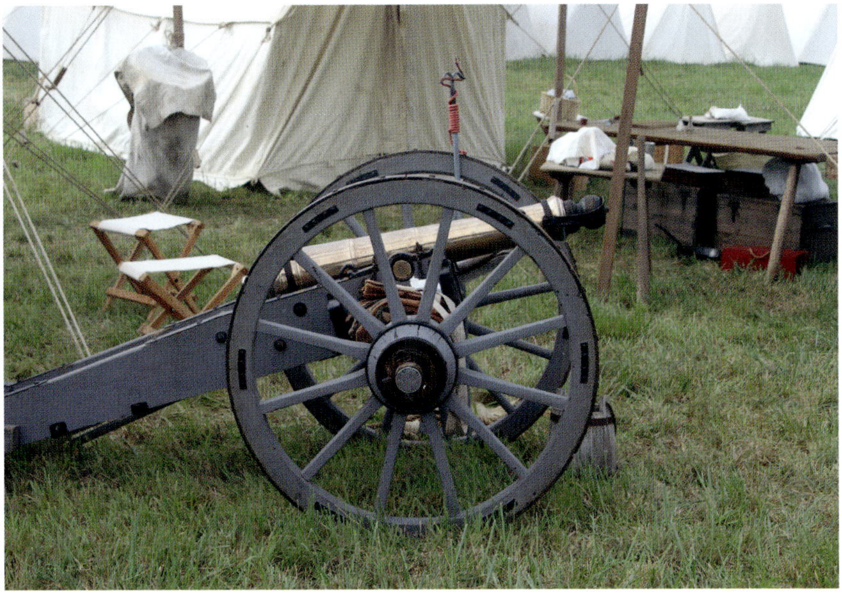

▶ Like the American artillery, most British pieces were of small caliber. Most British battalions were accompanied by two such pieces. (Author's collection)

opponent. The monotonous and repetitive drill created a soldier who reacted to orders with predictable speed and precision. British generals lost several battles during the American Revolution, but not because of a lack of discipline in their ranks.

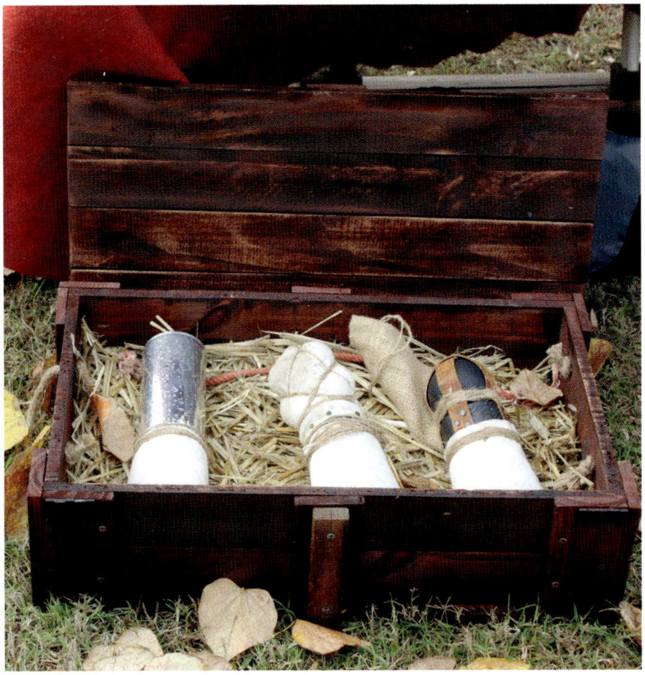

▼ Both armies used primarily three types of artillery rounds—solid shot, canister shot, or grape shot. (Author's collection)

The officers who led these men achieved their positions through either social rank or money. Officers purchased commissions, rising through the ranks from subaltern to colonel, requiring either the death of an officer, an officer's retirement, or the sponsorship of a higher-ranking officer or government patron. Many officers owed their position to someone else. This system created officers devoutly loyal to certain colonels or generals, but who sometimes undermined others within the army. Military competence played little role in the promotion of officers. Officer corps service was a respectable career that offered both status and the potential for advancement.

British Flank Companies

The elite soldiers of the eighteenth-century were assigned to the flank companies of their regiments. Throughout most of the Revolution, flank companies rarely served with their parent regiments and instead "brigaded" together to form battalions of light infantry or grenadiers, depriving the regiments of their best men.

The tallest and strongest men in the regiment made up grenadier companies. Originally, their function was to throw primitive grenades into fortifications, but grenades were no longer in use by the Revolution. The grenadier's uniform included a short sword and a tall bearskin cap instead of the cocked hats worn by the battalion men. The light infantry company consisted of fit men who functioned as rangers or scouts. They cut their coats short (for fast movement and to avoid entanglement in rough terrain), wore leather caps and red waistcoats, and carried small cartridge boxes and hatchets.

Like their comrades, grenadiers and light infantrymen were armed with muskets, although at least some British light infantry were armed with short rifles. Only a small number of these weapons were sent to North America, and there is evidence that each light company received some, though not enough to arm the entire company. While only a few British light troops were so armed, all of the Hessian jaegers (the German equivalent of light infantry) were armed with short jaeger rifles.

British Brigade of Guards

The Brigade of Guards was a special composite force made up of 1,000 men chosen by lottery from the three regiments of Foot Guards. Fifteen men from each of the Guard's 64 companies were selected to serve in America. The army had three regiments of Foot Guards during the eighteenth century: the First Guards (also known as the Grenadier Guards); the Second (the Coldstream Guards); and the Third Guards (the Scots Guards). All three were stationed in London or Westminster as bodyguards for the King. The Brigade of Guards was divided into two battalions of 500 men each and, unlike other British regiments, retained its flank companies while on campaign. The Guards functioned like a light infantry unit in America and used common-sense, flexible tactics when faced with heavy gunfire.

British Artillery

The British organized their field artillery into four battalions of eight companies each. The 4th Battalion of the Royal Artillery Regiment was deployed to the colonies in 1775. Hard service over the next two years reduced the strength of the battalion, and 300 Loyalists from New York were recruited when it became difficult to find suitable replacements. Howe took all eight companies to Pennsylvania.

The men of the Royal Artillery were clothed in dark blue rather than the traditional red, and artillery officers were promoted through merit rather than through the purchase of commissions. Given the scientific aspects of artillery, its officers were among the most highly trained in the service. The Woolwich Military Academy taught mathematics, engineering, and chemistry to prospective artillery officers.

Field guns ranged in size from large 24-pounders to small 3-pounders. The latter light brass cannons became popular for their mobility in the rough terrain of North America. Since 12-pounders required many horses to haul them, and maintaining horses in North America was difficult, the British preferred 6-pounders and 9-pounders. It was customary to allot two guns (known as "battalion guns") to each infantry regiment. The maximum range of the most powerful piece in the British artillery was about 2,000 yards, but no field gun was considered effective beyond 1,200 yards (and many of the smaller caliber much less than that). The guns were capable of firing solid shot, grape, or canister.

British Cavalry

The British had heavy cavalry within its service, but North American terrain precluded its use. As a result, light cavalry in the form of the 16th and 17th Light Dragoons were dispatched to America. Only the 16th was with Howe during most of the Philadelphia Campaign. Each regiment consisted of six troops (the equivalent of an infantry company), each of which contained three officers, four noncommissioned officers, and 38 privates. Few of these units were at full strength.

British Logistics

Regulations called for the British army operating in North America to be provisioned from England. The most important provisions included beef, pork, bread, flour, oatmeal, rice, peas, butter, and salt. Less important provisions, such as cheese, bacon, suet, fish, raisins, and molasses, also found their way to the colonies. Many types of vegetables, including potatoes, parsnips, carrots, turnips, cabbages, and onions, also were dispatched by sea, although they were not always fresh or edible when they reached the men at the front. Most of these vegetables were intended for soldiers recovering in hospitals. Onions, sauerkraut, porter, claret, spruce beer, malt, vinegar, celery seed, and brown mustard seed were used as anti-scorbutics to help ward off scurvy.

Provision trains required healthy horses in large numbers, which in turn required tons of fodder—a precious commodity the British sought to obtain from the countryside, which in turn required even more horses to haul it. Howe estimated he would need at least 3,662 horses, and all their requisite supplies, for his Philadelphia campaign. Exactly how many horses he left with from New York is unknown, but we do know many died and many more became ill during the difficult voyage to the Chesapeake.

By the time of the American Revolution, England had long had a standing army, and had long recognized the need for a different kind of support system for it. Each company had an authorized quota of women. The return for the British army in New York for May 1777 showed one woman present for every eight men in the ranks. The presence of women reduced desertions, and they performed work like mending, cooking, nursing, and laundering. The women traveled with the baggage wagons on the march and did not accompany the men directly.

German Auxiliaries

In an attempt to bolster the British war effort, King George III hired German forces to serve with his army. Great Britain was a global empire, with military commitments across the world in places like Gibraltar, India, Canada, the Caribbean, the American colonies, and of course, the home islands. British military manpower was stretched to its limits when the American Revolution began in 1775.

The German soldiers sent to North America were not mercenaries in the traditional sense, but rather armies from another country hired for use in the colonies. The soldiers were not paid by Great Britain directly and received nothing more than their regular army pay and rations. Instead, England paid the various German princes for the use of their troops. German officers commanded the German soldiers, and they were not subject to British military discipline.

Six German rulers hired out their soldiers to Great Britain: Frederick II, Landgrave of Hesse-Cassel; William, his son, the independent Count of Hesse-Hanau; Charles I, Duke of Brunswick;

Frederick, Prince of Waldeck; Charles Alexander, Margrave of Anspach-Bayreuth; and Frederick Augustus, Prince of Anhalt-Zerbst. Because the German troops sent to North America hailed from separate principalities, they were not all "Hessians," though traditionally they have been referred to by that name.

Unlike their British counterparts, Hessian officers were well trained. They attended Collegium Carolinum to study languages, engineering, and mathematics, becoming experts in military cartography, tactics, and logistics. Promotion was achieved through merit and often in the field for outstanding service. Many of the officers boasted years of field experience.

Enlisted Hessians were recruited in a process designed to serve the needs of their rulers. Those whose civil occupations were deemed indispensable, including skilled artisans, farmers owning more than fifty acres, and anyone making a major contribution to the economy, were exempted from service. Everyone else was encouraged to enlist, especially the sons of poor peasant families. Jaegers tended to be sons of gamekeepers and foresters, while most artillerymen grew up in the cities as sons of industrial workers. Soldiers were paid more than servants and unskilled farm workers, thus encouraging enlistment. Military families were exempted from onerous taxes. Others, like school dropouts, bankrupt tradesmen, and the unemployed, were all but forced into the army.

Both British and Hessian regiments were short of officers, which affected their command and control in battle. British regiments did not have enough officers in part because of the American habit of targeting officers in battle, but illness and

▼ The British army was supported by hired troops from German principalities—primarily Hessians. (Author's collection)

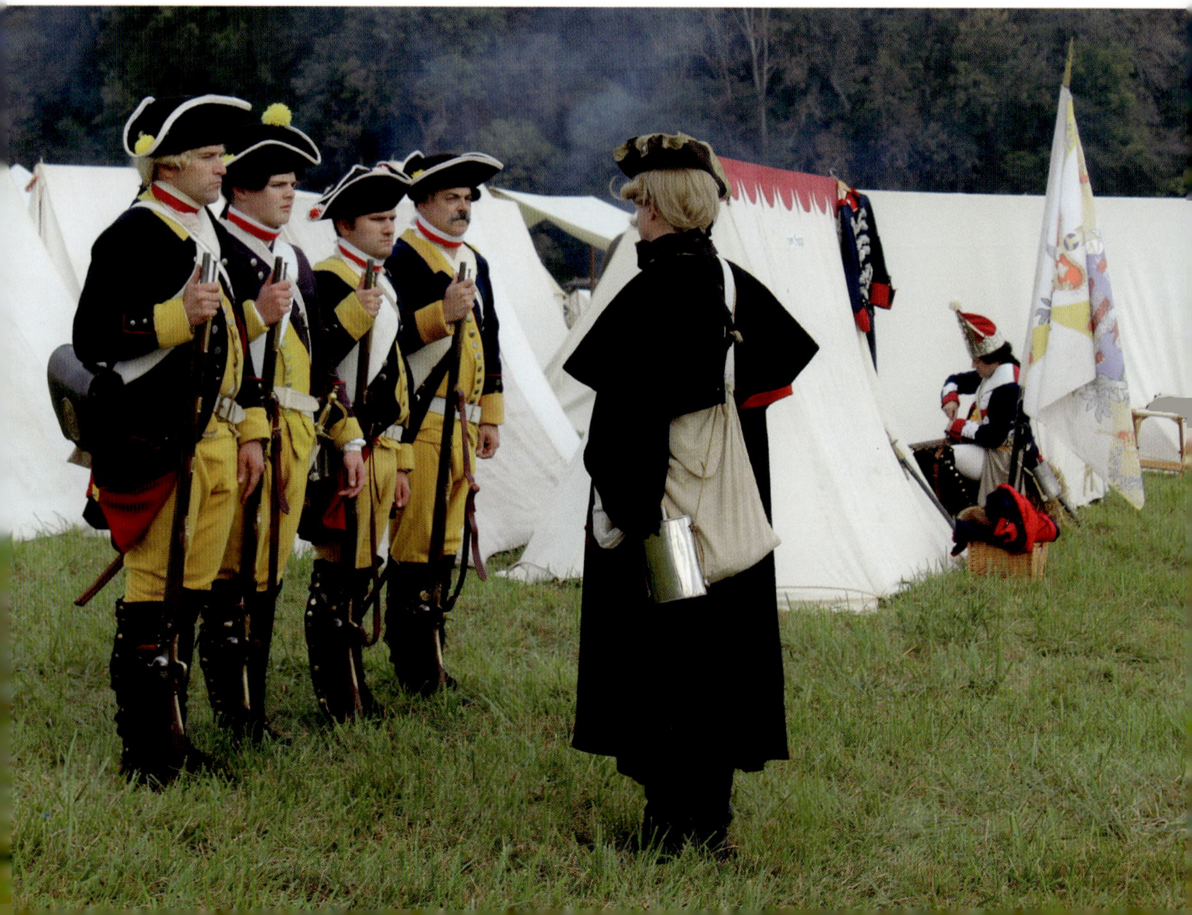

exhaustion associated with campaigning also took a toll. Hessian regiments were organized with a higher soldier-to-officer ratio, which put them at an immediate disadvantage. Sickness and battle casualties also took their toll on the regiments. Replacing both officers and men was difficult at best with more than 3,000 miles separating them from home.

Unlike British regiments, Hessian regiments typically contained five companies—four line companies and a grenadier company. At full strength, they contained 524 men. At the request of the British, the Hessians were asked to "brigade" their grenadier companies much as the British had done. The Hessian Grenadier Brigade for the Philadelphia Campaign was formed from the grenadier companies of twelve regiments. Each grenadier battalion was supported by two 3-pound artillery pieces. The grenadiers carried a .72 caliber Prussian-style musket.

This reproduction of the famous painting 'Mrs. Murray's strategy' by Percy Moran shows senior British officers being entertained to cake and wine as their enemy slipped away to safety undetected. (Library of Congress)

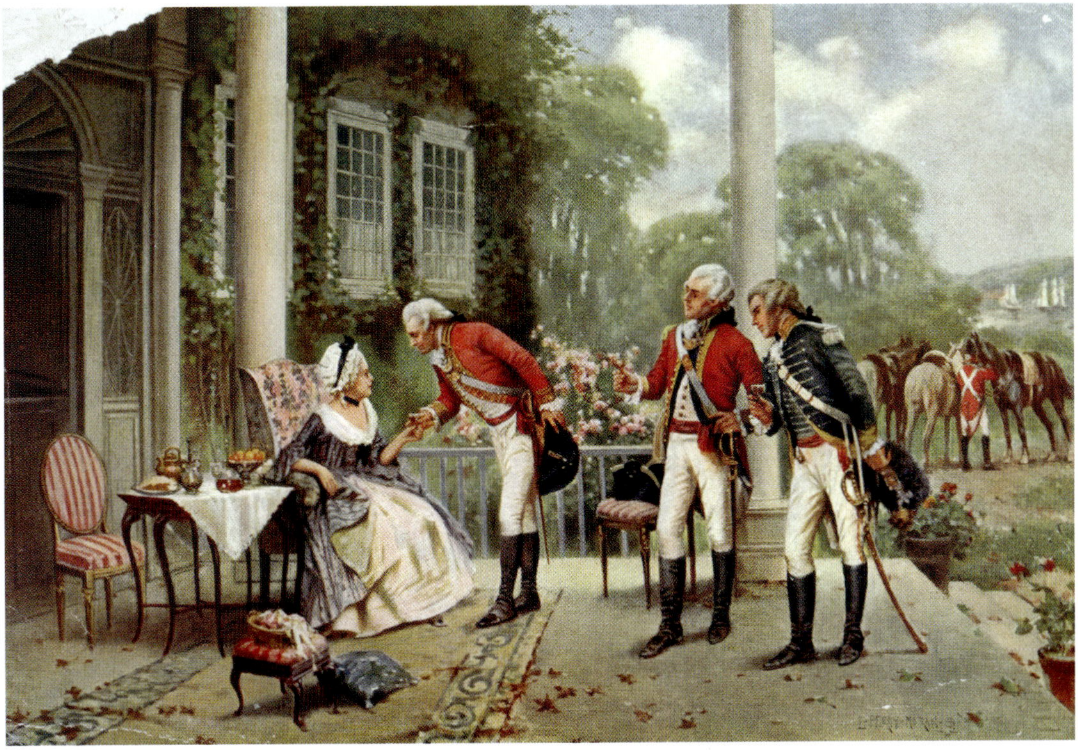

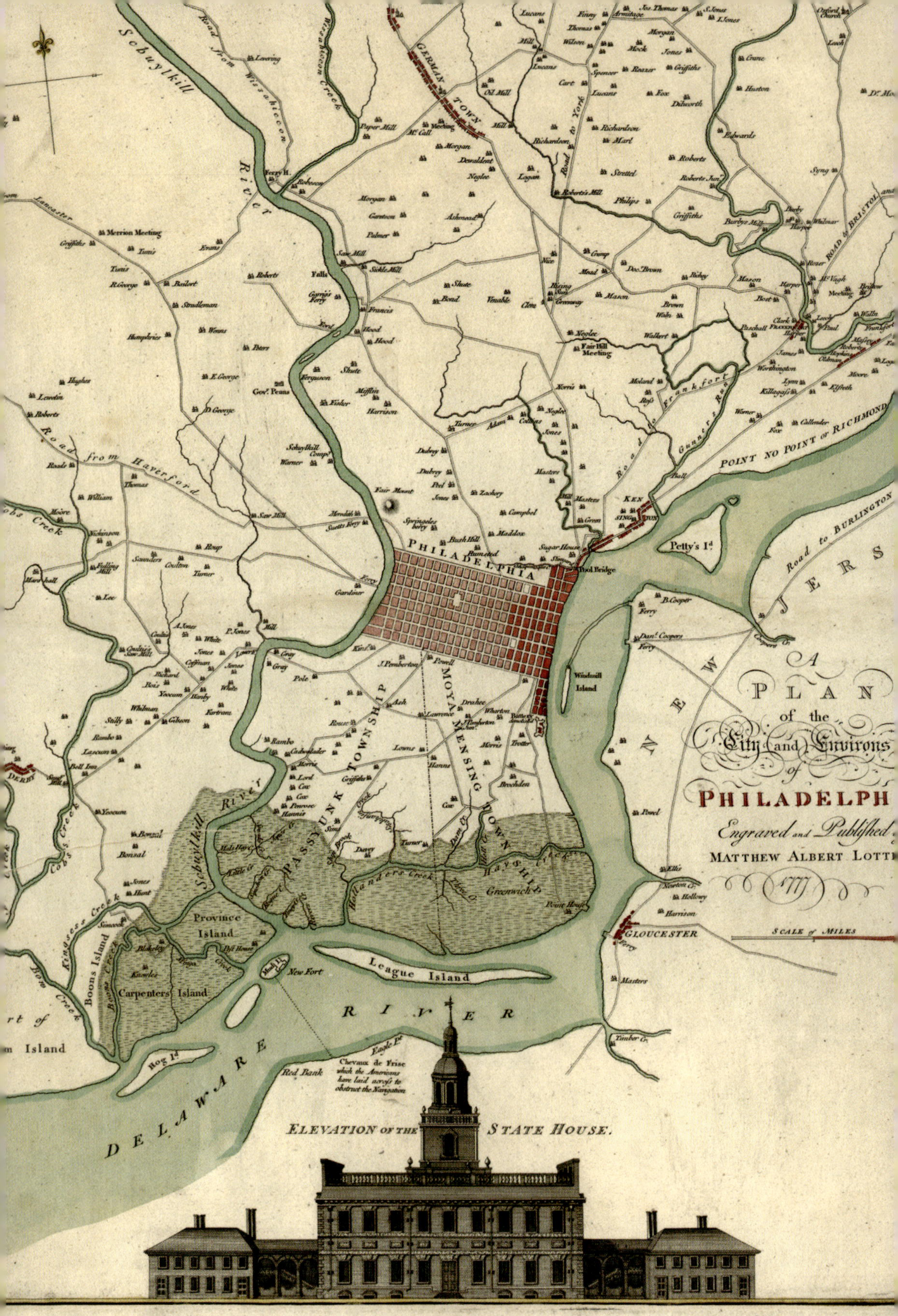
A PLAN of the City and Environs of PHILADELPHIA
Engraved and Published by MATTHEW ALBERT LOTTER
1777
SCALE of MILES
ELEVATION OF THE STATE HOUSE.
PHILADELPHIA
Schuylkill River
DELAWARE RIVER
NEW JERSEY
GERMAN TOWN
MOYAMENSING TOWNSHIP
PASSYUNK TOWNSHIP
Province Island
Carpenters Island
Boons Island
League Island
Petty's Id
Windmill Island
Hog Id
Mud Id
New Fort
Red Bank
Chevaux de Frise which the Americans have laid across to obstruct the Navigation
GLOUCESTER
KENSINGTON
POINT NO POINT or RICHMOND
Road to Burlington
Road to Bristol
Road to York
Road from Haverford
Road from Lancaster
Road from Wissahickon
Wissahickon Creek
Cobs Creek
Kingsess Creek
Gunners Run
Frankfort
Hollanders Creek
DERBY
Falls
Fair Hill Meeting
Merrion Meeting
Sugar House
Draw Bridge
Fair Mount
Bush Hill
Gov.r Penns
Schuylkill Compy
Timber Cr.

First Moves

Philadelphia was the largest American port, the colonial seat of government, and the fourth largest city in the entire British Empire. Although established less than a century earlier, the city grew more rapidly than the older cities of Boston and New York. The founding Penn family's offers of lucrative land deals, coupled with the province's Quaker tolerance of all faiths, contributed to the heavy and steady influx of immigrants to both the city and picturesque surrounding countryside. Within the Empire, only Dublin, Edinburgh, and London had larger populations.

Philadelphia was laid out in a grid pattern, with (mostly numbered) north-south streets running parallel to the Delaware River, and east–west streets named after trees and other plants. Streets were 50 feet wide, paved with cobblestone, and lined with sidewalks of brick or flagstone. Other than a scattering of church steeples and other cupolas, no building was taller than four stories. By 1777, the city of 30,000–40,000 citizens boasted more than 5,000 houses and 3,000 other buildings including warehouses, merchant facilities, and small workshops. These mostly red-brick structures were erected within one square mile. The city extended eight blocks west from the Delaware River. If the suburbs of Northern Liberties and Southwark are included, the boundaries were 14 blocks north-to-south from Callowhill to Christian Streets. Beyond the organized streetscape were verdant fields and farmland, stands of trees, and a sprinkling of country houses.

◄ A plan of the city and environs of Philadelphia 1777. (Library of Congress)

Politics divided the population. The Scotch-Irish Presbyterian Protestants favored American independence. Members of the Church of England, or Anglicans, were divided between loyalty to the Crown and support for their homes and livelihoods. Protestant Germans, who composed about half of Philadelphia, were neutral for religious reasons or supported the war effort. Members of the large Quaker contingent preferred neutrality but their default position was passive loyalty to the crown. The small number of Jews, Irish and German Catholics kept a low profile.

Flour and lumber exports made the region quite wealthy. The flour industry alone demanded the production of thousands of barrels annually, which in turn required sawmills to make the barrel staves, forges to produce iron straps for the hoops, and coopers to assemble them all. Barrels were also shipped to the West Indies for the transportation of sugar, molasses, and rum. These same lumber and iron businesses were also capable of producing war materials for the American army. During the war, most of the trade goods entering the colonies through Philadelphia came from the West Indies in the form of booty captured by privateers.

Being the largest port in British North America, Philadelphia had a large working-class population of rough dockworkers and laborers, as well as hundreds of small, independent craftsmen such as leatherworkers, shoemakers, printers, carpenters, and smiths of all kinds. Transportation of goods into and out of the city required porters, carters, draymen, and teamsters—tough, able-bodied characters who quenched their thirst at the more than 150 licensed taverns in the city. Others were more comfortable patronizing illegal taprooms populating back alleys and waterfront areas.

The lower Delaware valley and the farmlands to the south and west were rich centers of agricultural output and manufacturing that made a major contribution to the American war effort. The mid-Atlantic region supplied grain, horses, cattle, sheep, forage, cloth, lumber, and flour for the Continental Army. There were more than two dozen flour mills in the area. Five gunpowder mills in the area produced most of the army's ammunition. Uncounted local iron forges and furnaces supported the war by manufacturing cannon, cannonballs, horseshoes, wagon parts, shovels, and swords. German artisans farther inland produced the coveted Pennsylvania rifle. Salt, a precious commodity in any age without refrigeration, together with other sundries such as soap, candles, medicines, and blankets were all produced in the Philadelphia region. The area had long been renowned for its paper mills, whose products were necessary for Continental money, regimental books, writing paper, and small arms cartridges.

The port was both a shipbuilding facility and a major hub for the importation of

Joseph Galloway, 1731–1803

Prior to the war, Philadelphia aristocrat Joseph Galloway was one of the most powerful politicians in Pennsylvania and a member of the First Continental Congress.

When Galloway took his seat in the First Continental Congress in 1775, most members hoped for reconciliation. Once Congress pushed for independence Galloway fled Philadelphia to New York City, where the main British Army was located. Using his social standing, Galloway worked through Ambrose Serle, secretary to Admiral Richard Howe, and gained an audience with General Howe. Howe consulted with Galloway during the planning stages of his campaign to capture Philadelphia. When the British troops began their campaign in the late spring of 1777, Galloway was with them.

(National Portrait Gallery)

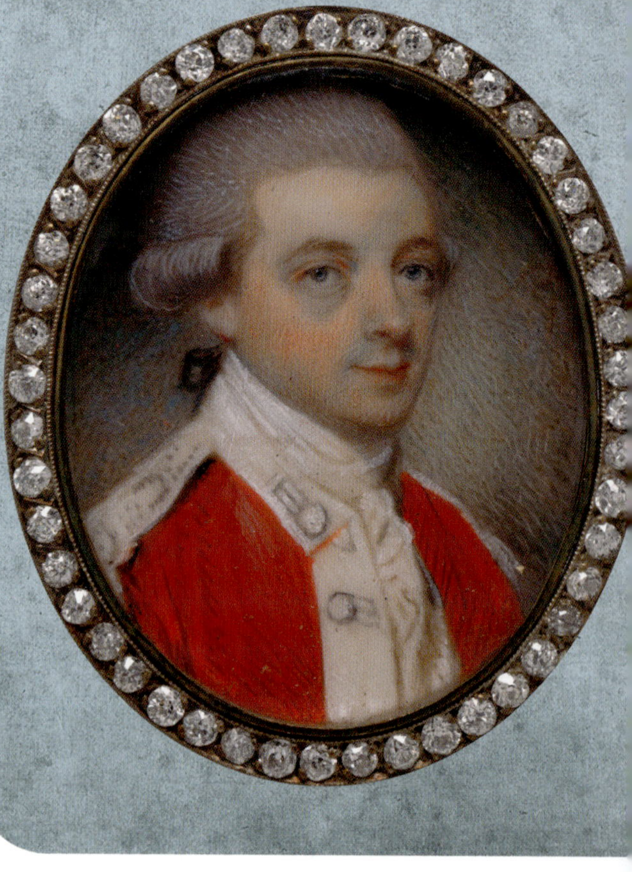

goods key to American military success. What little foreign trade Americans were able to nurture during the war was principally channeled through Philadelphia. Large quantities of French weapons and gunpowder were smuggled in from the Caribbean, while rice and other foodstuffs, together with liquor, tobacco, and indigo, arrived from the Chesapeake region. Philadelphia's shipyards turned out small and large vessels for military purposes. In March of 1777, a foundry opened on the waterfront opposite Old Swedes Church to produce brass cannon. Even the yard of the State House (today's Independence Hall) doubled as a muddy artillery park. By 1777, the signs of war were visible everywhere in and around Philadelphia. Howe had good reason to want to wrest it from Washington's grasp.

From the outside the city appeared to be solidly behind independence. A closer look revealed that more than half the population was disinterested in war or loyal to the King. The large population of Quakers in Pennsylvania made it unique among the colonies. Belief in nonviolence kept them politically neutral. While many agreed with the patriot cause, the vast majority refused to take up arms or support the war in any way. Likewise, Pennsylvania supported Loyalists within its borders. The combination of Quakers and Tories put the patriots of Pennsylvania in the minority.

Joseph Galloway, former speaker of the Pennsylvania Assembly, had led General Howe to believe that the Loyalists there would rise up to assist him. Galloway claimed that up to ninety percent of Pennsylvania's citizens were loyal to the Crown, and informed Howe that they would reaffirm their allegiance to the King should a British army march upon Philadelphia. Howe was convinced. The people in the middle colonies, he argued, were "disposed to peace, in which sentiment they would be confirmed, by our getting possession of Philadelphia, I am, from this consideration, fully persuaded, the principal army should act offensively on that side, where the enemy's chief strength will certainly be collected."

Opening Moves

Following his successes at Trenton and Princeton in late December 1776 and early January 1777, Gen. George Washington spent the next six months around Morristown, New Jersey, building a new army nearly from scratch. During the long and arduous process, Washington harassed British outposts scattered across northern New Jersey in a series of raids and skirmishes. Fortunately for him, British Gen. William Howe was more concerned with strategic planning and writing letters to London then with what he considered the minor doings of the Continental Army.

Between January and June 1777, the small-scale raids and skirmishes were the only military operations witnessed in northern New Jersey. The American Revolution had devolved into something more closely resembling a guerrilla war than the more traditional European-style of combat. Happily for Washington and the American cause, this form of warfare continued for the next four months, giving the general the precious time and space he needed to rebuild his weakened army. The stress built up during the extended off-tempo low-intensity war simmered through the spring of 1777 until it boiled over into the savageness exhibited later in the campaign.

General Howe intended to capture Philadelphia as rapidly as possible and return to New York to join forces with

Gen. John Burgoyne and the northern army yet showed no sign of urgency to actually do so. Defeating Washington in New Jersey and then marching to Philadelphia offered Howe the best chance to take the colonial capital and leave in time to aid Burgoyne in New York.

William Howe finally lurched into action in June by ordering an expedition to Middlebush, New Jersey. The British commander decided his best bet was to attempt the overland route to Philadelphia in the hope of luring Washington down from his mountain stronghold. Timing was crucial to the British plan, and the army could have moved weeks earlier when the winter rains stopped and the warmer weather dried the roads. Howe, however, did not move into northern New Jersey until June 13. To the disbelief of officers in both armies, the British army stopped after a march of about ten miles and established camp the day after reaching its destination. Not only did the army stop its advance, but Howe ordered fortifications erected. By remaining stationary, Howe intended to draw Washington down from the high ground and offer him battle on the relatively flat country east of the mountain range. To Howe's dismay, Washington refused to take the bait.

The failure to lure the Americans into a fight flummoxed Howe, whose army of professional soldiers was being stymied by Washington's ragtag collection of militia, frontiersmen, and Continental Regulars. No one believed Washington's force was formidable, including Washington himself. His was not the army of veterans that would come to life hardened and molded in the grueling campaign still ahead of them, followed by the reckoning that would take place at Valley Forge that winter. Four days ticked past as Howe waited in frustration for Washington to move. Other than light skirmishing and the launching of small raiding parties to plunder the countryside, Howe accomplished nothing. By remaining idle during perfectly good weather, Howe had effectively removed his army from the war effort.

Howe gave up the game and returned to New Brunswick on June 19 as elements of the Continental Army followed, skirmishing fitfully with his rear guard.

Major General William Alexander, 1726–1783

William Alexander (Lord Stirling) was one of Washington's senior commanders. He was born in 1726 in New York. He began the war as a colonel in the New Jersey militia and in 1776 was appointed brigadier general and captured in the fighting on Long Island. Stirling rejoined the colonial effort and served with Washington at Trenton.

(New York Public Library)

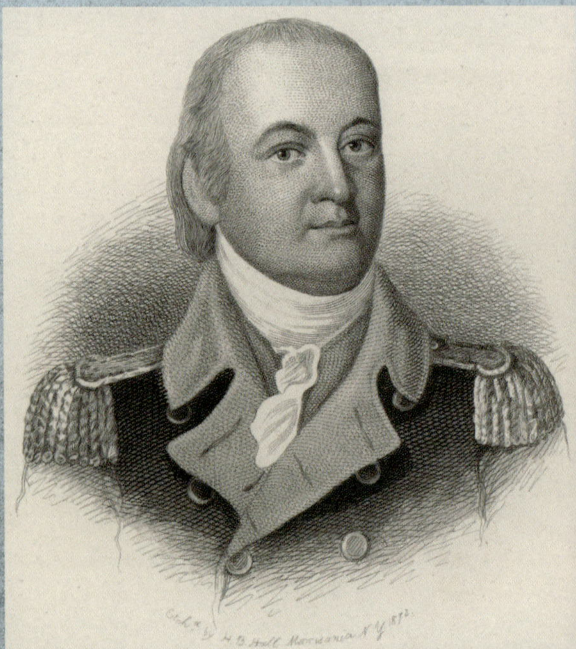

Howe's half-hearted attempt in New Jersey was as baffling then as it is today. Even though he was on a tight schedule, he moved thousands of troops ten miles, went into camp and constructed earthworks, waited four days, and returned to his starting point a week later. Most historians attribute Howe's actions to a failed effort to pull Washington from the mountains for an open-field fight. However, Washington had never so obliged his enemy. In fact, Washington rarely fought a battle under his enemy's terms. The more logical explanation is that Howe never intended to assault Philadelphia by marching through New Jersey. He would reach his objective by using the British fleet to transport his army.

Battle of Short Hills

On June 22, Howe retired farther to Amboy, New Jersey, to load his army and its baggage for the voyage to the Delaware River. The Americans pressed Howe's rear guard, harassing the tail of his column. Washington's willingness to come down off the high ground and pursue Howe's retreating army, however, provided the British general with the opportunity he had been seeking. The Continental Army

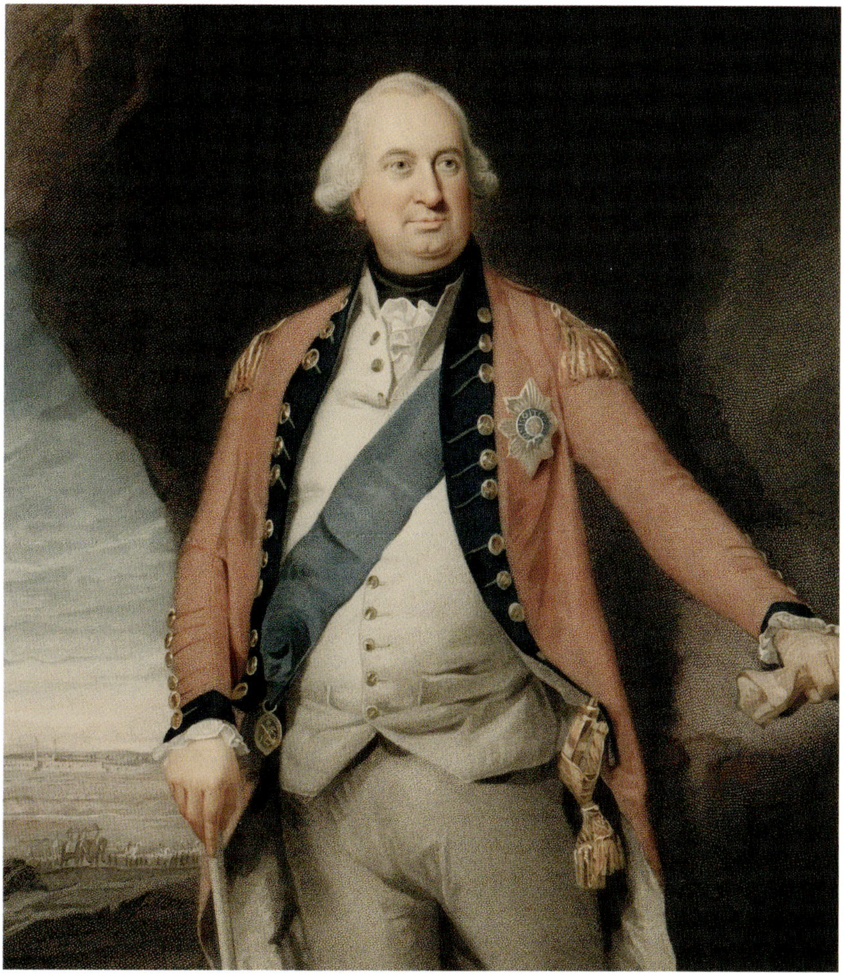

▶ Lieutenant General Charles Cornwallis, 1738–1805. Lord Charles Cornwallis took part in the battles of Long Island, the second battle of Trenton, and Princeton. One teenage Philadelphia resident described Cornwallis as "of the ordinary height, square built, one of his eyes was habitually closed, vulgarly termed cock-eyed." (Yale University)

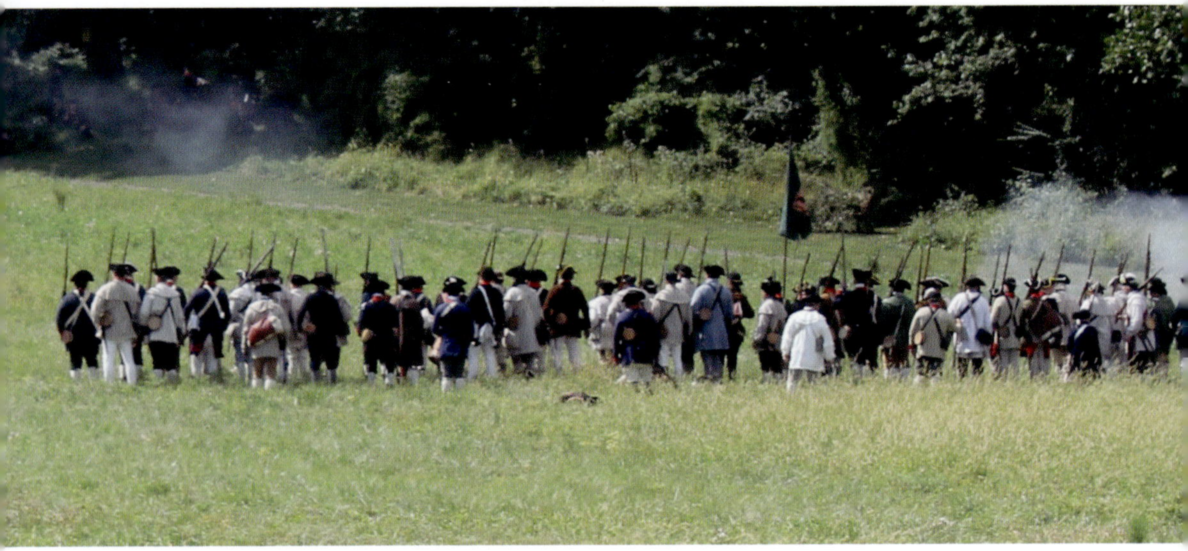

▲ Washington often chose defensive ground rather than launching an attack against the British army. (Author's collection)

was on more engageable terrain and Howe had his chance to attack. He did just that on June 25 by turning and assaulting Major General Lord Stirling's isolated and heavily outnumbered American division of some 2,500 men. Stirling took up a position on Washington's left flank at Short Hills, several miles north of New Brunswick.

In the middle of the night on June 25, Charles Cornwallis led a column toward Short Hills by way of Woodbridge with the intention of cutting Stirling's division off from the mountain passes. Another column led by Gen. John Vaughan, with Howe in accompaniment, moved back toward New Brunswick before turning north toward Scotch Plains. Much like the strategy he had used on Long Island the previous August, Howe was trying to catch a portion of Washington's army in a pincer movement and destroy it. The front of Cornwallis's column engaged Stirling's pickets at sunrise.

Stirling waged a well-crafted fighting withdrawal and took up a strong defensive position in the area of Ash Swamp and Scotch Plains. By the end of the day, Stirling had been driven back after losing three artillery pieces in the process, and nearly being captured himself. The Battle of Short Hills bought precious time for Washington to move the balance of his army into the hill country to deny Howe the opportunity of the larger pitched battle he so craved. Howe had been unable to bring Washington to battle, but his short-lived romp across the Jersey countryside had made one thing clear: the large and often lumbering British army could move about the countryside, plundering as it went, and there was little Washington could or would do about it. After driving away Stirling and his division, the British troops moved on the road to Westfield. The lack of drinkable water, coupled with a miserably hot and humid mid-Atlantic summer day, resulted in the death by sunstroke of several British soldiers.

Unbeknownst to Washington, the same day Stirling was fighting Cornwallis at Short Hills, Burgoyne's troops from Canada reoccupied the fortifications at Crown Point, New York, at the southern tip of Lake Champlain. Burgoyne's campaign was well underway; the same could not be said for Howe's operation.

After the mauling Stirling's men received, Washington refused to offer Howe battle on

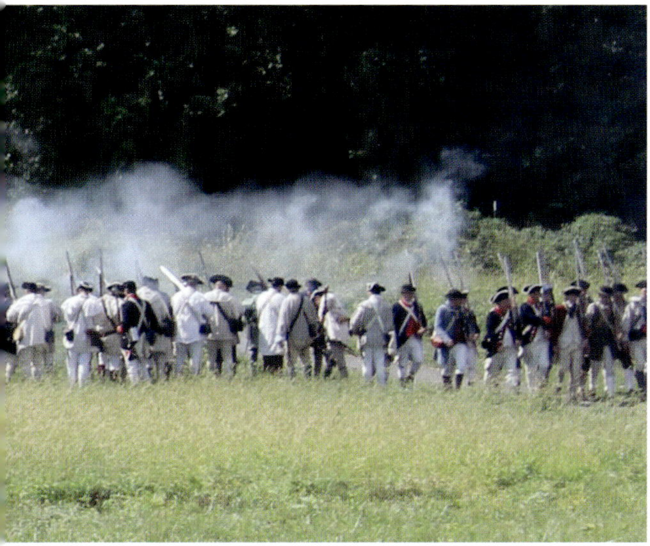

the open plains, choosing instead to pull his men back into the mountains. Howe's maneuver had almost worked. He inflicted serious damage upon an American division, and nearly lured Washington into an open-field fight. Whatever the impact upon morale, Washington knew better than to waste his army in a pitched fight against the cream of the British army. By June 28 Howe was back in Amboy, his attempt to defeat Washington in northern New Jersey at an end. On the last day of June, Howe removed the last of his troops from New Jersey and returned to Staten Island, New York. He and his command were right back where they had started nearly a year earlier before their attack on New York City. The city and its environs, together with Newport, Rhode Island, remained under British control, but Howe's withdrawal allowed Washington and his Continental Army to assume complete control of New Jersey.

The Sea Voyage

Early July found most of Washington's Continental Army back in the mountains around Morristown. The position provided Washington with the option of shifting north to block the Hudson River, or south to protect the capital. The next move was up to Howe. Determined to use his fleet to reach Philadelphia, on July 8 the British general began the arduous process of loading his army onto transport ships. Howe believed he could ascend the Delaware River and gain Philadelphia and still aid Burgoyne in a timely fashion. He also believed that moving by sea would freeze the Americans in place until Washington realized where Howe was going.

By the time Howe finished the loading process on July 9, he had filled some 260 ships with 20,000 soldiers, support personnel, artillery, horses, and everything else he needed to launch a major campaign. Rather than depart immediately, however, Howe left his men and animals bobbing in the harbor for several days confined in tight overheated quarters aboard stuffy transports.

Washington was aware Howe was loading ships for a campaign and decided to get a jump on him by moving to the New Jersey–New York border in anticipation of an ascent up the Hudson. The army moved north on July 12. Leaving New Jersey wide open for Howe to make an overland forced march for Philadelphia was a bold decision. Howe failed to recognize or exploit the opportunity. The deliberate British general was finally ready on July 20. He ordered the large British armada to sail out of New York harbor, leaving behind General Henry Clinton and the city's garrison of 7,400 troops. American observers along the New Jersey coast speculated the fleet was turning south, but at this point Howe's target was still an open question. The lack of a Continental Navy hampered Washington, who was forced to rely upon spotters scattered along the coastline to locate the ships and relay information. Howe could be headed north to Boston or Canada or south to any number of port cities. Until reliable intelligence arrived, Washington had no choice but to mark time in northern New Jersey.

Howe's voyage promised to be long and slow, for the prevailing summer winds along the Atlantic coast tend to blow north—the opposite direction Howe's fleet was heading. The journey was a miserable experience for man and beast alike. The heat and humidity were stifling and brisk winds buffeted the ships. Frequent late afternoon thunderstorms added to the general misery of the voyage. The weather proved so uncooperative that it took the fleet a week to travel only 150 miles to Cape May, New Jersey. Washington, meanwhile, concentrated near Ramapo, New Jersey, a position from which he could march to the Hudson Highlands or move rapidly to Philadelphia.

On July 26, spotters along the New Jersey shoreline sighted a large portion of the British fleet heading south near Little Egg Harbor, New Jersey. Washington was already beginning to hedge his bets and had been slowly moving south, inching toward Morristown with four of the army's five divisions. When news of the fleet found its way to Washington, there was little doubt Howe was heading for Philadelphia. On July 28 the leading elements of Washington's legions reached the Delaware River.

The final days of July arrived with the British fleet tacking into the Delaware Bay to assess the current conditions and intelligence about Washington's army. When the news reached Washington about 24 hours later, he ordered the army to cross into Pennsylvania to block a move against Philadelphia. Almost simultaneously, the Howe brothers made what was perhaps the most critical decision of 1777 aboard bobbing ships in Delaware Bay.

At 10:00 a.m. on July 30, Capt. Andrew Hamond reported to Admiral Richard

Admiral Lord Richard Howe, 1726–1799

Admiral Richard Howe was Gen. William Howe's older brother and in command of the British fleet in North America. Howe joined the navy at 13 and served throughout the War of the Austrian Succession and the Seven Years' War. Like his brother, the admiral was not unsympathetic to the American cause, which may have influenced how he employed his naval power. It was mostly his responsibility to open the Delaware River to British shipping after disembarking his brother's army in northeastern Maryland.

(New York Public Library)

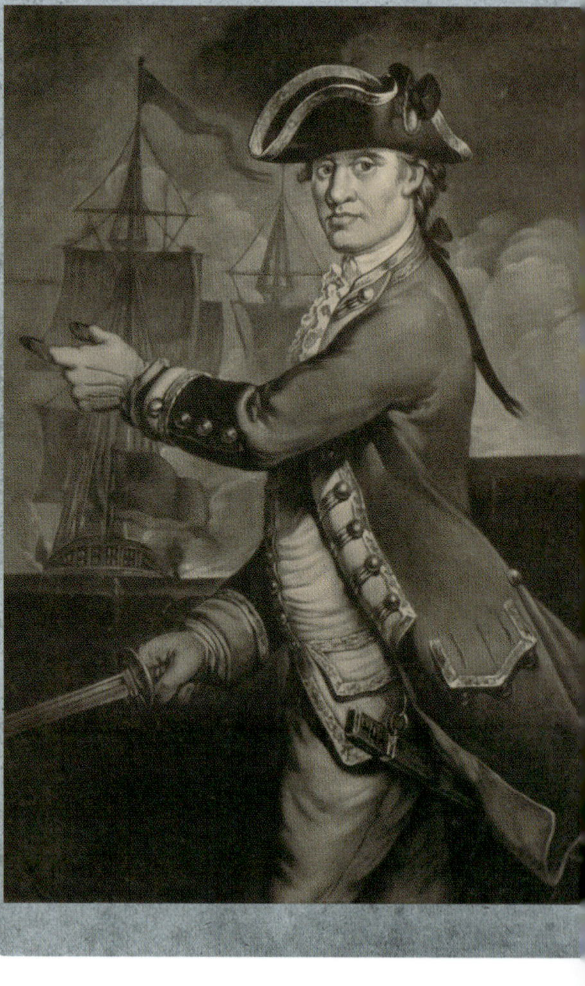

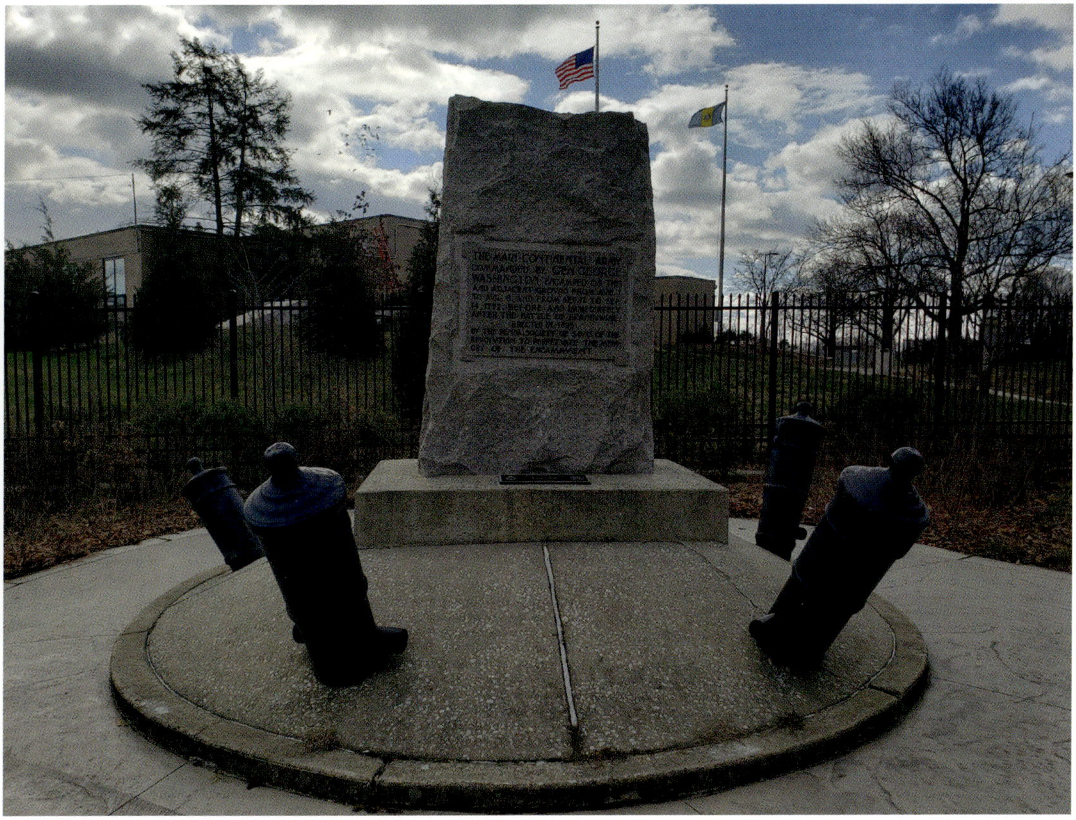

▲ 1895 marker in the Germantown section of Philadelphia denoting the camp site of Washington's army in early August 1777 and again after the Battle of Brandywine. (Author's collection)

Howe's flagship HMS *Eagle* to meet with the Howe brothers. Commander of the HMS *Roebuck*, Hamond commanded the blockading squadron in the Delaware Bay and was presumably was the best informed about local conditions. Hamond was shocked to find the general still asleep. A short time later the two Howes and Hamond met in the admiral's cabin. One of the first questions posed was whether Hamond knew the location of Washington's army. The army, he replied, was across the Delaware heading for Wilmington. His intelligence source is not known, but Hamond's assessment was false. Perhaps one brigade was across the river, but the rest of Washington's army was strung out across northern New Jersey. Howe's most recent dispatch to Lord George Germain, however, stated that he would ascend the Delaware River only if Washington remained in northern New Jersey. If he had entered Pennsylvania instead, Howe was going to revert to the plan to ascend the Chesapeake Bay. Hamond's incorrect report made Howe's decision for him.

The British general and admiral acted upon incorrect information that Washington's entire army was across the Delaware and approaching Wilmington, Delaware. They were also told that fortifications had been constructed along the shores of the Delaware and various obstructions had been placed in the river to halt the fleet. Fortifications that would play a major role in the campaign were unprepared. Fort Mifflin, just south of Philadelphia, lacked a garrison. Opposite that position, Fort Mercer in New Jersey was yet to be constructed. The river defenses

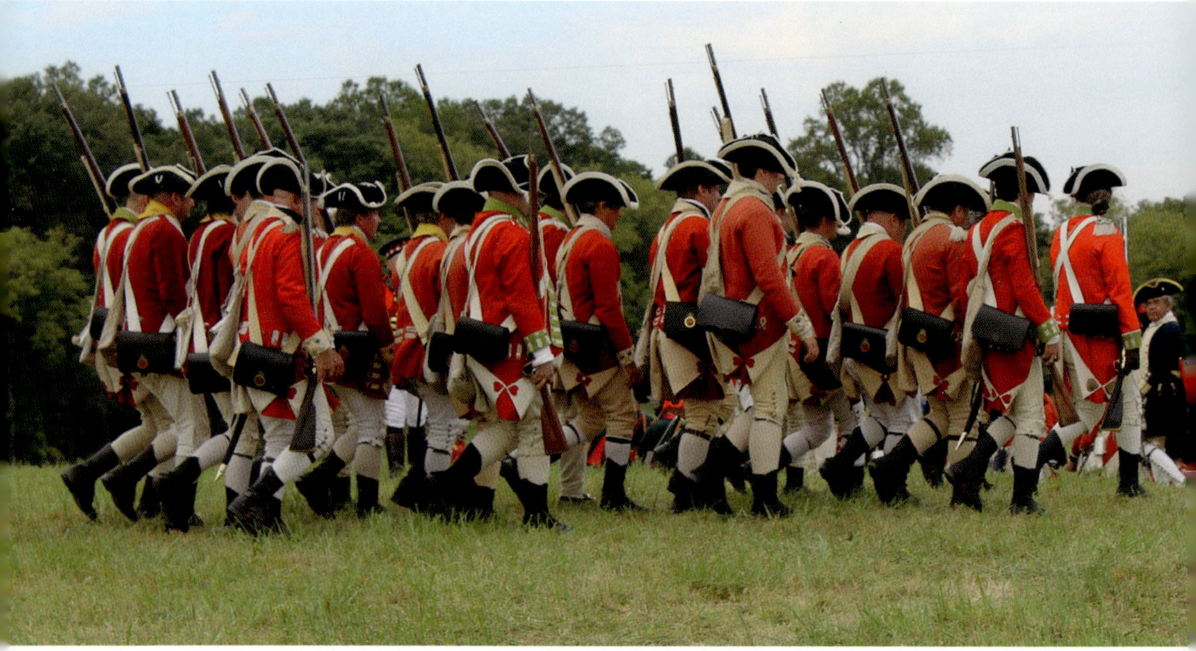

▲ 18th century battle formations were unwieldy for long marches. Both armies used formations such as this for lengthy marches. (Author's collection)

and a small naval militia were of trifling concern when the most important city in North America was essentially undefended. The Schuylkill and Brandywine rivers that stood between the army and the colonial capital would have to be crossed, but they could be forded at numerous locations. Although William Howe was informed that Washington's army was west of the Delaware River, little if any of the Continental Army had yet to arrive in Philadelphia. There was a clear and open path for the British to the American capital.

Despite easy access to Philadelphia, approximately 90 miles by ship, Howe decided to sail south to Chesapeake Bay, where he could put his troops ashore unmolested. The move, he also stressed, would threaten backcountry settlements such as Lancaster and York in Pennsylvania. On July 31, the fleet headed back to sea. Howe later claimed the move farther south benefited John Burgoyne by drawing Washington away from the Hudson River Valley. In reality, the moment William Howe gave the order to steer toward the Chesapeake, he eliminated any possibility of aiding Burgoyne.

By the beginning of August, the British fleet was moving south along the Delaware coast. The move left Washington with a conundrum. Was Howe making for the Hudson River or was his objective one of the port cities farther south? By August 10, Washington shifted the army to the banks of Neshaminy Creek north of Philadelphia and closer to the Delaware River in case he needed to rush back to the Hudson Highlands. There was little more he could do until definitive intelligence arrived confirming the location of Howe's fleet. Washington may well have smiled had he known that British fleet had reached the entrance to the Chesapeake Bay after suffering through terrible storms. Fresh food and water had run out on many transports and horses were dying by the score and being tossed overboard. When news of Howe's location, if not his army's condition, arrived on August 21, Washington scrambled to move the scattered elements of his army into a position to confront Howe south of Philadelphia. Washington started inching towards northern Delaware to block Howe.

Howe was going for Philadelphia and would approach from the southwest. There terrain was cut with several creeks and rivers that would slow, but not stop, Howe's access to the city, including the Red and White Clay Creeks, the Brandywine, and the Schuylkill. Washington was concerned that Howe would march into the American interior and threaten the major American supply depots at Lancaster or Reading. There was no real choice: he would have to advance toward Howe.

British Landing

On August 24, Washington paraded his troops through Philadelphia en route to Delaware. It was time to block Howe's approaches to the capital. The next morning, Washington crossed into Delaware. On the morning of August 25, as Washington deployed outside Wilmington, Delaware, William Howe's army began offloading along the Elk River in northeastern Maryland.

Now that Howe had landed, making a connection with the Delaware River was imperative. Throughout the war the British were in short supply of land transportation. Howe's logistical concerns compounded because many of his horses had died during the voyage. It was vitally important for British armies to operate in the field near navigable rivers so the Royal Navy could resupply them. This operational conundrum affected Howe's decision-making throughout the campaign. Had he landed in northern Delaware at the end of July, he would have had his connection with the Delaware River. Now, Howe was barely back on land and he had no choice but to find and operate along the Delaware River—ignoring his reason he initially provided for delaying the campaign for another month by shifting his army farther south. Howe would never seriously threaten those backcountry settlements.

On August 28, the British advanced from their landing site, brushing aside American militia and plundering the countryside. The initial move overran the commercial trading village at Head of Elk, Maryland. By the end of August Howe was devastating the countryside in northeastern Maryland in search of badly needed supplies, including fresh horses and reinforcements. Contrary to Howe's belief, Loyalists had little interest in flocking to his standard. Howe later claimed that the real reason he could not support Burgoyne's army was the failure to recruit Loyalist support. Excuses for abandoning Burgoyne were growing larger with each telling.

Action at Cooch's Bridge

By the beginning of September, men under William Howe itched for action. They had spent several weeks cooped up on ships and the last several days conducting a fitful and frustrating advance into northeastern Maryland. Howe was as ready as he would ever be to risk a battle. He had been avoiding a pitched confrontation, but the campaign season was rapidly winding down and there was precious little to show for it. Unfortunately for Howe and the British cause in North America, the reports of American victories on the northern front were accurate, and Burgoyne's situation was rapidly deteriorating.

Cooch's Bridge carried the main road to Wilmington across Christiana Creek just east of Iron Hill in northern Delaware. Some of Washington's officers believed Christiana Creek offered a better defensive position than Red Clay Creek, but the only men Washington had there were William

Maxwell's light infantry and some militia. On the east side of the creek was a road system and open terrain. On the west side around the base of Iron Hill were woods that offered excellent terrain for ambushes and skirmishing with the enemy. Lastly, the Christiana was a deeper and better defensive moat than the Red Clay.

When Maxwell moved into the area, his men not only occupied Iron Hill but also extended themselves about a mile south along the road leading to Aiken's Tavern. The terrain was studded with ambush positions. At the intersection of the King's Highway (the road to Wilmington) with the road to Aiken's Tavern, just west of Cooch's Bridge, stood the Cooch grist mill, and on a small rise nearby stood the family home of Thomas Cooch. The family, however, was long gone, having fled to Pennsylvania to escape the dangers of warfare.

Howe would have to deal with Maxwell's outpost in order to reach Washington's main army. He did just that on September 3, pushing 450 jaegers and 1,300 light infantry in a series of flanking movements against 1,000 Americans under William Maxwell. In an effort to outflank the American positions on Iron Hill, the British moved to the south of that position and headed toward Aiken's Tavern. Crossing the Mason–Dixon line (surveyed between 1763 and 1767) into what originally had been the three lower counties of Pennsylvania, the British easily outflanked Maxwell's light infantry.

Hessian Jaeger Capt. Johann Ewald was ordered to take six mounted jaegers and

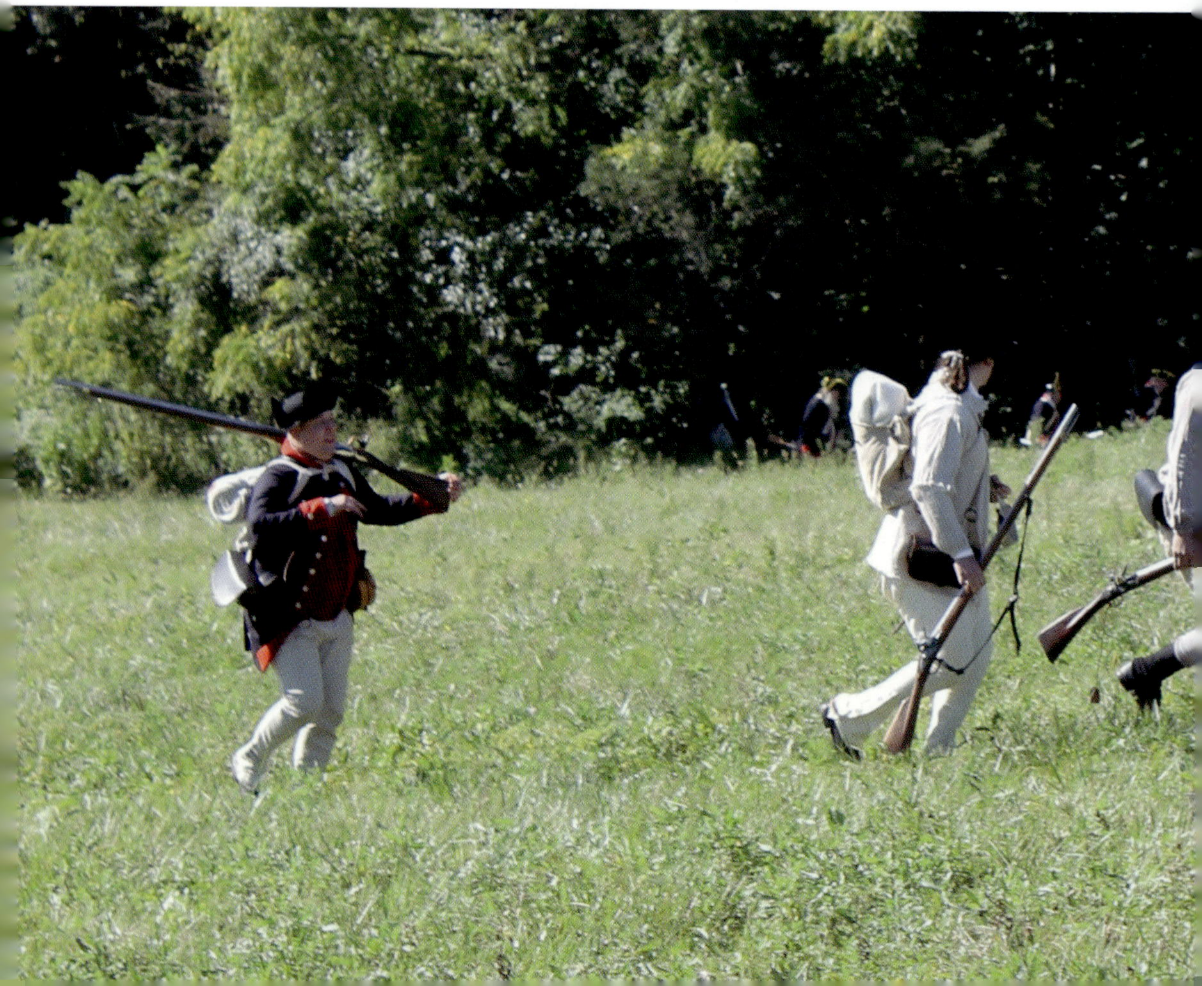

ride north toward Iron Hill to determine whether the Americans had reacted to the British movement. They had not gone far when an American detachment ambushed the seven men. A volley of gunfire rippled from behind a hedge, killing or wounding all six of Ewald's mounted jaegers. Ewald's normally calm horse was wounded in the belly. Ewald called forward the foot jaegers still some distance behind him.

A running two-mile fight developed as some 400 jaegers pushed north toward Cooch's Mill and the bridge spanning Christiana Creek. Foreshadowing what would occur eight days later along the Brandywine, Maxwell, through a series of small ambushes carried out by his novice light infantry, slowed the British advance. Iron Hill towered above the surrounding countryside as the jaegers approached the mill, the high ground studded with Maxwell's Continentals. Alerted to the fighting, Howe rode to the front to observe the unfolding situation. Once he understood what was transpiring, he ordered the jaegers to assault the hill.

The protracted combat included a two-front fight. While some of Maxwell's men were indeed upon Iron Hill, others had run across Cooch's Bridge and were fighting from the opposite side of Christiana Creek. Late in the engagement, Howe pushed forward additional elements to support the exhausted jaegers. The British 1st Light Infantry Battalion attempted to come up on the left flank, but was slowed by swampy ground. The British 2nd Light Infantry Battalion arrived on the jaegers' right, followed by the British grenadiers. It was the arrival of these fresh troops that allowed the jaegers to dash across the bridge and drive the Americans away from Christiana Creek.

The two bodies of troops that faced each other that September day consisted of men who intended to take advantage of cover and pick off their opponents. The result was an unexpected and difficult slog for the Jaegers. The fitful fighting lasted some seven hours before Maxwell's men ran out of ammunition and fled across the bridge and eventually back toward Wilmington, leaving the British in command of the banks of the Christiana River. Despite its length, the combat resulted in fewer than 100 casualties combined for the two armies. The engagement at Cooch's Bridge was not a major affair and had no effect on the outcome of the campaign or the war. However, by brushing aside the Americans, Howe eliminated the threat against the

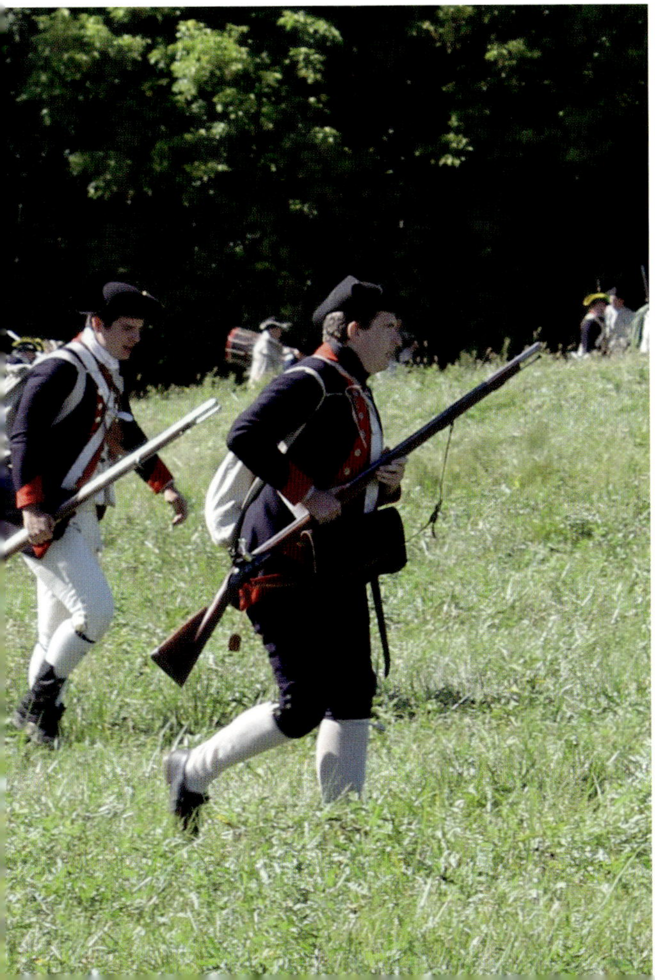

◀ Upon defeat, Washington's army often left a battlefield in scattered groups. (Author's collection)

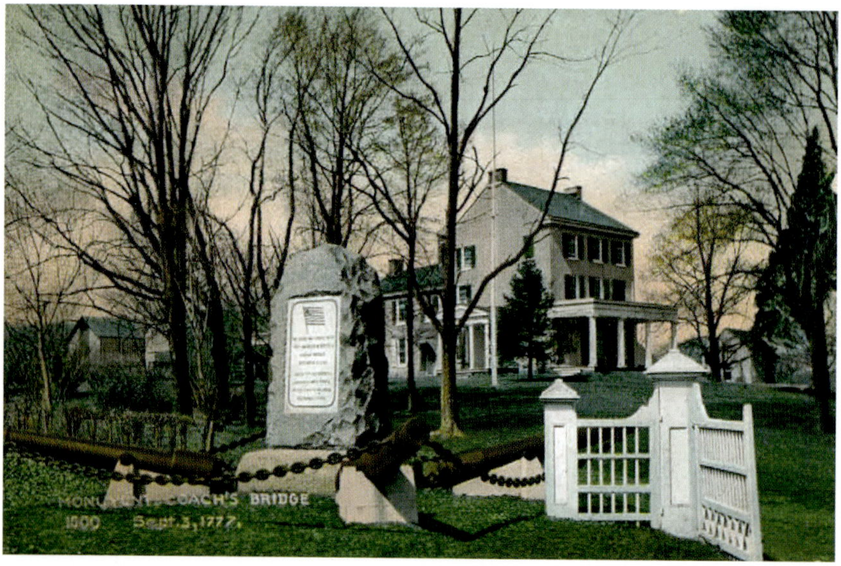

◀ Monument, Cooch's Bridge. (Delaware Public Archives)

new British camp at Aiken's Tavern and cleared Iron Hill of enemy troops. The battle, which carried Howe one step closer to Philadelphia, was the largest land engagement in the history of Delaware. Once he achieved his success, however, Howe settled down for another five days to pillage the countryside. Feeding his army was imperative; providing for it in a hostile land was a constant problem.

Following Cooch's Bridge, Washington convinced himself that Howe would take the main road into Wilmington. He lined his army behind the Red Clay Creek with a defense in depth. Since Howe never resorted to frontal assaults, Washington's thinking is a mystery. At Long Island, White Plains, Short Hills, and Cooch's Bridge, Howe utilized flanking movements to avoid a bloody attack. Given his history, Howe's next move was predictable. On September 8, he resorted to what he did best, and gained the Pennsylvania border ahead of Washington. By late morning, the bulk of Howe's army was camped on the hills around Hockessin, Delaware, well above Washington's right flank.

Outgeneraled yet again, Washington scrambled to get his army in motion and into a blocking position to protect Philadelphia. In the middle of the night, Washington pulled the Continental Army from northern Delaware, marched north, and by the next day began moving into positions on the east side of the Brandywine River near Chads's Ford in Pennsylvania.

Between the evening of September 9 and the morning of September 10, Howe's army moved north parallel to Washington's position and camped about six miles west of the American army at Kennett Square. Washington had spent the long summer months attempting to hinder British movements with militia and other troops while seeking a favorable opportunity to make a stand should one become necessary. The terrain along the Brandywine River provided him with exactly that.

Brandywine

The Battle of Brandywine was the longest and largest single-day engagement of the war. The fighting on September 11, 1777, is also a study of contradictions. Washington hoped a stout defense along the rolling terrain hugging the Brandywine River would bar British access to Philadelphia. His goal was to defend its various crossings and prevent Howe from gaining access to the east bank.

Although Washington had his troops in position east of the Brandywine a full day before the fighting began, he failed to gather all the intelligence needed to execute his defensive battle plan. He intended to use the river to block Howe's advance, yet remained almost completely ignorant of the surrounding terrain and road network and failed to identify and guard all the fords available to the British. There was a lack of reconnaissance patrols. Even more alarming was that no one in a position of authority thought to speak to the many local residents serving in the Continental Army.

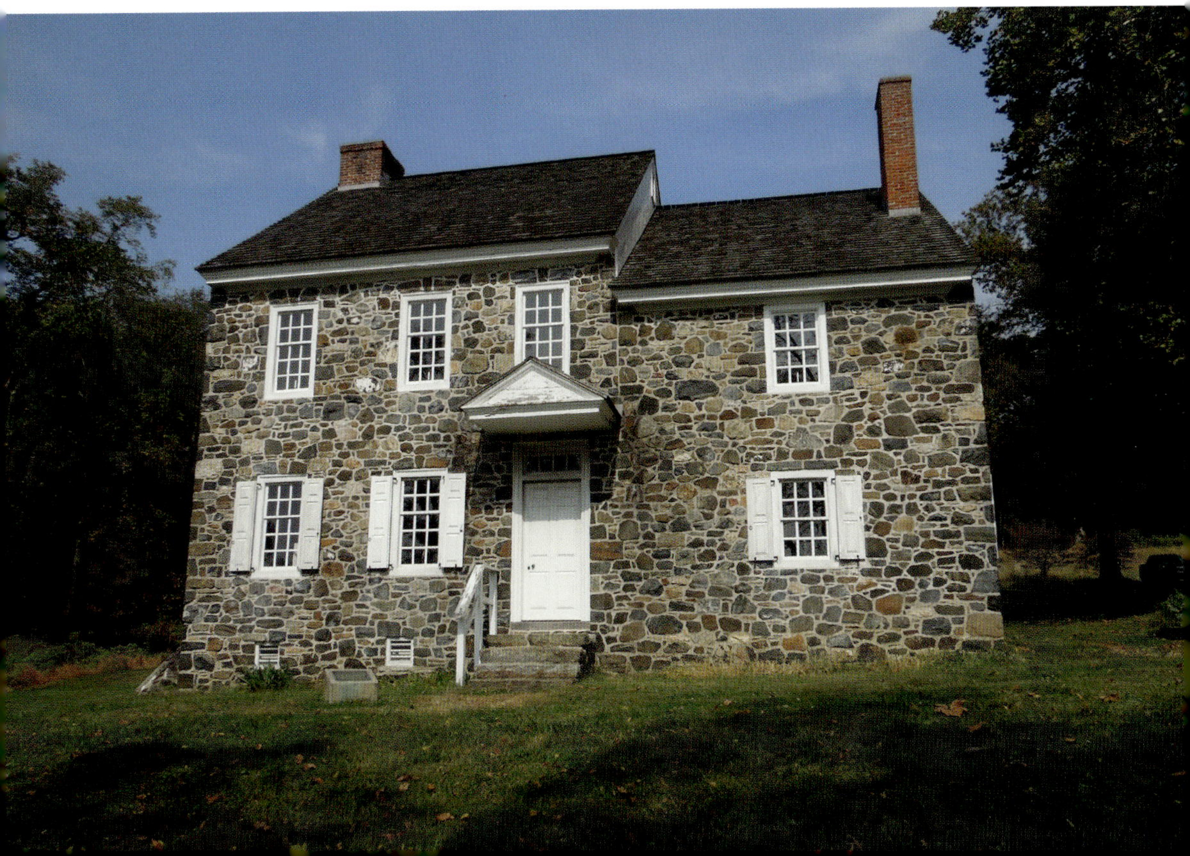

▼ Benjamin Ring House. Today, this structure is located within Brandywine Battlefield State Historic Site. Washington made his headquarters here during the battle. (Author's collection)

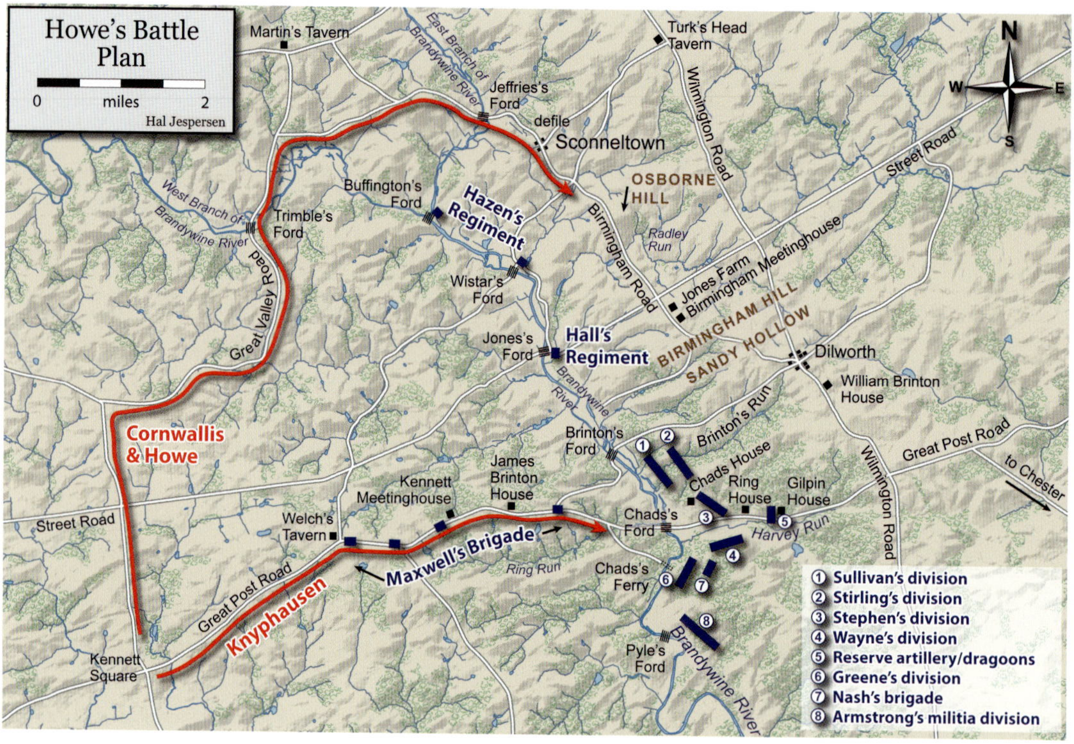

While Washington prepared for battle with little terrain knowledge and even less help from the locals, William Howe made his plans with the advantage of both. Pennsylvania loyalist Joseph Galloway and others provided Howe with everything he needed to know about local terrain conditions and the road network. Washington's position east of the Brandywine limited Howe's options. A frontal assault against the American positions would be too costly and the men hard to replace. Howe, who strove to avoid direct assaults, preferred sending a diversionary force forward against the center of an enemy's main position to pin him in place, and a strong column on a flanking march to turn his enemy out of his position.

Howe had used just this tactic repeatedly and just recently against Washington, but the Virginian had not yet taken the lesson to heart and was consistently unprepared for Howe's predictable maneuverer. Brandywine was merely a repeat of Howe's performance on other fields. He sent Wilhelm von Knyphausen's division ahead to pin Washington in place and executed a wide left hook under the command of General Charles Cornwallis that surprised the Americans by appearing beyond their vulnerable right flank.

At dawn on September 11, William Howe split his army and sent them out two different roads from Kennett Square. Knyphausen's diversionary column marched east on the Great Post Road toward Chads's Ford on the Brandywine and Cornwallis marched north on back roads toward unprotected fords beyond Washington's right flank.

Aware Howe camped in Kennett Square prior to the battle, Washington dispatched a light infantry force and local militia under William Maxwell west of the Brandywine to skirmish with and delay the British

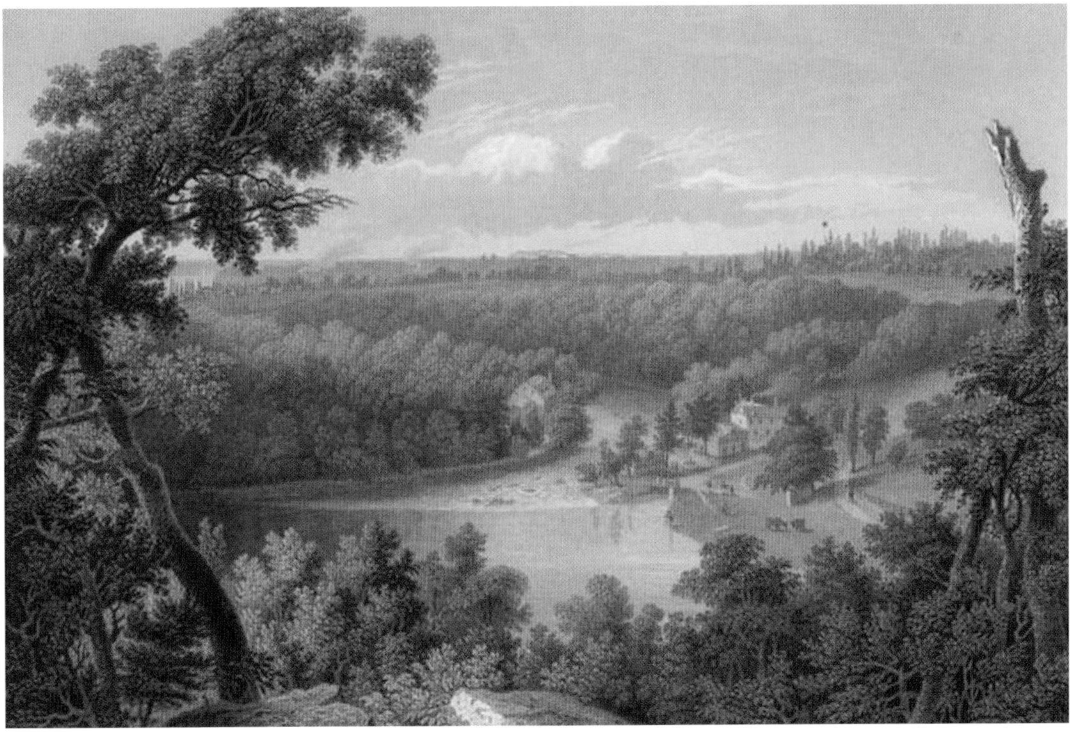

▲ Early print showing the Brandywine Battlefield. (New York Public Library)

approach to Chads's Ford. Knypahusen encountered this force at 6 a.m. resulting in a running fight similar to the fight witnessed on the Concord Road in 1775 as Maxwell conducted a fighting retreat. Most heavily engaged for Knyphausen were the Queen's Rangers and Patrick Ferguson's British riflemen. The Rangers were an American Loyalist unit while Ferguson's men carried a uniquely designed breech

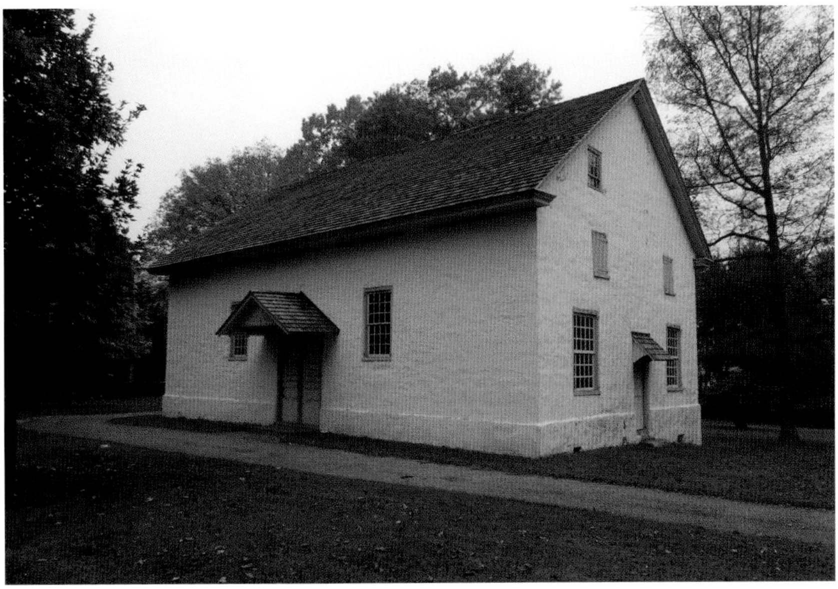

▶ A 2013 view of the Kennett Meetinghouse. In addition to being the site of an American ambush on the morning of September 11, 1777, a Quaker meeting was taking place inside while the fighting opened around it. (Author's collection)

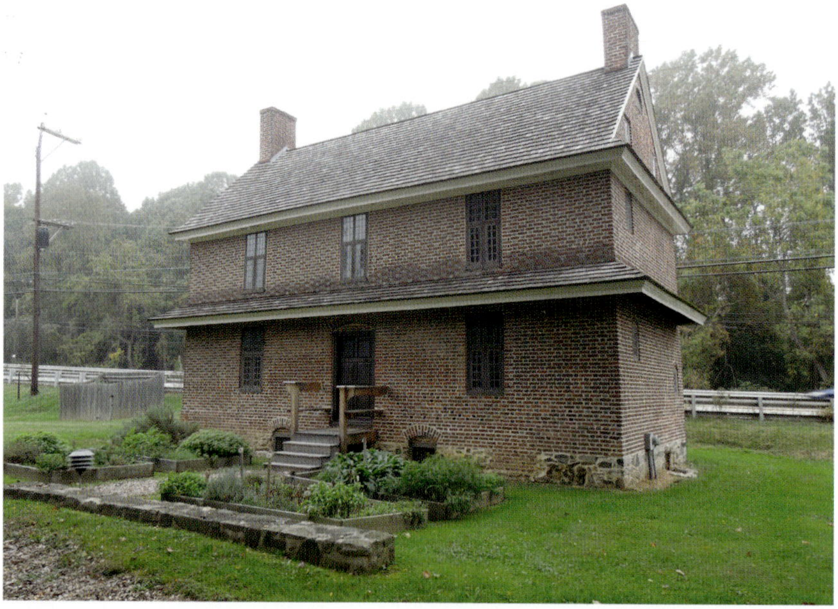

◄ A 2013 view of the James Brinton House along the route of the British advance. At the time of the Brandywine battle the Great Post Road passed by the front side of this home. Today, U.S. Route 1 passes behind the structure. (Author's collection)

▼ A modern view of the John Chads House. An American artillery position was located on the hill to the right rear of the house. Washington came under British artillery fire while in the yard of the house with some of his staff. (Author's collection)

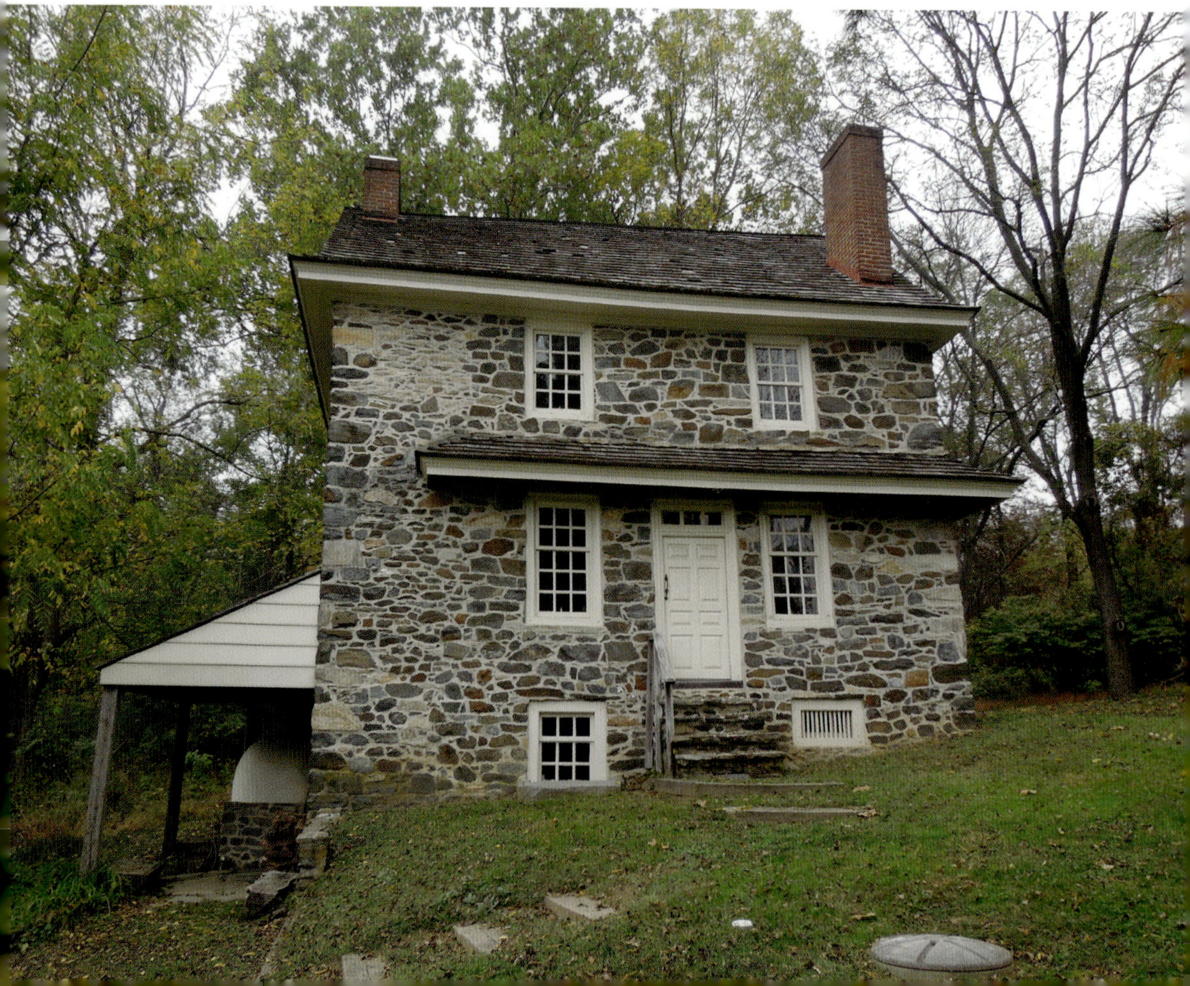

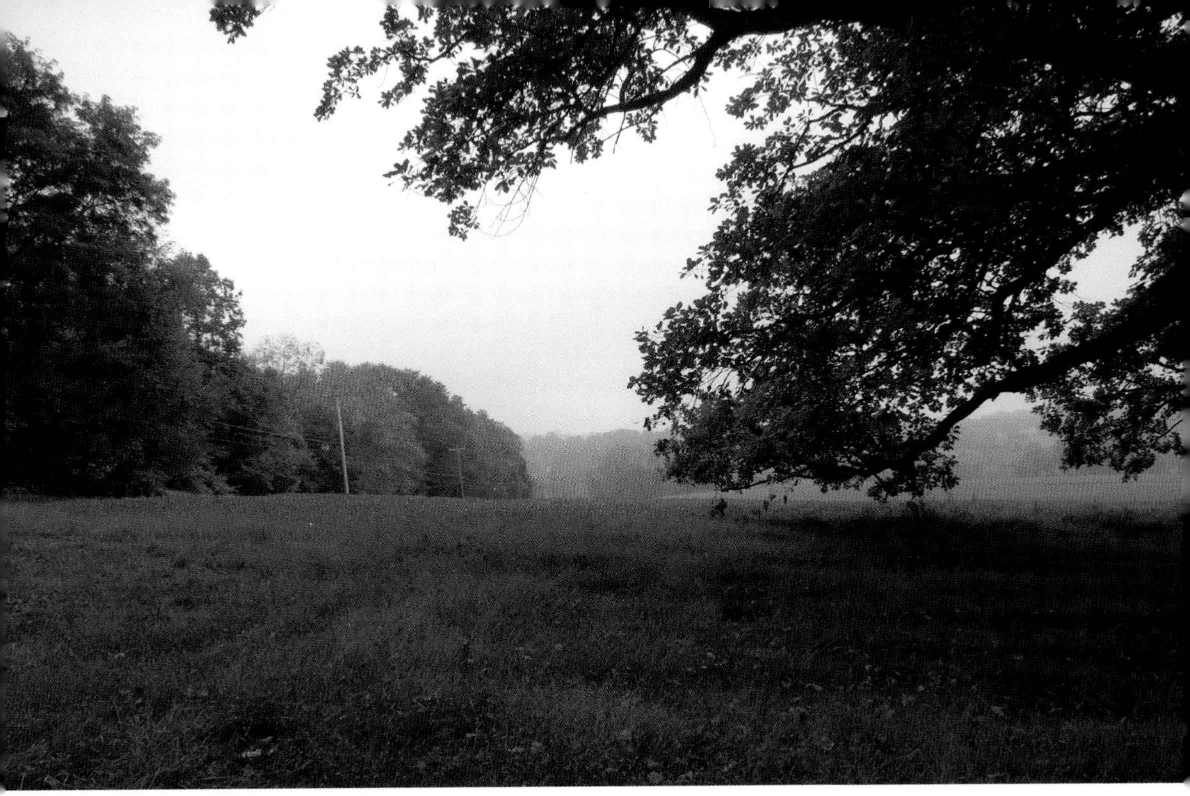

▲ Osborne Hill view. This modern view looks south from the British position on Osborne Hill toward Birmingham Hill, the tree line on the horizon. (Author's collection)

loading rifle. While the loyalists suffered heavy casualties in this fight, Ferguson's men suffered few casualties thanks to the advantage of reloading while lying down. After advancing at a snail's pace over three hours, a final clash just west of Chads's Ford followed, Maxwell withdrew the last of his men across the river granting Knyphausen control of the west bank of the river.

For the next five hours the area around Chads's Ford saw desultory artillery fire and fitful skirmishing as Knyphausen demonstrated hoping to prevent Washington from sending troops to his vulnerable right flank. Meanwhile, Cornwallis continued his lengthy seventeen mile flank march to turn that American flank. Throughout these hours conflicting intelligence reports arrived at Washington's headquarters as he vacillated about what move to make on the military chess board.

At one point, Washington felt he did in fact face less than half the British army at Chads's Ford and ordered an attack across the river to crush Knyphausen and hopefully defeat Howe's army in detail. The risky manoeuvre was just developing with increased intensity in the fighting along the river when fresh intelligence arrived indicating there was no British flank movement occurring. Washington panicked knowing his army was not strong enough to launch a frontal assault against the entire British army and called off the movement at Chads's Ford. Just as the Americans were returning east of the river, yet another intelligence report arrived at Washington's headquarters confirming the British flank movement. More importantly, the head of Cornwallis's column had already penetrated Washington's right rear. The time was nearly 2 p.m.

Washington discovered the move too late to prevent it—a glaring failure of intelligence gathering. To his credit he shifted the bulk of his army to oppose it and conducted a dogged defensive action that cost Howe dearly. Howe's success that day can be evenly credited to his good generalship and Washington's failures.

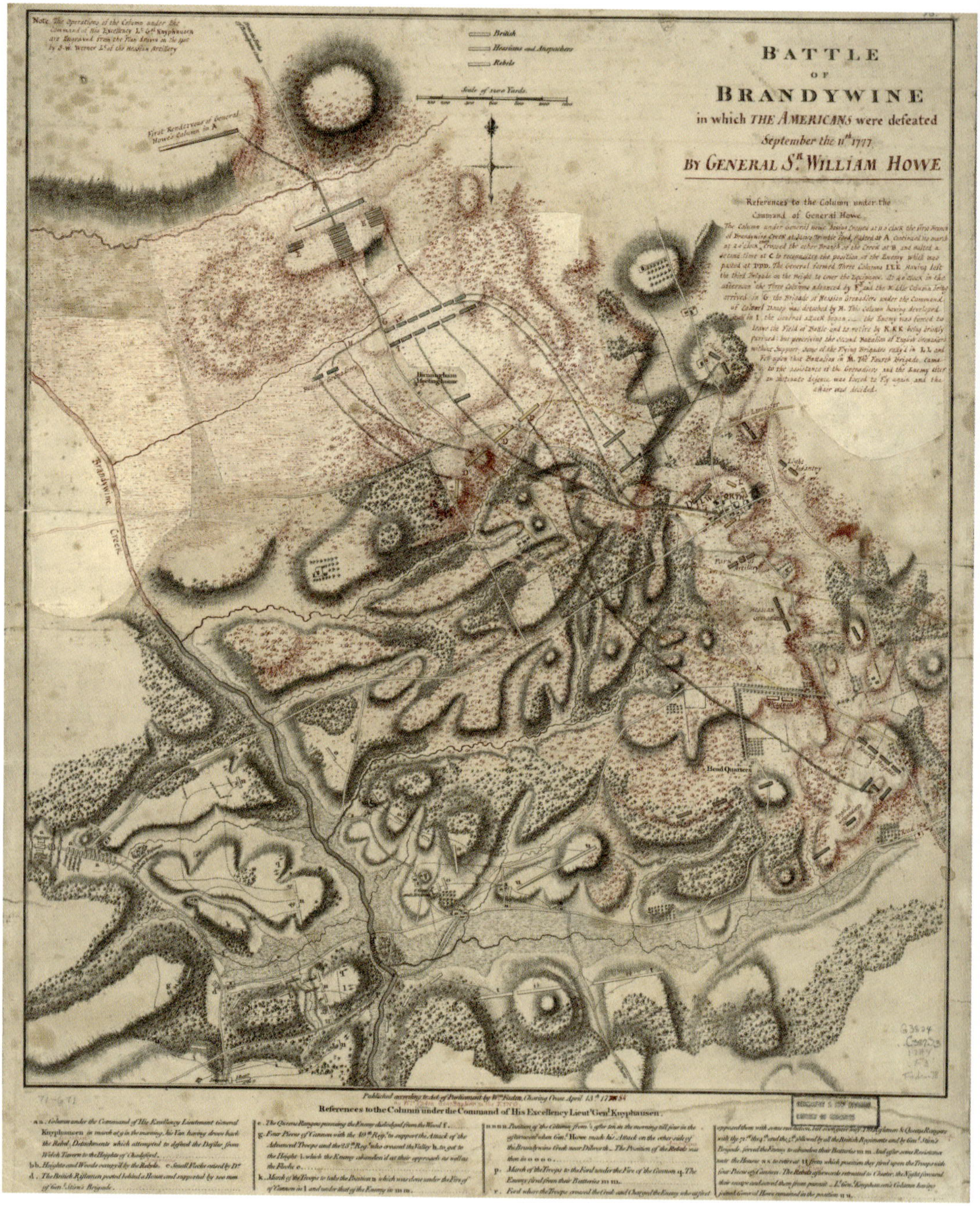

▲ Map of the Battle of Brandywine, 1784. (Library of Congress)

Washington rushed three of his divisions to the north to confront this new threat—John Sullivan's, Lord Stirling's, and Adam Stephen's. These 5,300 troops deployed on Birmingham Hill hoping to block the British from crushing Washington's army. They faced the elite of the British army including British and Hessian grenadiers, British Light Infantry, Hessian jaegers, and the British Brigade of Guards. Nearly 9,000 British and Hessian troops aligned themselves about a mile from the new American position.

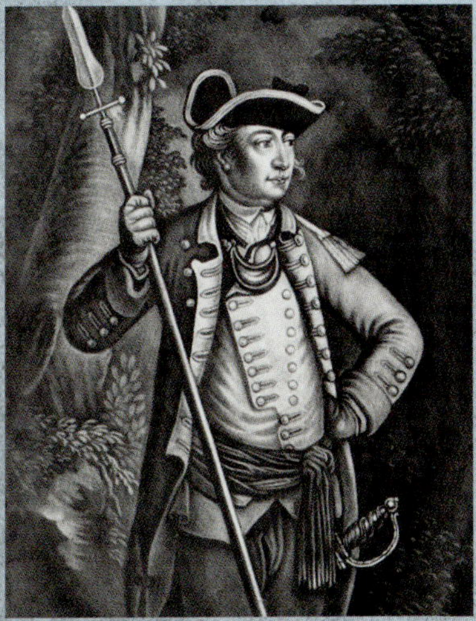

Major General John Sullivan, 1740–1795

John Sullivan studied law and served as a major of militia before the war. In June 1775 he was appointed brigadier general in the army, took part in the Canadian operations, and was promoted to major general in August 1776. The British captured Sullivan during the battle of Long Island, and General Howe used him as a pawn in the contemplated peace negotiation by sending him as an errand boy under parole to speak with Congress. They exchanged Sullivan in September in November 1775. When Gen. Charles Lee was taken prisoner in northern New Jersey, Washington put Sullivan in command of Lee's division and he performed well at Trenton.

(Metropolitan Museum of Art)

▼ A modern view of the cemetery wall at Birmingham Meetinghouse. The 3rd Virginia Regiment defended this position as the British approached from the right side of the photograph. (Author's collection)

By 3:30 p.m. the British launched their attack and despite excellent defensive terrain, the American line was overwhelmed over the next hour. Initially, the center and right of the American line under Stirling and Stephen respectively held as their artillery fire slowed the British advance. However, on the American left, a poor decision while realigning Sullivan's division proved catastrophic as the British Brigade of Guards crushed the American division while in the middle of moving. The elimination of Sullivan's division from the battlefield allowed the British grenadiers to

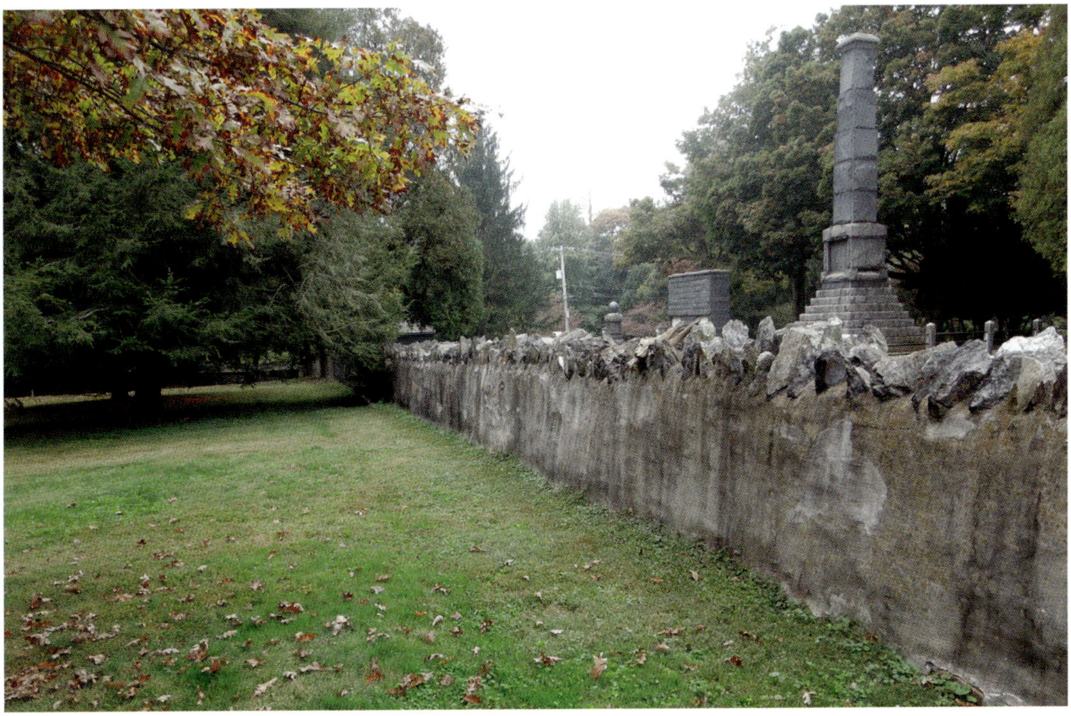

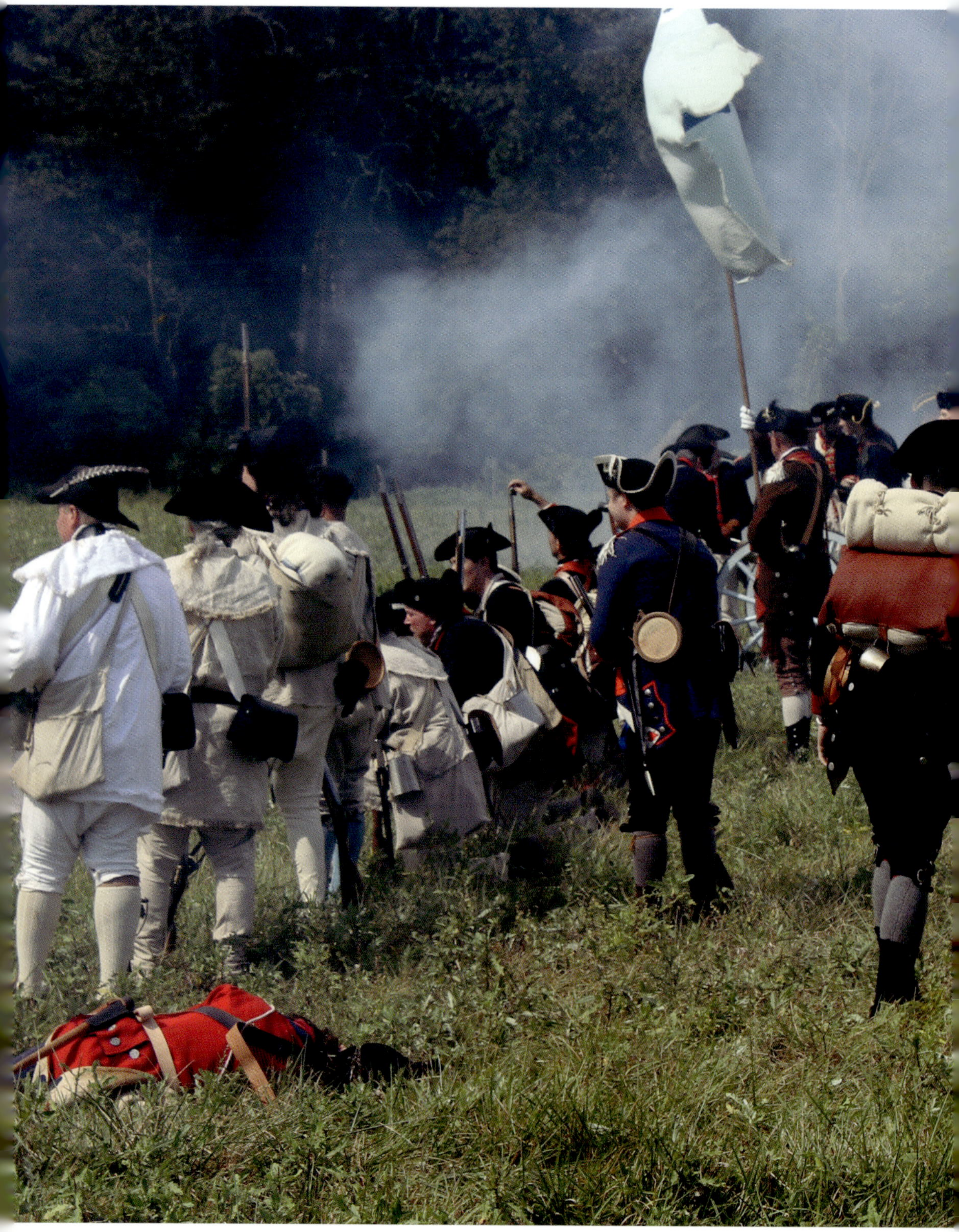

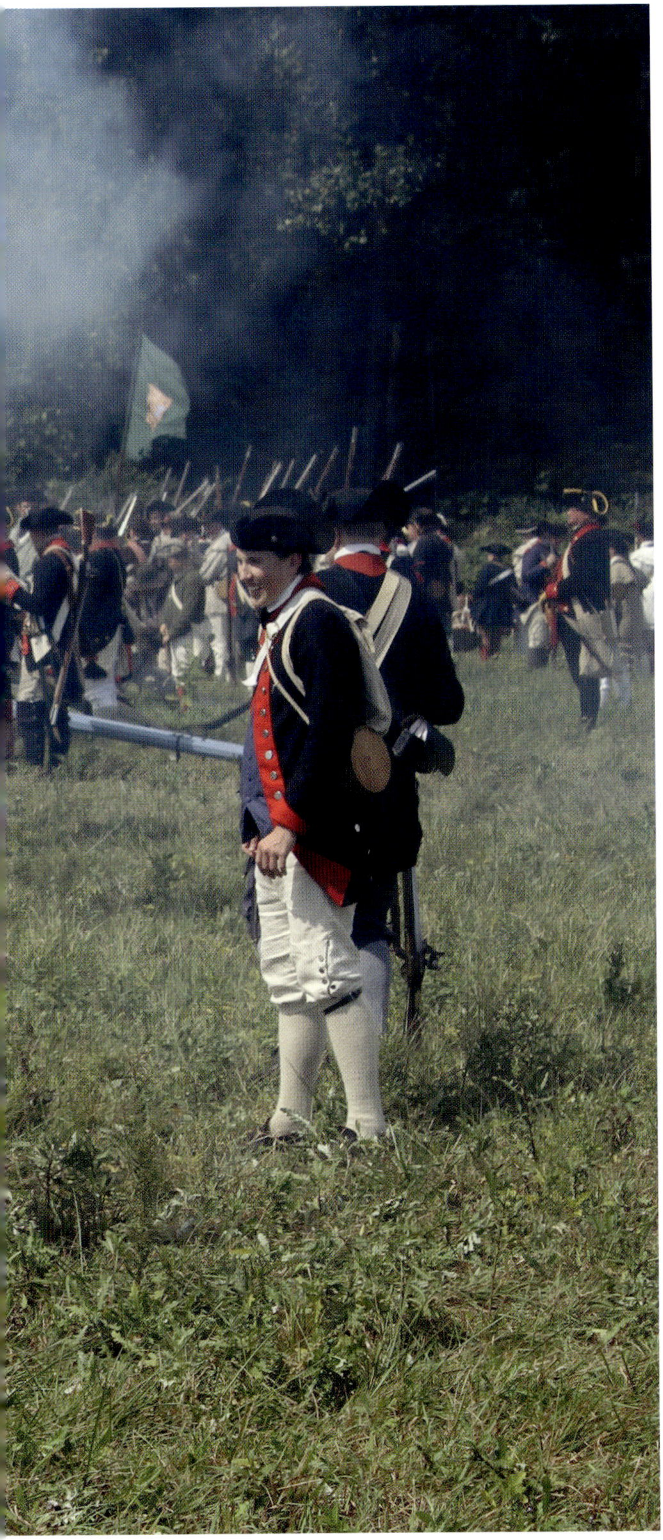

turn the flank of Stirling's division and in turn the British light infantry to turn the flank of Stephen's division. The American line fell like dominoes. At one point in the fighting, the Marquis de Lafayette arrived on the scene hoping to sturdy the wavering American line. Lafayette, a major general holding no command at Brandywine, hoped he could help but received a severe leg wound removing him from the war effort over the next two months.

With the American line broken on Birmingham Hill, the remnants of the three American divisions now fled across farm fields to their south with the British in pursuit. John Sullivan managed to patch together a force for a rear guard and conducted a fighting retreat with the assistance of two artillery pieces commanded by Henry Knox. Meanwhile, realizing the threat to his right flank, Washington ordered Nathanael Greene to rush his division from Chads's Ford to that front. Greene arrived about 5 p.m. about a mile south of Birmingham Hill on the reverse slope of another ridge. Sullivan managed to rally a number of units around Greene's fresh division forming a formidable front to guard the avenue of retreat. As the new American front was hidden from British view and with the sun setting, the pursuing British troops crossed the ridge line into a large ambush that devastated a battalion of British grenadiers and the 4th British Brigade. Greene's evening action allowed the survivors of Cornwallis's attack to retreat safely.

Meanwhile, hearing the sounds of battle to the northeast, Knyphausen launched his own attack across Chads's Ford. Because Washington pulled four divisions away from Chads's Ford to confront Cornwallis, Knyphausen's 6,800 men

◀ Americans fighting in a compact formation. (Author's collection)

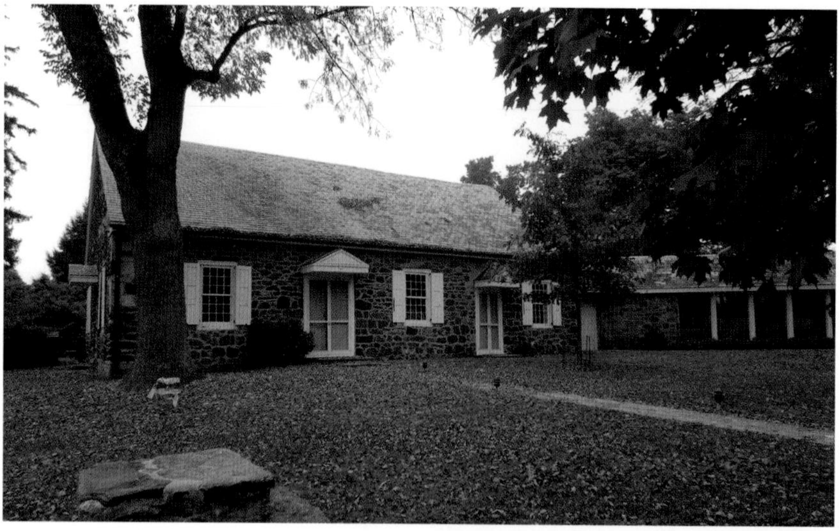

◄ A modern view of the Birmingham Meetinghouse. The cemetery with its surrounding wall sits to the left rear of the building, which was used as a hospital in the bloody battle's aftermath. (Author's collection)

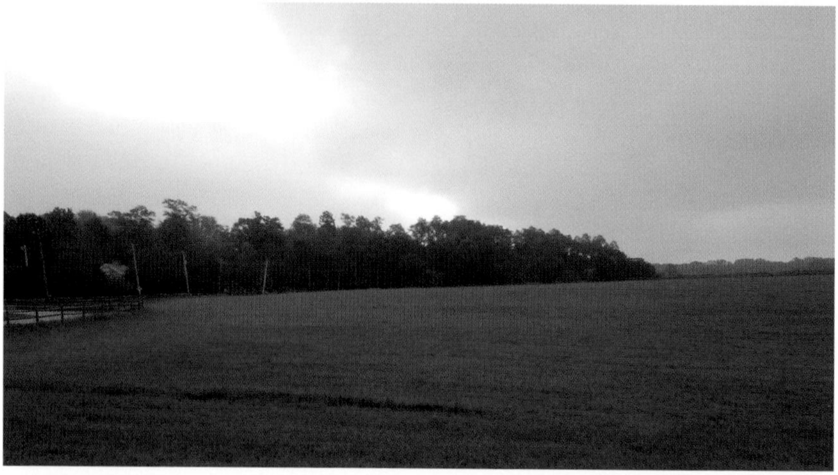

◄ This modern view looks south through the eyes of the British advance toward the American line on Birmingham Hill. Lord Stirling's Continental division was in position where the modern fence line visible in the distance stands today. (Author's collection)

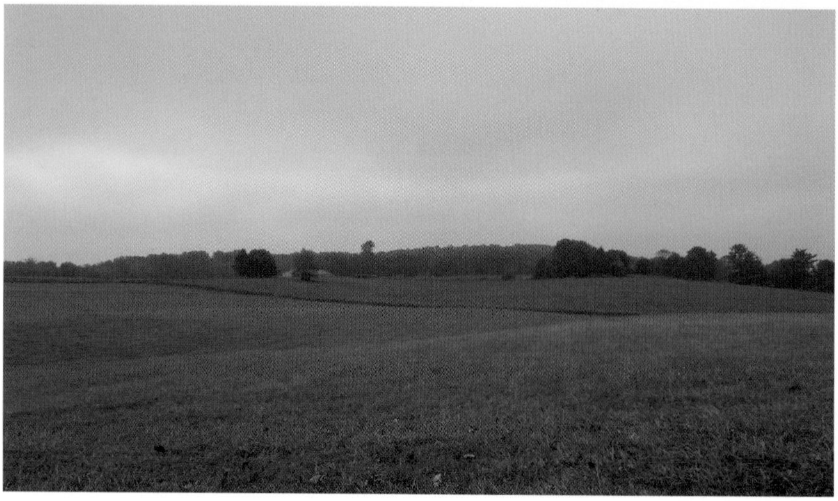

◄ This modern view looks west across the northern slope of Birmingham Hill. The British grenadiers advanced from the right side of this image and advanced across the rolling terrain toward Birmingham Hill off to the left. (Author's collection)

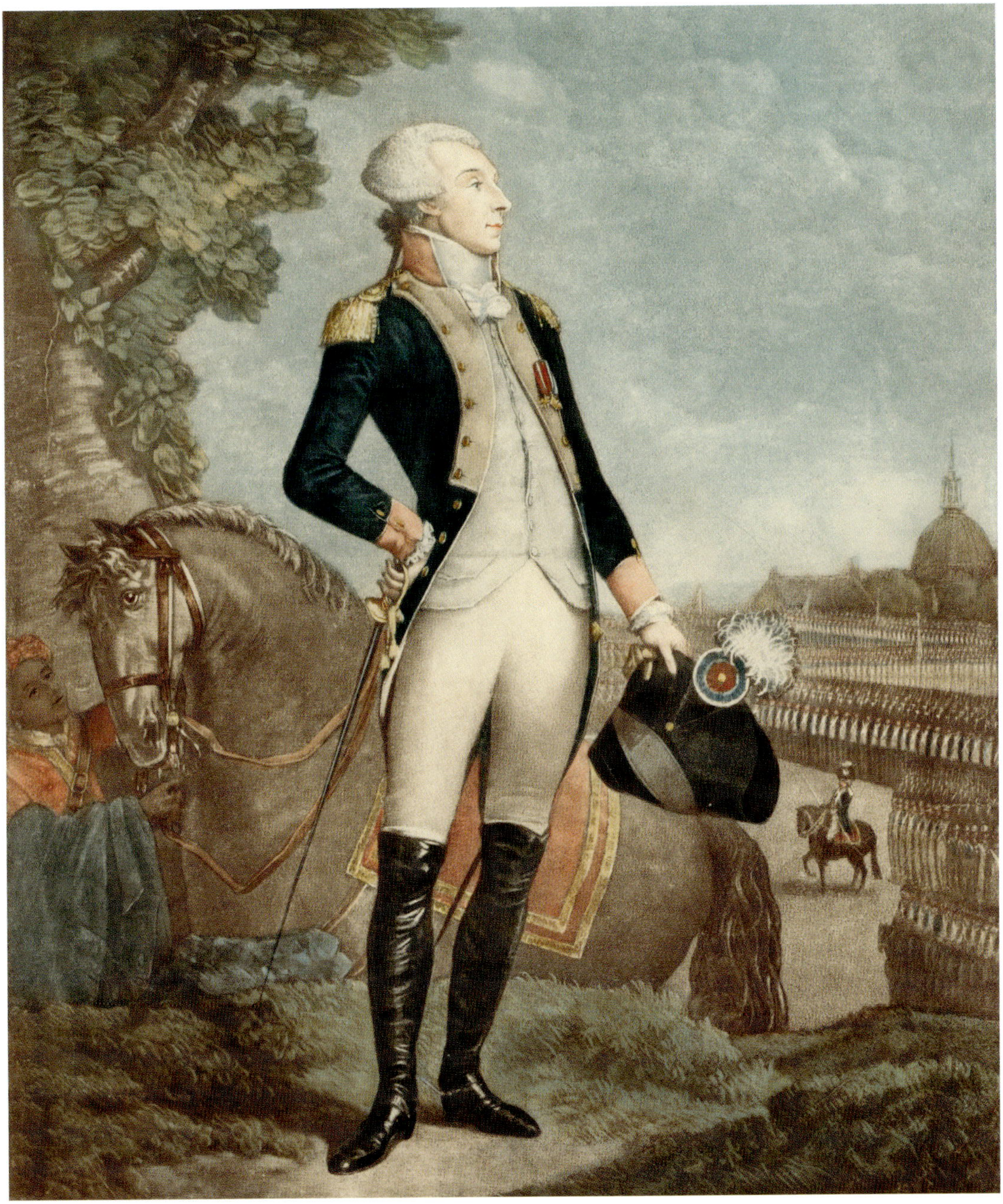

▲ Although baptized Marie Joseph Paul Yves Roch Gilbert du Motier, and hereditarily Marquis du Lafayette, Baron de Vissac, and Seigneur de St. Romain, he was better known as simply, the Marquis de Lafayette. At 16, he entered a pre-arranged marriage with the 14-year-old Marie Adrienne Francoise de Noalles, a member of one of the most powerful families in France, and became a member of the Free Masons. Lafayette became a captain in the Noailles Dragoons in 1775, and later that same year his wife bore him Henriette, their first child. Fascinated by the upheaval on the other side of the Atlantic, on December 7, 1776, Lafayette signed an agreement with Silas Deane, the American army commissioner in Paris, to serve as a major general in the Continental Army. The next year, Lafayette bought his own ship and sailed for America, accompanied by Baron Johann de Kalb and a dozen other French officers. (National Portrait Gallery)

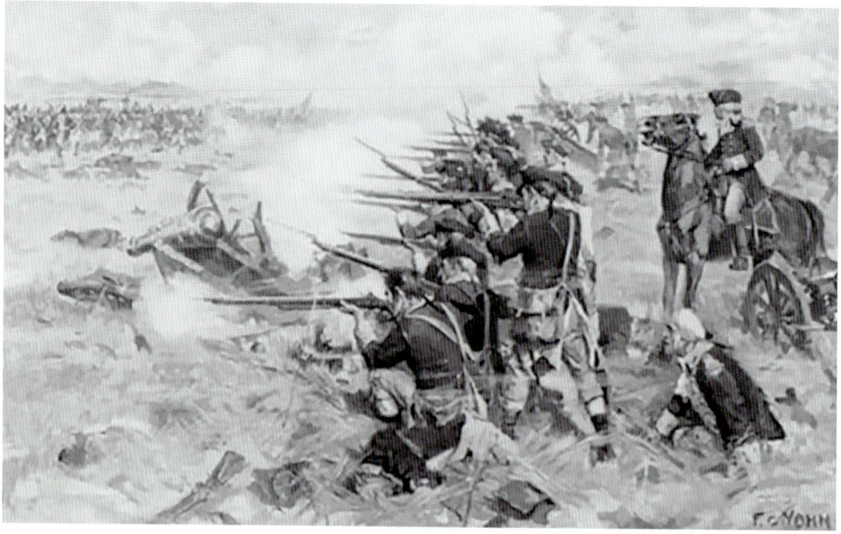

◄ 1898 Depiction of the Battle of Brandywine, by F. C. Yohn, 1898. (Library of Congress)

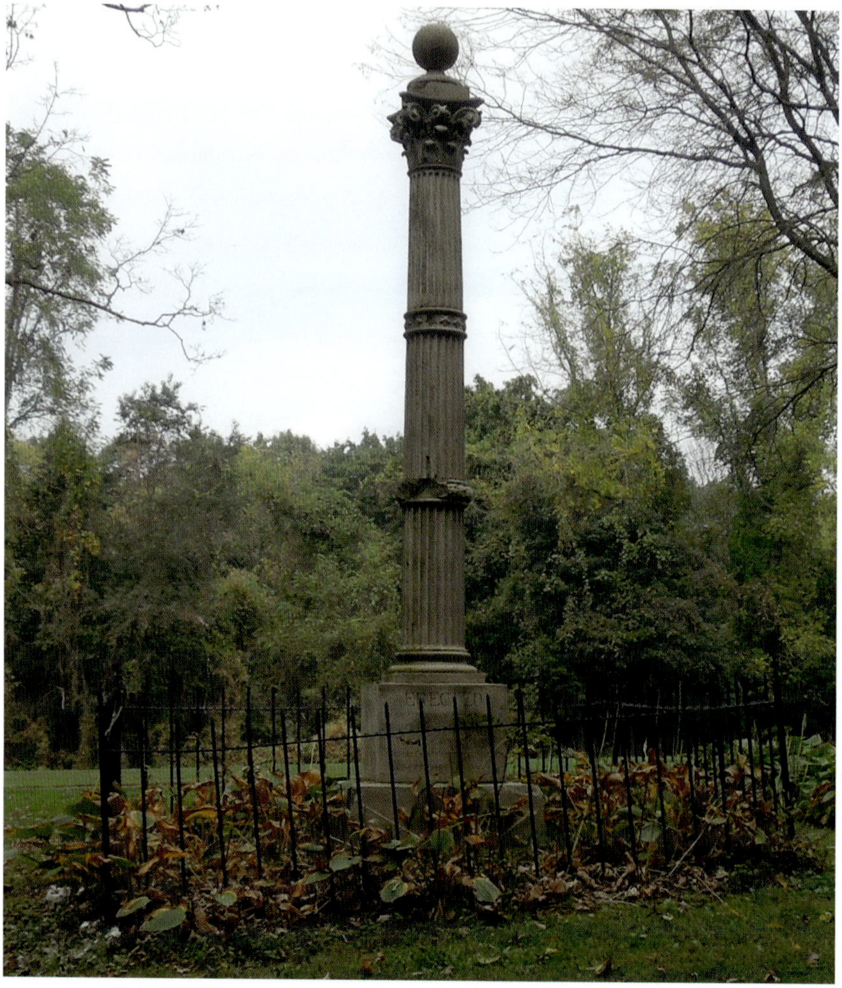

◄ This modern view depicts the Lafayette memorial shaft that was erected in 1895 on the crest of Birmingham Hill. The monument was intended to mark the location of Lafayette's wounding. Given our understanding of the battle today, however, the shaft is almost certainly in the wrong location. (Author's collection)

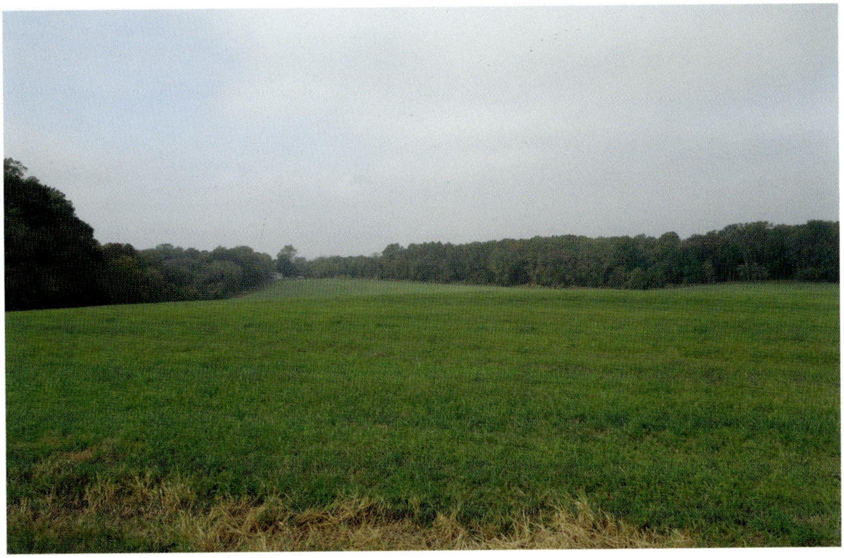

▶ This modern view looks north from Adam Stephen's position on the edge of Sandy Hollow. The British light infantry and Hessian jaegers assaulted from the tree line visible in the distance. (Author's collection)

only faced Anthony Wayne's division and Maxwell's troops that fought all morning—perhaps 3,000 men. Heavily outnumbered, Knyphausen easily pushed back Wayne and Maxwell. Thanks to gathering darkness, Wayne managed to conduct a fighting retreat keeping the avenue of retreat open for the army just as Greene had done.

Although the Continental Army had suffered a tactical defeat along the Brandywine, Washington's men fought remarkably well. The result was some 1,300 casualties, with 300 killed, 600 wounded, and 400 missing or captured. British losses approached 600, with 93 killed and nearly 500 wounded. Fortunately for the

Major General Nathanael Greene, 1742–86

Nathanael Greene was not a healthy man. He was born in 1742 into a Rhode Island Quaker family and suffered a childhood accident that left him with a life-long limp. He also suffered from asthma and endured a painful spot in his right eye from a smallpox inoculation. None of these issues slowed him down. Greene sold toys to earn money to buy books and was the owner of an iron fabrication business before the war. After serving with a Rhode Island militia company, he was commissioned a brigadier general in 1775 and given command of all of the state's troops. His first field test was the successful defensive action at Harlem Heights in September 1776, one of the few bright spots of the New York Campaign. Greene offered bad advice and was responsible for the disaster at Fort Washington, but redeemed himself by leading a wing of the army well at both Trenton and Princeton.

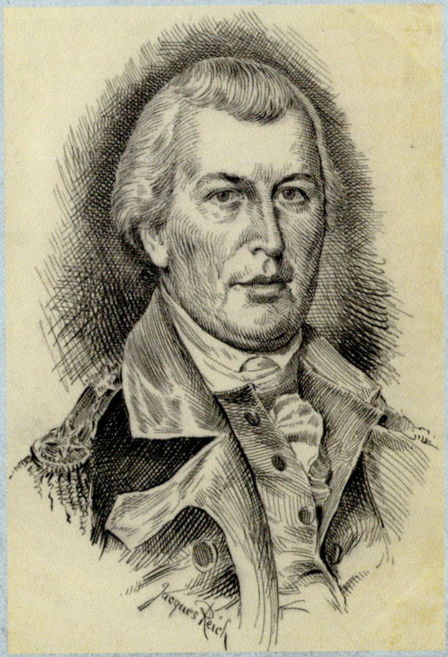

(National Portrait Gallery)

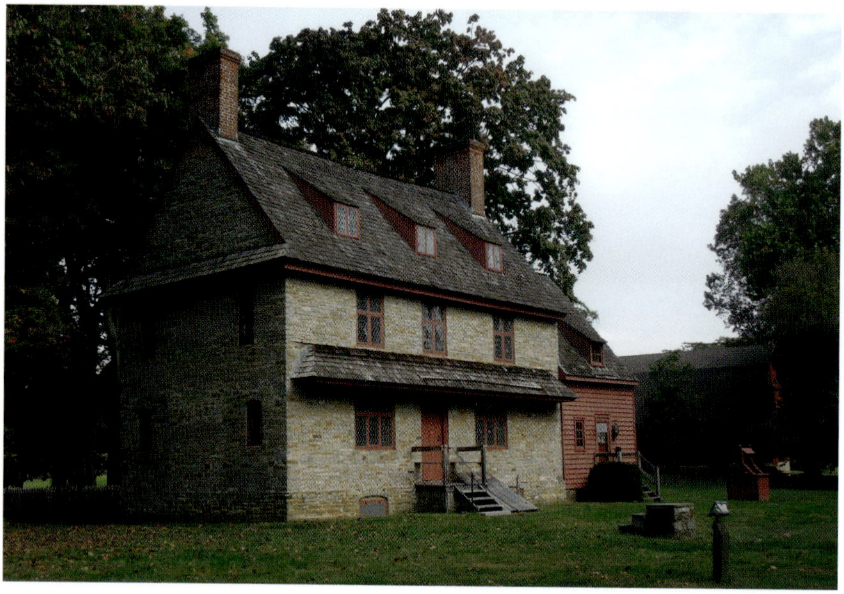

◀ A modern view of the 1704 William Brinton House. General Washington rode into the yard of this house with several members of his staff at a critical moment during the early evening fighting on the northern portion of the battlefield. (Author's collection)

Americans Howe was hampered by a lack of mounted troops, which prevented him from pursuing his defeated enemy.

Washington's retreat from the battlefield did not end the fighting for the city of Philadelphia, but the battle along the Brandywine would prove to be the major engagement of the 1777 Philadelphia Campaign. What did the fighting and bloodshed waged in the rolling hills of the

▼ This modern view looks north across the fields towards Dilworth. The British lines advanced across these fields toward Greene's hidden position. (Author's collection)

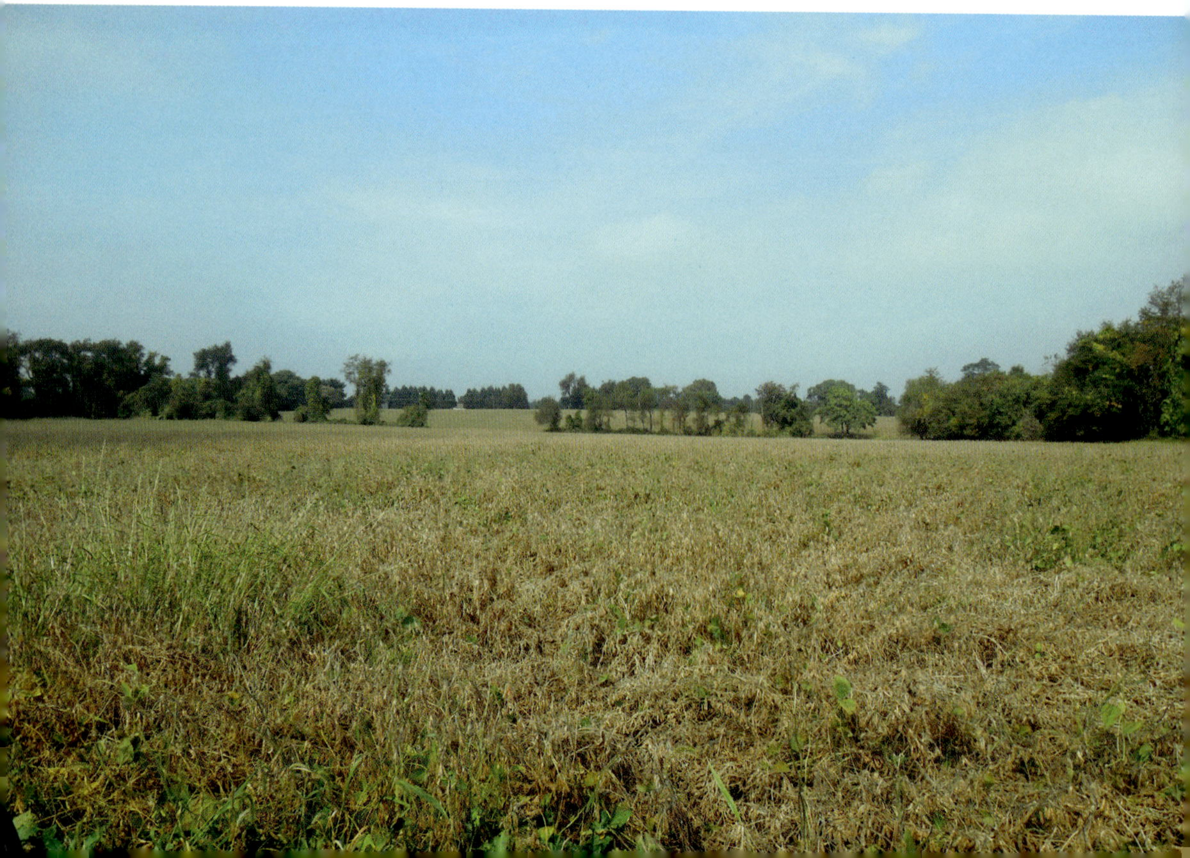

Brigadier General Anthony Wayne, 1745–96

The bombastic Anthony Wayne became a colonel of the 4th Pennsylvania Battalion, which he commanded at Fort Washington during the New York-area campaign of 1776. Wayne took part in the Canadian expedition and was put in command of Fort Ticonderoga in upper New York. In February 1777, he was promoted to brigadier general while commanding a portion of the Pennsylvania Line at Fort Ticonderoga before joining the army at Morristown. Wayne was placed in command of the First Pennsylvania Brigade of Benjamin Lincoln's division. When Lincoln was detached to serve under Horatio Gates during the Saratoga campaign, the 32-year-old Wayne took over temporary command of the division.

Anthony Wayne (National Portrait Gallery)

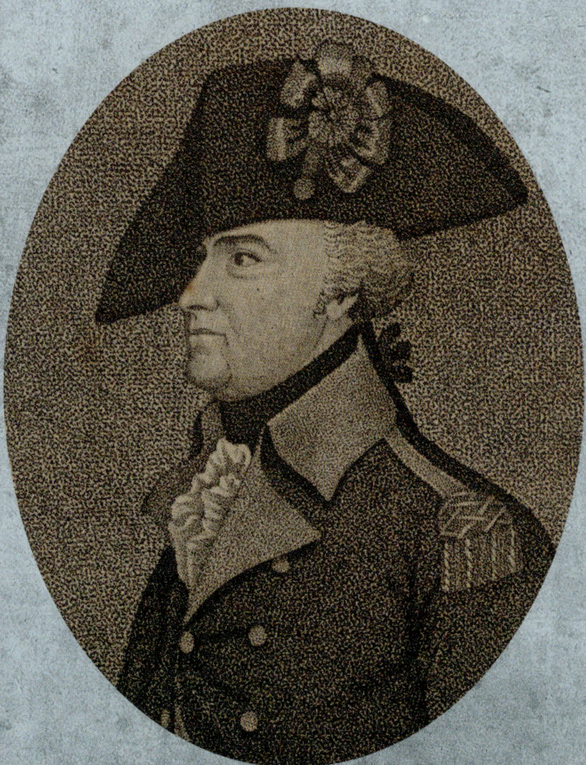

Brandywine River valley mean to the cause of American independence? The men who participated in the battle and those who simply lived during that time left a variety of opinions in the immediate aftermath of the fighting.

Despite losing the battle, many American officers remained optimistic. "Notwithstanding we gave the Enemy the ground," wrote Gen. Nathanael Greene, "the purchase has been at much blood, this being by far the greatest loss they have met with since the commencement of the War. From the circumstances and from several accounts of people that has seen the field of action," Greene continued, "there must have been a terrible carnage among his [Howe's] troops. I expect the next action to ruin Mr. How totally." General Weedon agreed with Greene's assessment when he penned, "Such another victory would establish the Rights of America and I wish them the honor of the Field again on the same terms." "Our people behaved well," Henry Knox wrote to his wife, "but Heaven frowned upon us in a degree. We were obliged to retire after a very considerable slaughter of the enemy; they dared not pursue a single step."

While a number of officers remained hopeful that overall strategic conditions would improve, several realized that tactical mistakes had been made on the 11th of September. Washington knew almost immediately what had gone wrong. "Unfortunately the intelligence received of the enemy's advancing up the Brandywine, and crossing at a ford about six miles above us, was uncertain and contradictory," he wrote John Hancock, "notwithstanding all my pains to get the best." Perhaps Col. Aaron Ogden of the New Jersey Line offered the best summation of the general understanding of how the September 11 combat evolved as it did: "This battle, in all probability was lost and won by th[e] contrary intelligence."

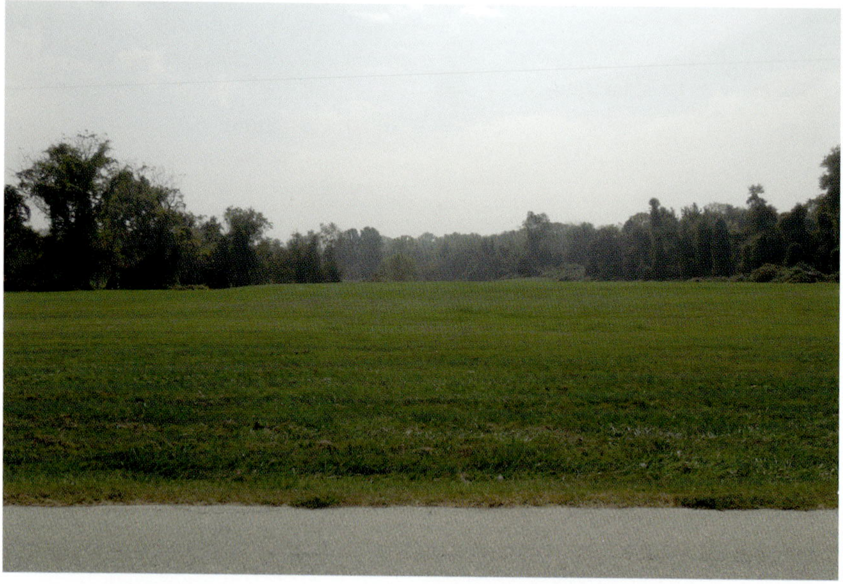

◄ This modern view looks toward Nathanael Greene's American line. The British advanced south across these fields toward the distant tree line. (Author's collection)

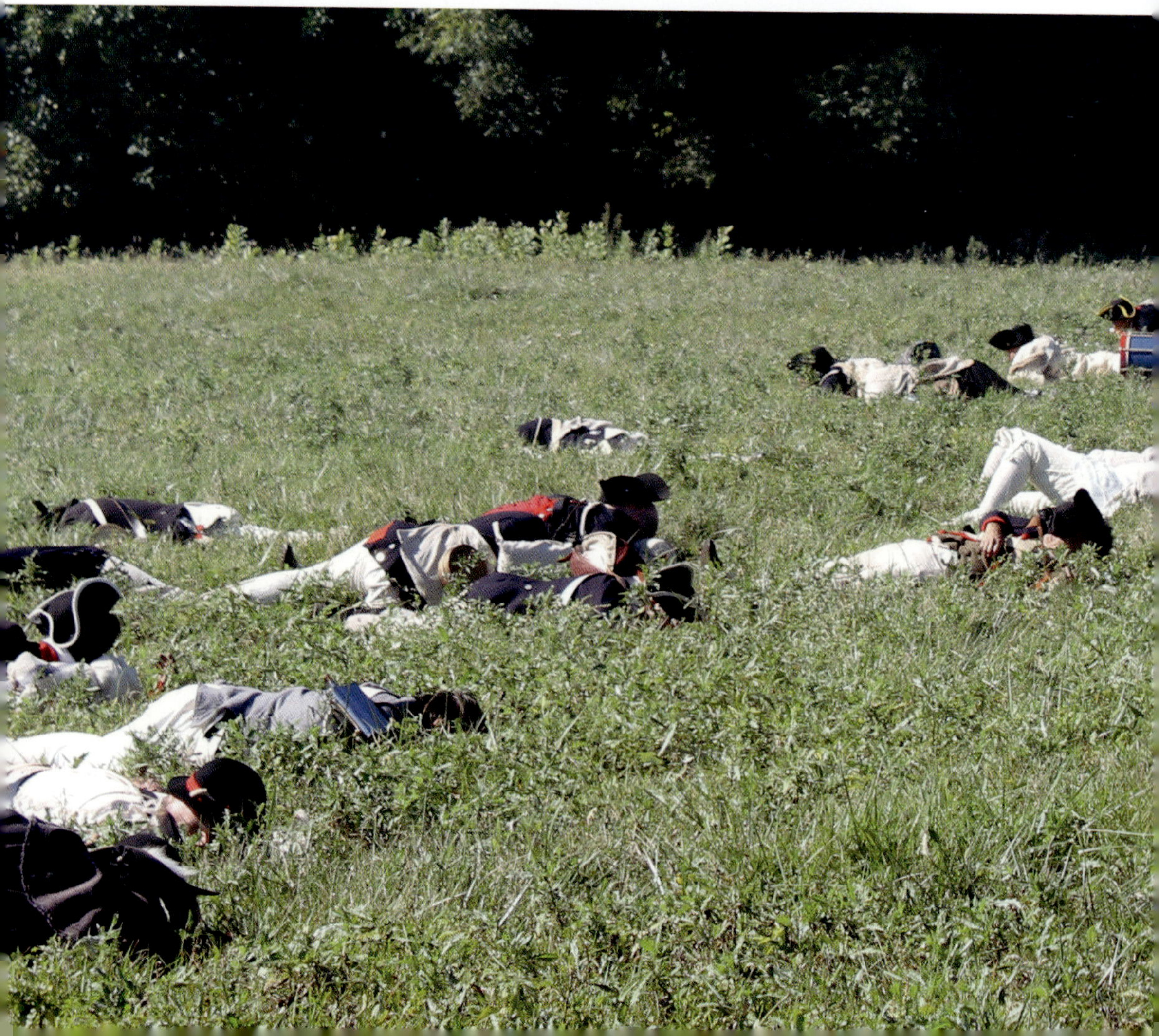

As the months and years slipped past, others waded into the controversy and passed judgment on Washington's military abilities. "Certainly no General ever planned his battles more judiciously," wrote Thomas Jefferson not long before his own death but many years after Washington had died. "But if deranged during the course of the action, if any member of his plan was dislocated by sudden circumstances, he was slow in readjustment. The consequence was that he often failed in the field."

Many British and Hessian officers expressed praise for the Continental effort and Washington's management of the battle. William Howe's aide, Capt. von Muenchhausen, praised the American effort: "As far as I can tell, Washington executed a masterpiece of strategy today by sending columns from his right to his left wing in the beginning... Soon after this Washington withdrew from his left wing... All this was done with great speed and especially good order."

Regardless of their impressions of the Continental Army and Washington, many British officers were impressed with Howe's strategy that day. Von Muenchhausen had nothing but praise for his commanding officer: "We all admire the strong and unexpected march of General Howe, and the special bravery, which the English showed in the battle, and I am convinced that everyone in Europe would admire General

▼ Following the battle, American dead and wounded left behind had to be handled by the British army. (Author's collection)

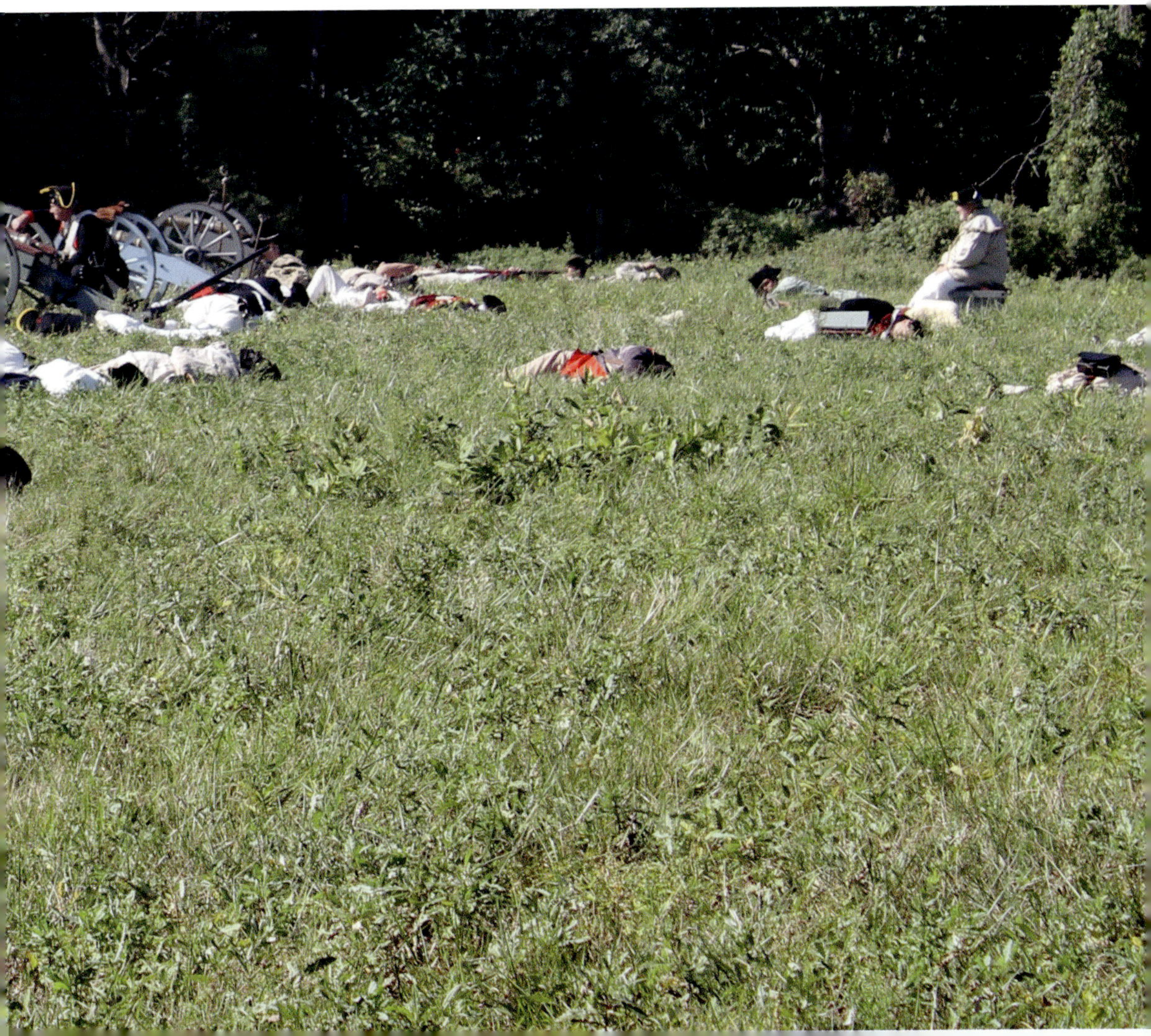

Howe if they were as familiar with all of the obstacles he faces, as we are." However, some British officers believed Howe let an opportunity slip through his grasp. "Had General Howe set out two hours earlier, or marched faster," asserted Hessian officer Capt. Johann Ewald, "Washington's army would have been caught between two fires." Ewald continued: "[S]everal good friends from headquarters assured me that this mistake was caused by the guides, who had declared the route shorter than we found it to be." British officer George Duke agreed with Ewald that the long march earlier in the day prevented a proper pursuit. "We only wanted a few more hours of daylight; if we had, it's the general opinion the rebellion must have been over, for they were all dispersed, some run one way and some another."

Everyone agrees Washington suffered a tactical defeat along the Brandywine. Despite having been defeated and outmaneuvered by Howe at least five times prior to September 1777 (Long Island, White Plains, Short Hills, Cooch's Bridge, and along Red Clay Creek), Washington was somehow unprepared for its use at the Brandywine. Howe's tactical success was more the result of Washington's failure to learn from his mistakes than his brilliance. The young Continental Army that would mature that winter at Valley Forge fought remarkably well. Maxwell's newly formed light infantry brigade conducted the difficult delaying action during the morning as Washington requested. The three divisions that shifted to the right flank (Stephen, Lord Stirling, and Sullivan) quickly found good defensive ground

▼ A modern view of the memorial stone to the battle dead buried at Birmingham Meetinghouse. (Author's collection)

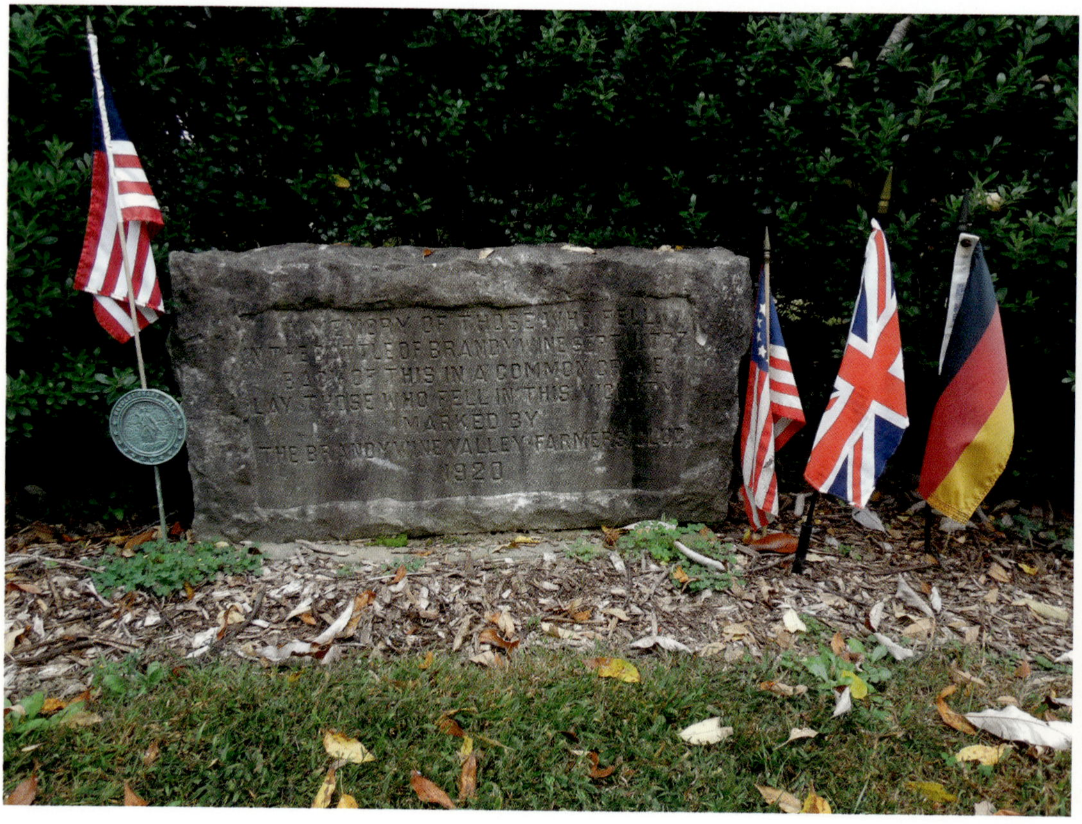

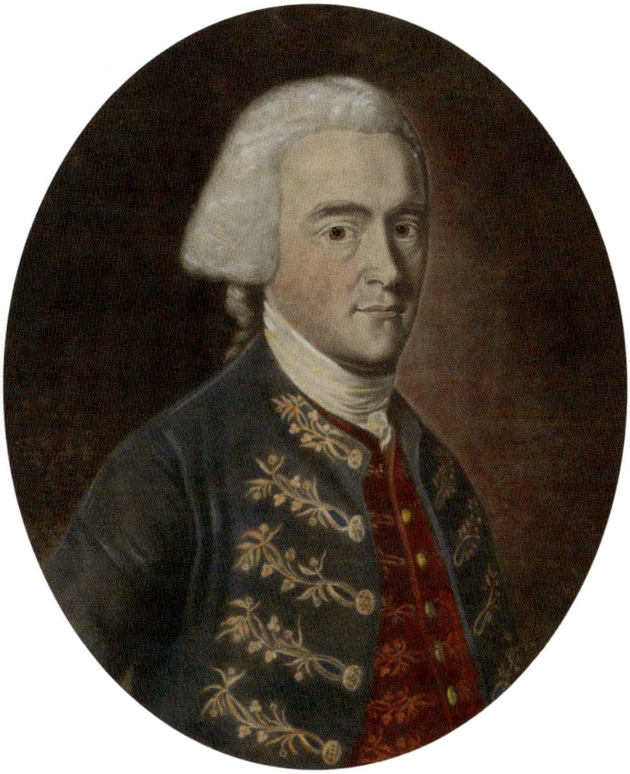

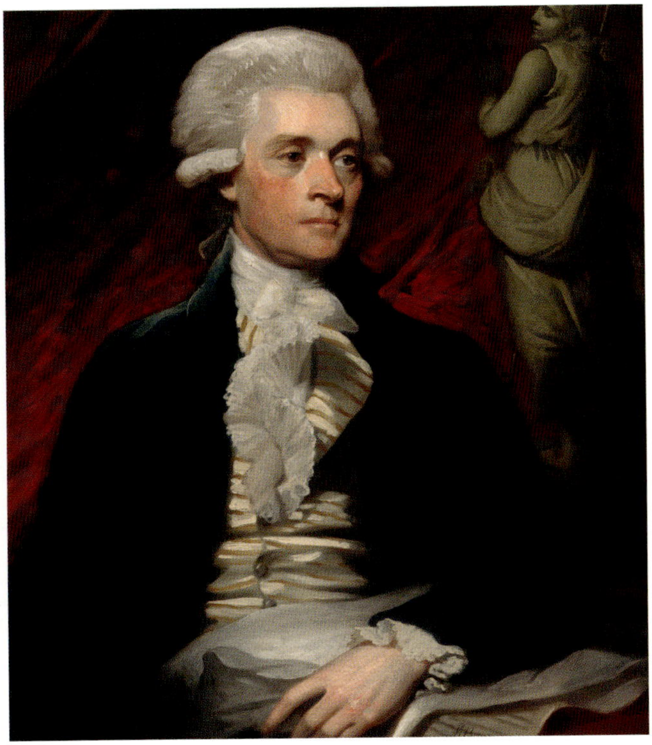

on Birmingham Hill. They defended it well until Sullivan's command on the left was caught by the British out of position (more by luck than design) and broken. Outmanned and then outflanked, the remaining defenders were driven away. That evening, Nathanael Greene's division and Anthony Wayne's command on the American left stood against heavy numbers and held the roads to Chester open for the army. Given the circumstances, the Continentals did their job about as well as anyone could have expected.

The most obvious failure experienced by the American army was its intelligence-gathering operation by the light dragoons and militiamen, the lack of local scouts, and the interpretation of intelligence once it was received. Washington's inability to gather reliable information about the region in which he was operating haunted him all day. Knowledge of the fords and other terrain features could have made the difference. In this regard Washington failed the army; the army did not fail Washington.

By contrast, despite operating in hostile territory, Howe's army succeeded in getting all the information it needed to achieve its main goal of flanking the American army and driving into its rear. The veteran British and Hessian soldiers under Howe's command performed brilliantly—they did all that was asked of them. General Knyphausen's column created the diversion that confused Washington into thinking he was facing the entire British army opposite Chads's Ford. The men comprising Cornwallis's division not only completed a grueling flank march, but went on to fight and crush an American line holding a formidable position. Any mistakes

▲ For most of the 1777 campaign, John Hancock was the president of Congress. (National Portrait Gallery)

◄ Thomas Jefferson. (National Portrait Gallery)

by Howe's men resulted from a lack of mounted troops.

General Howe did little to interfere with Washington's efforts to regroup in the immediate aftermath of the battle. For four days, Howe kept most of his army on the battlefield instead of launching a vigorous pursuit. In truth, Howe's army was exhausted. The soldiers had endured a long tedious voyage, followed by hard marching and prolonged combat with sustained casualties. They were in no condition to drive ahead, and had earned a much-needed rest. The army needed to establish a bridgehead at Wilmington, Delaware, to evacuate the injured, the seriously ill, and the collected provisions to a safe garrison town. Insufficient wagons and the paucity of healthy horses hampered Howe's operational ability and it took several days to accomplish these tasks.

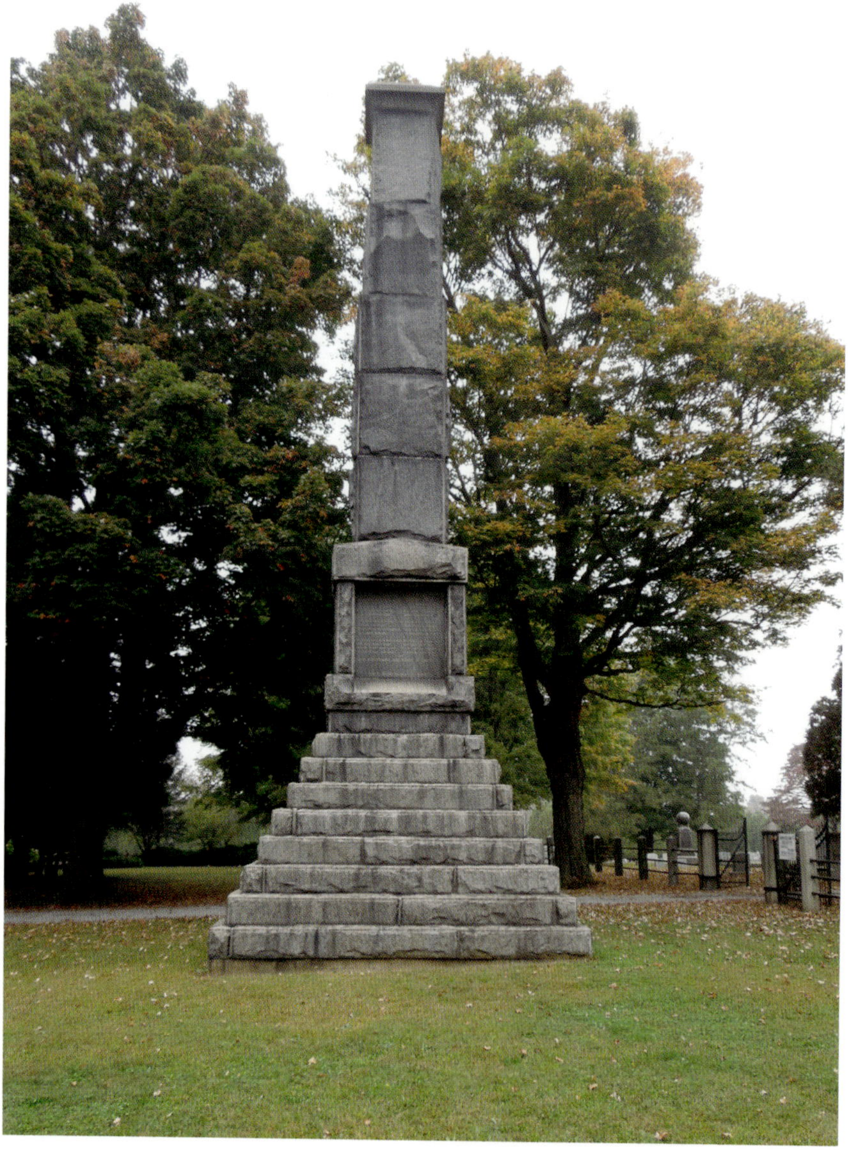

◀ A modern view of the monument honoring the Marquis de Lafayette and Casimir Pulaski. Erected in 1900, the memorial is located in Lafayette Cemetery adjacent to Birmingham Meetinghouse. (Author's collection)

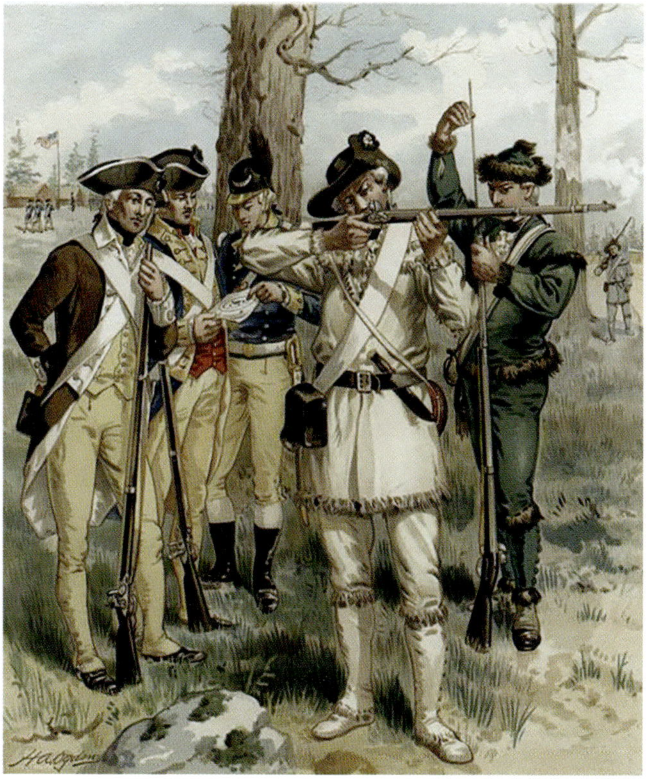

▲ Miscellaneous organizations Continental Army, 1776–1779 (New York Public Library)

Washington needed to find fresh defensive ground to protect Philadelphia from Howe's victorious army. The only remaining natural barrier was the Schuylkill River. After retreating to Chester, Pennsylvania the night of the battle, the Continentals left Chester and crossed into the outskirts of Philadelphia near Germantown. Moving the army north of the Schuylkill River put Washington behind the last natural barrier between the British and Philadelphia. The river was swift-flowing but shallow in many spots. As a defensive barrier, the Schuylkill was less than ideal. If defending the numerous fords across the Brandywine had been difficult for Washington, then defending the fords across the Schuylkill, which were more spread out, would prove a Herculean task. Somehow Washington would have to protect every ford and potential crossing point if he was going to defend the Schuylkill river line.

Fighting for the Schuylkill River

Moving into the Germantown area left Washington with a vexing conundrum. The Delaware and Schuylkill rivers form a peninsula, at the tip of which sat Philadelphia. He felt duty-bound to defend the capital, but he could not leave the critical supply depots at Reading and other places in the backcountry unprotected. Moving northwest to protect the depots would expose Philadelphia. Moving into position to protect Philadelphia exposed the supply centers upon which his army depended. It was now readily obvious that the loss at Brandywine made protecting the American capital nearly impossible. Protecting his storehouses had to take precedence over the most important city in North America.

While Washington wrestled with his options, and while most of Howe's army cleared the Brandywine battlefield and rested, elements of the British army probed ahead in search of the Americans. Howe sent a detachment south ten miles to

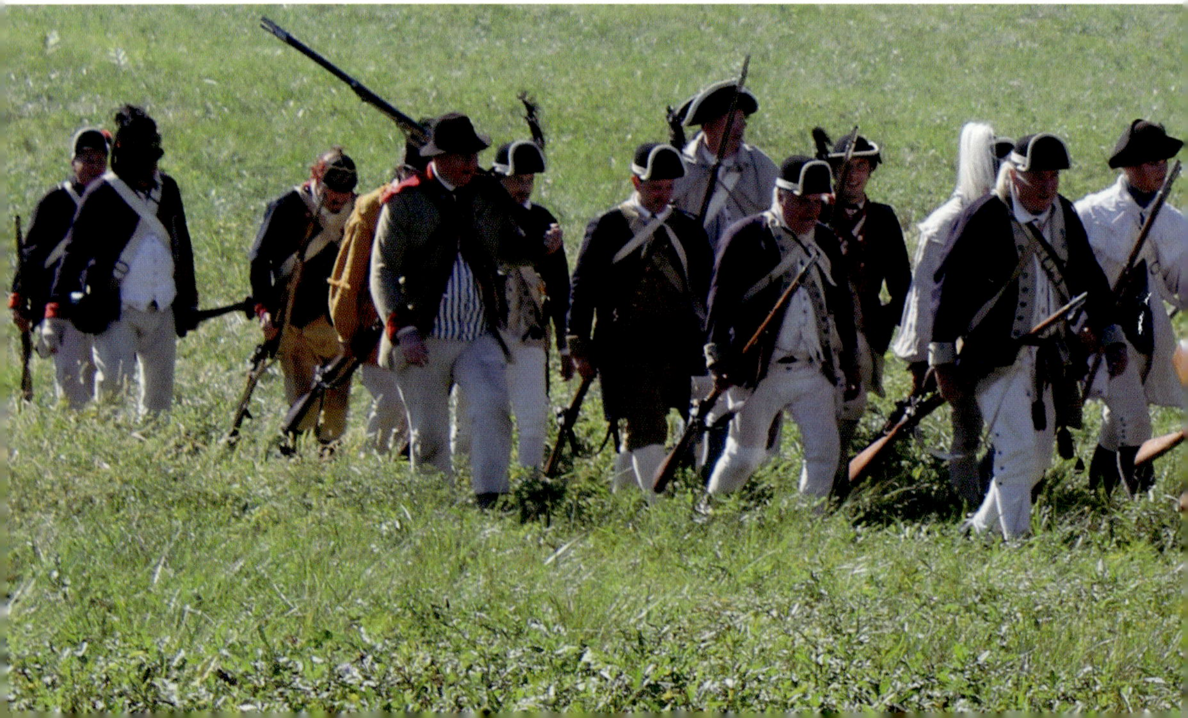

Wilmington, Delaware, to secure the town, establish a rendezvous with the fleet, and establish a hospital.

Most of Howe's army, meanwhile, remained idle. An aggressive pursuit of Washington's defeated army would have maintained the initiative, forced additional fighting on his terms, and likely crushed or further dispersed the Americans. Howe could have crossed the upper fords on the Schuylkill River with ease, cutting Washington off from his crucial supply depots. Earlier in the campaign, Howe told Lord Germain that he took the long route up the Chesapeake Bay so he could threaten those American storehouses, but his continued lethargy gave Washington the time he required to block access to them. Like his propensity for flanking operations, Howe had a history of unenthusiastic follow through after successful battles. Brandywine's aftermath was no different.

On September 14, Washington's army left the Germantown area and recrossed the Schuylkill River and moved to the Old Lancaster Road. By moving into the Great Valley, the army blocked the roads leading to the Schuylkill River. When the army finally halted the next day, the Continentals stretched along three miles of the Lancaster Road. Washington's army was strategically positioned to block a British advance to the Schuylkill River. Although the Americans had taken a roundabout route to get there, they were just ten miles from where they had fought at Brandywine four days ago. While the Great Valley could protect the approaches to the Schuylkill River, it did not protect Philadelphia along the Delaware River. The Delaware River was still vulnerable to the British navy then making its way toward the river after backtracking from the Chesapeake Bay.

Battle of the Clouds

While Washington contemplated how best to defend Philadelphia and weaken the British, information reached Howe that would prompt action. The American army was within reach, and Howe intended to move on that intelligence. On the night of September 15, he issued orders for the army to move into the Great Valley the following day. Rain had already moved into

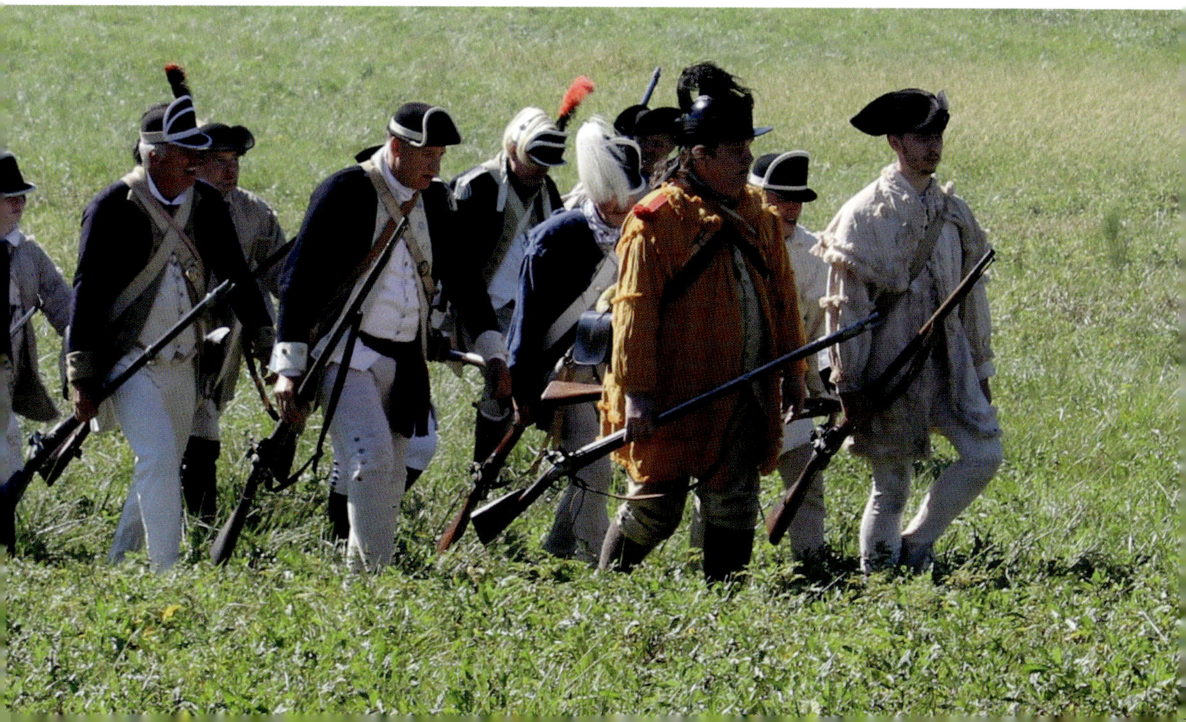

▼ Americans would have approached the Battle of the Clouds in formations like this one. (Author's collection)

the area, turning the rutted dirt roads of Chester County into a dense paste through which thousands of soldiers tramped. What Howe seems not to have known is that on the morning of September 16, Washington's army was moving from the Lancaster Road and ascending the South Valley Hill to block Howe from the Schuylkill River. The armies were once more on a collision course, and only five days after the conclusion of the largest battle of the American Revolution.

Howe, with the main body of the British army, left the Brandywine area and passed by the Turk's Head Tavern en route to Goshen Friends Meeting House to join forces with Cornwallis's column coming from the Chester area. The rain showers, which had been heavy but intermittent, were now blending into a nearly continuous downpour.

As the British columns were coming together at Goshen Meeting, Washington was moving his army into position on the South Valley Hill. The Continentals moved in two columns. Washington intended to march his army south from the Lancaster Road and deploy along the crest of South Valley Hill to block Howe's advance once these two columns deployed on the hill. Howe and Cornwallis hoped to catch Washington moving west along Lancaster Road along which the Continentals camped the night before—not south of that road. However, the two armies were marching towards each other.

The British easily pushed the lead elements of Washington's army off the South Valley Hill. As the majority of the Continental Army never started marching up the South Valley Hill, Washington was able to relatively quickly form a line on the southern slope of the North Valley Hill approximately three miles north of where the two separate actions known as the "Battle of the Clouds" occurred. The ammunition in American cartridge boxes, however, was being rendered useless by wind-whipped rain. If they were attacked, they would have no choice but to rely on bayonets, an unpalatable option that would have given the British a huge advantage. Other than some skirmishing and muddy maneuvering, the "Battle of the Clouds" ground to a halt without a major clash of arms. To the dismay of Howe and his subordinates, the driving rain of a nor'easter prevented Howe from exploiting his initial success.

Major John Howard of the 4th Maryland Regiment offered an insightful summation of the situation faced by Washington's army that day, and why the engagement ended in the manner it did. "The advanced parties had met, and were beginning to skirmish, when they were separated by a heavy rain, which becoming more and more violent, soon rendered the retreat of the Americans a matter of absolute necessity."

Washington gave orders to move to Yellow Springs ten miles distant on the other side of the North Valley Hill. When the army stopped to rest at Yellow Springs, the Americans dropped onto the soggy ground with little or no shelter to protect them from the cold driving rain. Most had thrown away their blankets during their retreat from Brandywine and so lacked even that meagre cover. While the American army slogged through that miserable night, the British took up camp wherever they happened to be when the action stopped. When the storm clouds cleared the next day, the path was clear to the Schuylkill River fords and an easy occupation of Philadelphia. If Howe chose delay as he had after Brandywine, perhaps Washington would have enough time to move into a blocking position north of the Schuylkill.

The early hours of September 17 found Washington's waterlogged army trudging into Yellow Springs, with most of its ammunition supply ruined by defective

▼ The young and opinionated Alexander Hamilton was born an illegitimate child in the Caribbean. He commanded a New York militia artillery battery throughout the 1776 campaign. His capabilities reached Washington's attention, and he added Hamilton to his staff as an aide-de-camp in March 1777. Hamilton's fluency in French helped Washington translate important documents. (National Gallery of Art)

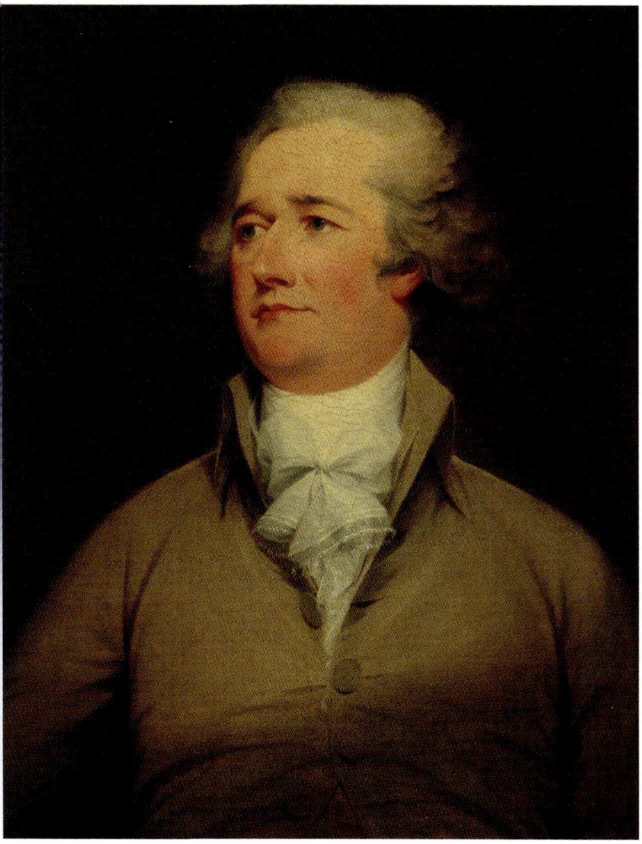

cartridge boxes. The Continental Army was essentially defenseless that morning, its members exhausted by their recent travails and in a foul mood. Washington had no choice but to distance his army from the British and find a new source of ammunition and other badly needed supplies. He decided upon Warwick Furnace in northwestern Chester County, where he could rest his army and obtain what it needed to fight again. Anthony Wayne's Pennsylvania Division remained behind to screen the rear of the army and keep a close watch on Howe.

After waiting out the rain, Howe had his army in motion on September 18. Howe's new position stretched for three miles along Swedesford Road facing Valley Forge. Howe intended to cross the Schuylkill River, but like every waterway in the region it was above flood stage. Washington knew his opponent wanted to move north of the Schuylkill and hoped to use the barrier to his advantage and make Howe pay for the effort. Washington ordered General Wayne to march his division into the British rear.

Valley Forge skirmish

The heavy rains turned the Schuylkill River into a rushing torrent, so it would be awhile before the British could cross. Howe instead set his sights on Continental supply depots south of the river. Three miles down the Valley Creek from the British camp sat Valley Forge, an ironworks and the site of an American storehouse. West of Valley Forge, several ironworks, such as Warwick and Hopewell Furnaces, were casting cannons and ammunition. The Valley Forge storehouses were convenient locations for finished goods and flour ground at local mills.

Henry "Lighthorse Harry" Lee and Washington's aide, Alexander Hamilton, were sent with a handful of dragoons to Valley Forge to rescue the supplies stored there. Lee approached from the west via Nutt Road, while Hamilton crossed the Schuylkill aboard a commandeered barge. The task proved impossible. A mere eight men and two rafts were available to move 4,000 barrels of flour, each weighing around 200 pounds, plus tons of iron goods. Not only would they need to make many trips across the river, but they would have to move all the materials 400 yards just to reach the Schuylkill. Howe also had something to do with it.

That evening, the British commander sent a column to seize the storehouse at Valley Forge. Lieutenant Colonel William Harcourt with two mounted squadrons of the 16th Light Dragoons, 200 dismounted dragoons, and three companies of light infantry pushed up Baptist Road to Gulph Road to gain access to the forge. Once the British reached Gulph Road, they moved cross-country over the hill to their left to get to Valley Creek, along which sat the forge complex.

One of the British shots killed Alexander Hamilton's horse in the boat, while an American round accounted for the only British casualty—the horse of Maj. Peter Craig, commander of the light infantry detachment. Lee and Hamilton escaped without injury, but two men in the boat were hit, one killed and one wounded. Without any serious opposition the British easily seized 4,000 barrels of flour and other items, such as soap, candles, kettles, tools, axes, and more. More important than seizing the complex, the British now controlled a critical road junction, explained Harry Lee, "with roads leading to Reading, the French Creek iron region, Lancaster, and several Schuylkill River fords."

Battle of Paoli

On September 19, General Wayne began his new assignment by marching his 2,200-man column out of Yellow Springs back into the Great Valley onto Lancaster Road. After passing the Admiral Warren Tavern, Wayne halted at the Paoli Tavern 10 miles east of Yellow Springs and just two miles behind the British camp at Tredyffrin. In front of Howe's army on the hills on the north side of the Great Valley were overflowing creeks and rivers, and his flanks exposed to various highways between Lancaster and Philadelphia. Wooded terrain clogged his rear. Wayne's division behind him would make Howes's ability to conduct a speedy retreat difficult, and perhaps impossible. Later, Wayne moved his Pennsylvania division back up the road toward Admiral Warren Tavern before turning left onto the high ground at the Warren Tavern. The only approach the British had to reach Wayne's new position was a path winding up from the Warren Tavern. Wayne had a good line of retreat and supply over a well-traveled road leading southwest to White Horse Tavern two miles behind the Continental camp. The new camp was in an open field surrounded by woods with roads passing on both flanks of the division. The British were aware Wayne was in the general vicinity of their camp, but did not know his exact precise whereabouts.

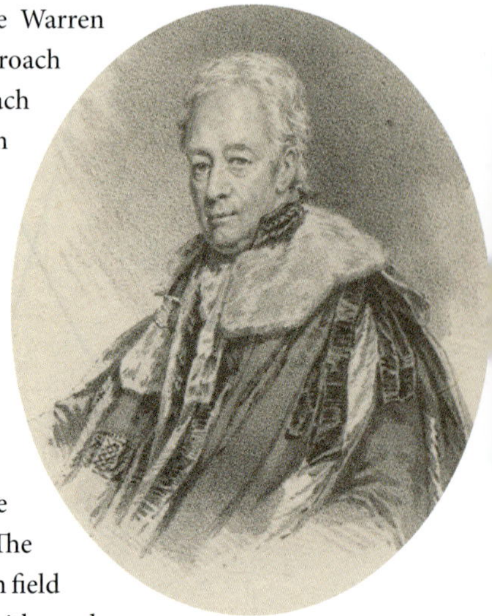

▲ William Harcourt commanded the 16th Light Dragoons during the Philadelphia Campaign. (New York Public Library)

On September 19, the same day Wayne shifted to a new camp, Washington had his main army on the move. Washington wanted to cross north of the Schuylkill River at Parker's Ford and move into a blocking position above its many crossings. With Wayne behind the British, Washington hoped to catch the enemy in a pincher movement and force him into battle on his own terms.

Most of the army camped along the east side of Perkiomen Creek after a gruelling 29-mile march. No one in Washington's Continental Army knew the American army under General Horatio Gates had won a decisive victory against General Burgoyne at Freeman's Farm the same day. The consequences of Howe's decision to campaign for possession of Philadelphia instead of moving north to join forces with Burgoyne were coming to fruition.

Washington's movement left Wayne in a terrible position. The main body of the Continental Army had increased its distance from Wayne, leaving him without immediate support and with Howe's main army between him and Washington. Wayne was operating under the impression that Washington would march back into the Great Valley once the army had been resupplied. Washington had sent a dispatch to Wayne informing him of the new plans, but neither general was aware that a British patrol had intercepted it, leaving both in the dark as to the true nature of the danger.

The Continentals moved from their camp along the Perkiomen Creek the next day to tramp between 10 to 15 miles and take up positions along the Schuylkill on a nine-mile front stretching from Gordon's Ford to Swedes' Ford. Just as he had done at Brandywine, Washington spread his army thin along a wide front to keep the British from crossing a natural barrier. Howe now had American forces of varying strength on multiple sides. Despite his defeat at Brandywine and the near-disaster at the Battle of the Clouds, Washington had once more managed to seize the initiative. Temporarily at a loss on how to proceed but hellbent to take Philadelphia, Howe pondered how to cross the Schuylkill.

Howe reached a decision on how to extricate his command from his predicament and achieve his objective. Before moving the main army to the Valley Forge area, he would deal with General Wayne. General Howe made his decision by early on the evening of Saturday, September 20. The problem behind him had to be eliminated so he could focus on Washington's troops north of the Schuylkill River and achieve his objective of capturing Philadelphia: Anthony Wayne's Pennsylvania division had to be destroyed.

Howe tapped Maj. Gen. Charles Grey to command the operation. Hoping to achieve complete surprise, General Grey ordered his men to remove their flints to prevent

▼ Battle of Paoli.

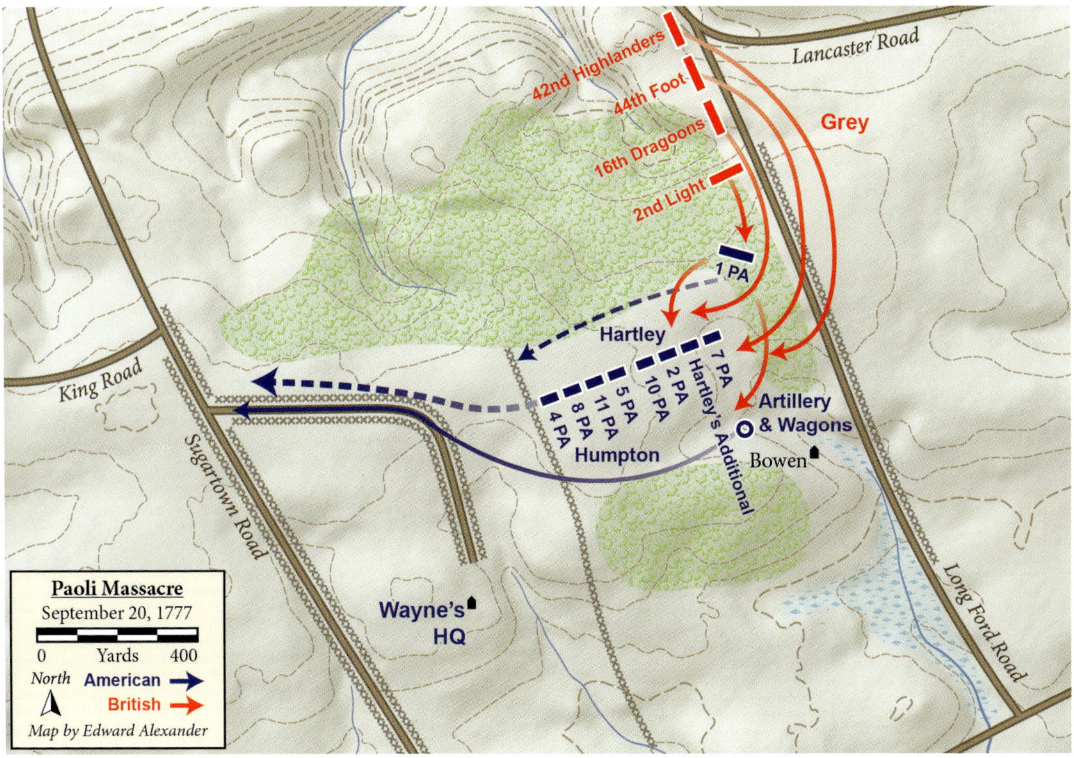

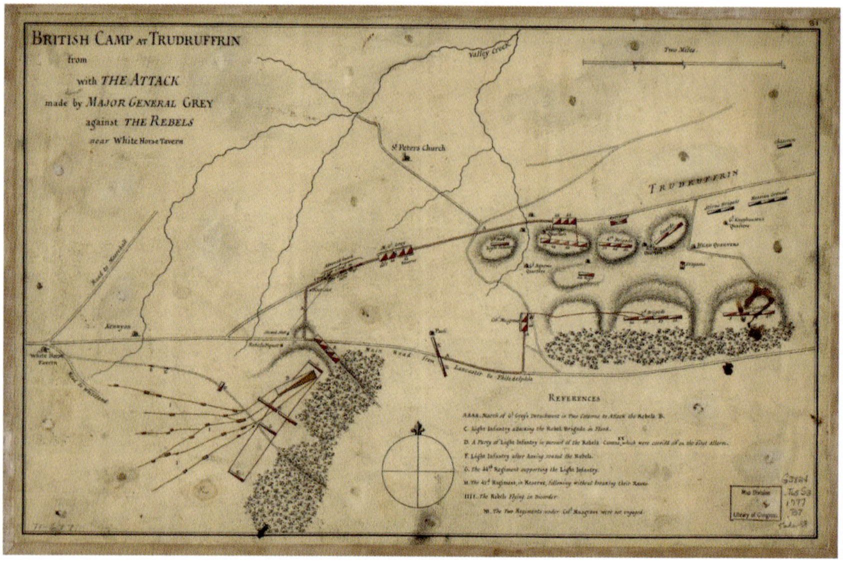

◀ Map showing the British attack at Paoli, 1777. (Library of Congress)

muskets from accidently discharging, and perform their dirty work with bayonets. Videttes rode into Wayne's camp and spread word of the British advance. The division formed on the parade ground in front of camp facing north. Wayne intended to move his division across the fields and get his men on the road to the White Horse Tavern before the British could strike his camp. The fitful small arms fire echoing in the distant signaled the British were coming toward Wayne's right flank. The Pennsylvanian ordered the division to file to the left (west) and head toward Sugartown Road and White Horse Tavern.

Before the infantry could move, however, Wayne needed to extricate his wheeled vehicles. They were simply too valuable to risk losing. Once these vehicles were moving down the road, the waiting infantry could leave. One of those wheeled vehicles overturned blocking the escape route. However, having overwhelmed

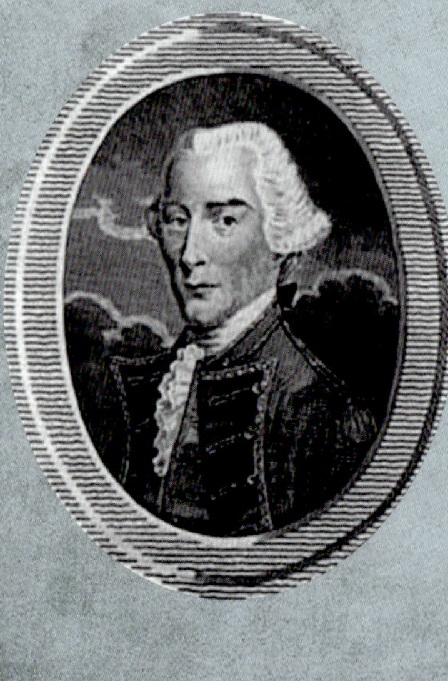

Major General Charles Grey, 1729–1807

The fourth son of 1st Baronet Sir Henry Grey, born in 1729, had no hope of inheriting his father's estates or titles and, though born just a mile from the North Sea, embarked on a career in the army. By the time of the American Revolution he had three decades of extensive military experience and was considered one of Britain's best commanders.

(Library of Congress)

Wayne's pickets, the British light infantry began to sweep into Wayne's camp. The British 2nd Light Infantry Battalion swarmed through Wayne's camp and surrounded the rear of the stalled column. Confusion spread through the ranks of Wayne's command. Farther up the stalled column, men scattered to save themselves, climbing over fences and into the woods. Many were caught by the pursuing British while still on the fences and bayonetted. The affair would go down in history as the "Paoli Massacre" because of a series of atrocities committed by Grey's troops. Pockets of Pennsylvanians attempted to stem the crimson tide from behind stout fences, but nothing they could do could stop the surge of British Regulars pouring through the camp.

Wayne had his men in column with enough time to extricate them from the approaching danger, but the order of

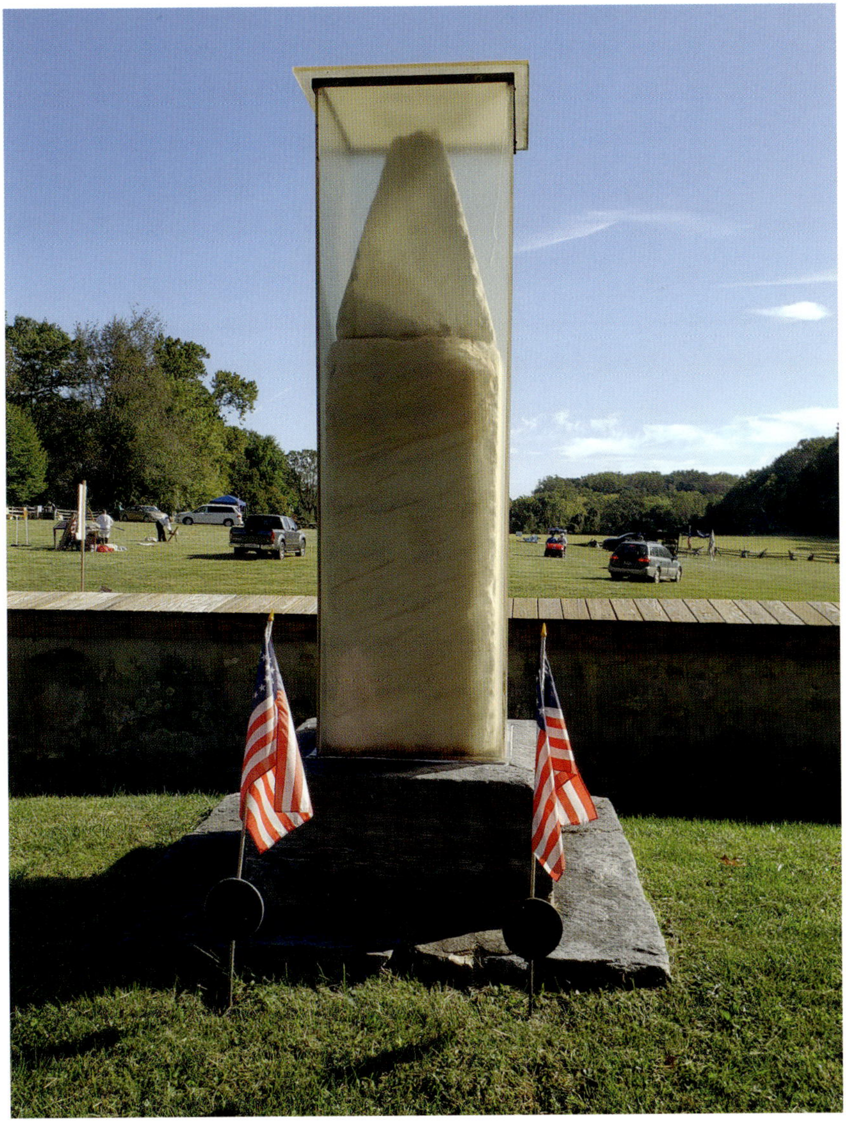

▶ 1817 Paoli Monument. This monument was erected on the 50th anniversary of the battle over the graves of Wayne's dead. (Author's collection)

march doomed his command at Paoli. Twenty-nine wheeled vehicles including artillery pieces and wagons had to move from the right side across the entire rear of the column, and then pass through a fence line to reach the Sugartown Road. In the darkness and with the approaching confusion of battle, it is no surprise that the movement took longer than expected. Once the confusion at the head of the column was dealt with and the fence laid low, the head of the column began to move.

Despite the close-quarter fighting and darkness, the British assault force lost only three men killed and nine wounded. The British rounded up between 70 and 80 prisoners, many of whom were suffering from multiple stab wounds. The horrific

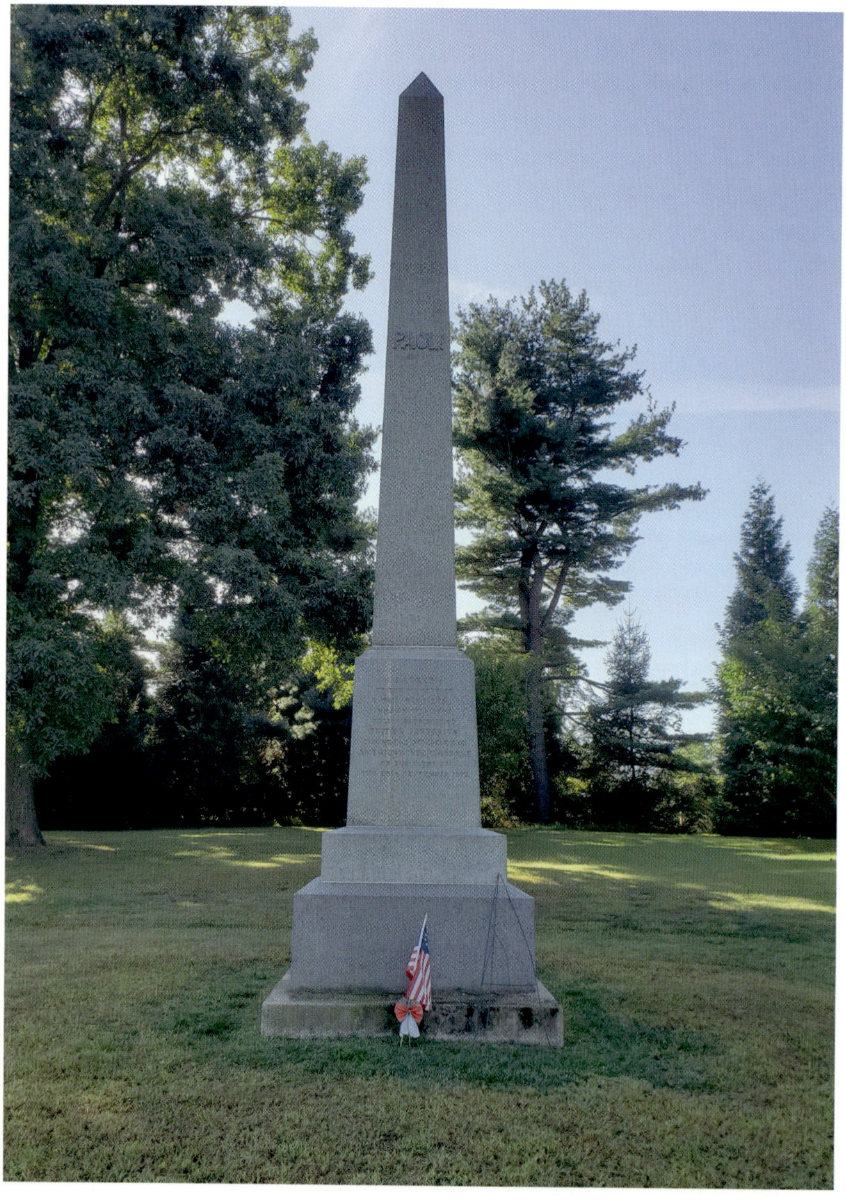

◄ 1877 Paoli Monument. This monument was erected on the 100th anniversary of the battle. (Author's collection)

condition of the wounded and the mutilated bodies of the dead infuriated the survivors, who swore to gain revenge in their next fight. Since Howe planned to cross the Schuylkill, Grey called off the pursuit and returned to the British camp by the Lancaster Road, leaving the American dead and many of the wounded in the fields where the fell.

Despite being taken by surprise and the brutality of the fight that followed, Wayne managed to extract most of his division, including all four of his precious artillery pieces. The officers and men, however, lost most of their baggage and personal effects. All told, he suffered about 300 killed, wounded, or captured, about 15 percent of his strength. The darkness, which shielded Grey's men during their advance and added to the terror of the sudden attack also aided the Continentals, though to a lesser extent. Grey did not know the exact location of Wayne's camp, and maneuvering men during a night attack was a confusing endeavor that helps explain why Wayne managed to extract so many of his men. Wayne's pride took a hit at Paoli and the resentment would simmer until he unleashed his pent-up frustration at Stony Point, New York two years later.

Crossing the Schuylkill

Once Grey's column returned from the successful Paoli operation, William Howe put his army in motion. With the threat that Wayne posed to his rear eliminated, Howe moved ahead with his plans to cross the Schuylkill River. The British army departed its camps, turned up the Baptist Road, bore left at Gulph Road into the Valley Creek watershed, and marched up Nutt Road. The column moved past the forge ruins on Nutt Road and as far as the bridge over French Creek in Charlestown Township before halting. With the army's left flank at French Creek and the right at Valley Forge, Howe had six river crossings in front of him. By the time Howe arrived the Continental Army stretched for nine miles and covered the Schuylkill River fords across from the British.

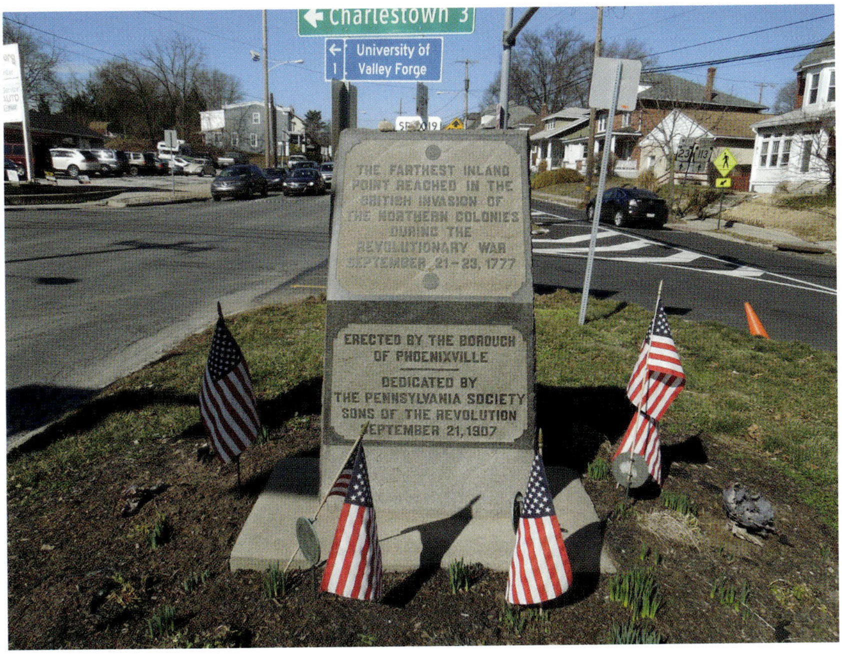

▶ 1907 marker in Phoenixville, PA denoting the furthest inland advance of the British army. The British, however, actually advanced beyond the location of this marker. (Author's collection)

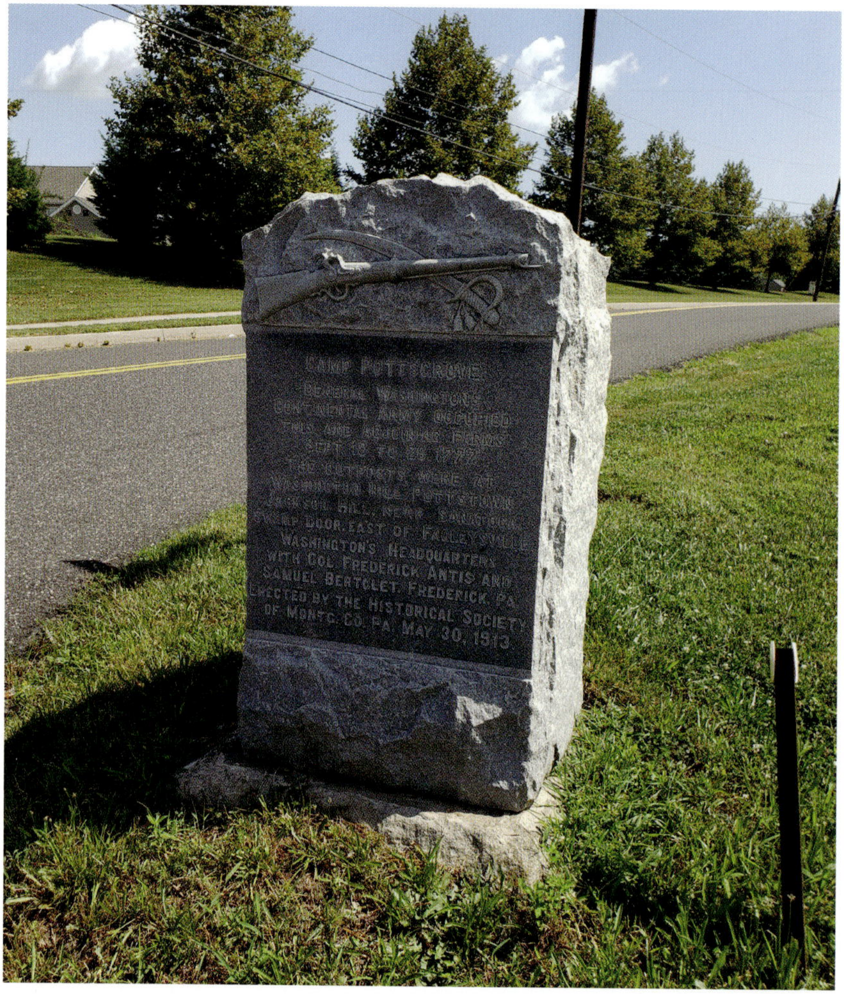

◀ 1913 marker in New Hanover Township, PA denoting the site of Washington's Camp Pottsgrove. (Author's collection)

Washington faced a Hobson's Choice, for the storehouses at Reading needed to be protected, but to do so would uncover Philadelphia, which, politically speaking, could not be surrendered without a fight. His choices were bleak: lose Reading and the supply depots of the Pennsylvania backcountry, or lose the colonial capital at Philadelphia. If he shifted troops to guard the city, Howe could seize the iron manufacturing region to the west. To the poorly supplied army, protecting those backcountry regions was more important than the psychological loss of Philadelphia. It was obvious, however, that Howe could move rapidly west, capture the Continental supply centers, and return for Philadelphia and win both major prizes. No matter what Howe decided to do, Philadelphia was all but lost. The Paoli defeat had indeed altered the strategic equation.

Howe's move seemed to signal that he was about to march toward Reading and the iron manufacturing region. Indeed, Howe had informed George Germain that he had utilized the water route to the Chesapeake earlier in the campaign to threaten the storehouses in the Pennsylvania backcountry. Any British move in that direction would force Washington to move accordingly, leaving Howe the option of reversing course and marching for lower fords of the Schuylkill River and into the capital city. Howe had utilized a flanking maneuverer to turn Washington's army at least six times, most recently at Brandywine just ten days earlier. His current move toward the American right flank appeared to be more of the same.

Convinced that Reading was Howe's immediate objective, on the evening of September 21 Washington pulled away from the river fords and shifted his army west to better protect the supply center. The risky movement exposed the lower fords of the Schuylkill River to the British. Other than some militia detachments, Washington's army was gone.

Having duped Washington into moving west away from the Schuylkill River fords, the British army crossed to the north side of the Schuylkill unopposed. The Brigade of Guards under Brig. Gen. Edward Matthew, led by its grenadier and light companies, formed the vanguard of the British column driving across the Schuylkill River that night. The water, recalled Grenadier John Peebles, came "up to a Gr[enadie]rs breetches pockets." Luckily for the British, the river passage was not challenged by American fire. The units crossed at Fatland and Richardson's fords under a bright moonlight that made for a challenging but not difficult passage. The British were now firmly positioned between Washington and Philadelphia. No more combat was needed to seize the colonial capital, but the fighting was far from over.

Howe was above the river and held all the strategic cards except one: he desperately

▼ View above the Falls of Schuylkill. (New York Public Library)

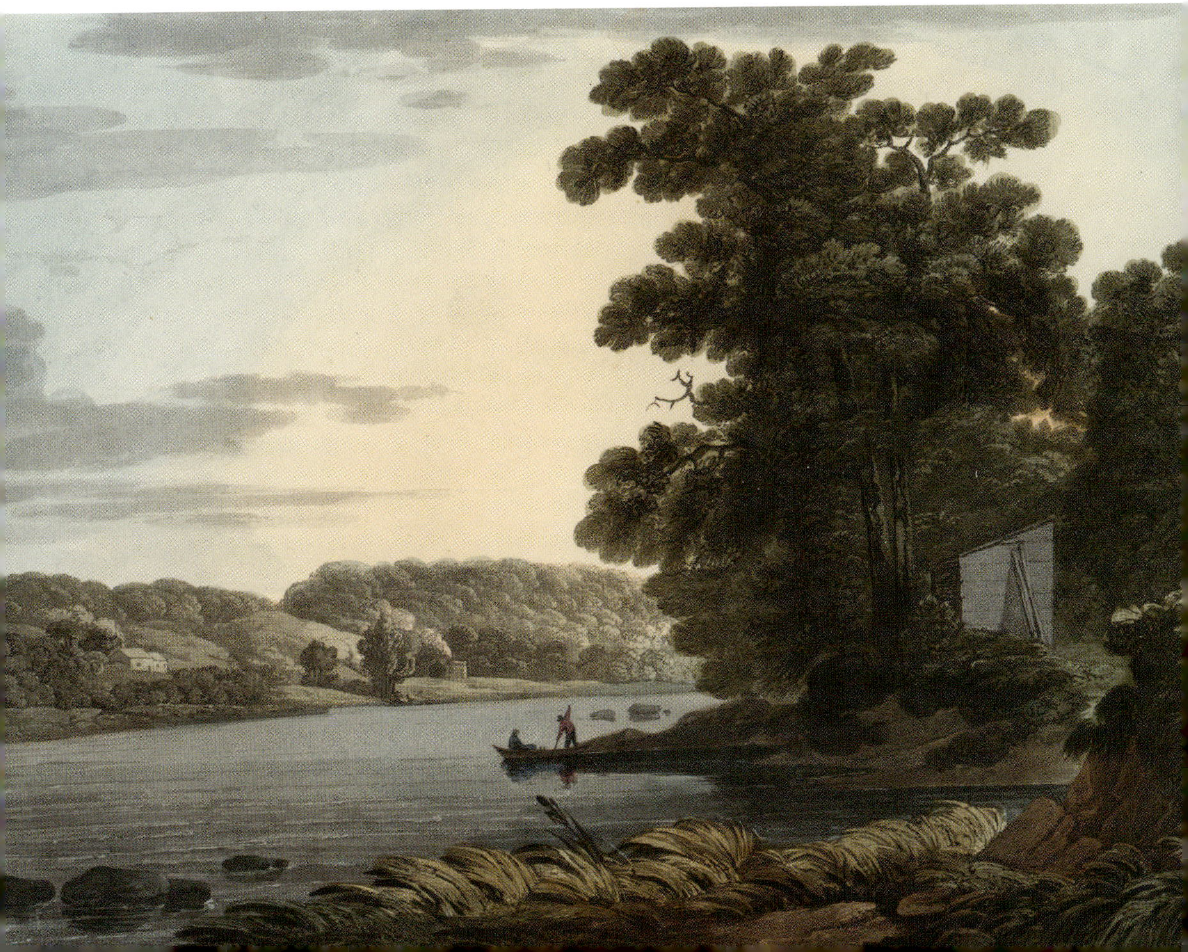

needed to be resupplied by the British fleet. The army officer, however, did not have a full understanding of the difficulties facing his naval officer brother. After the victory at Brandywine, Admiral Richard Howe needed to move the frigates and supply ships to the mouth of the Delaware. It would be several weeks before the fleet could return to the Delaware River from the Chesapeake. Sailing ships, however, are subject to the vagaries of wind, and unfavorable winds kept the resupply convoy and the balance of the fleet in the Chesapeake for another full ten days.

The Continental Army was now positioned near Pottsgrove (a region encompassing most of modern-day northwestern Montgomery County). The large-scale battle at Brandywine, skirmishes and engagements (including Paoli), and long marches and stretches without adequate food and supplies had worn down the army. The army, Washington informed Congress, was short of clothing, blankets and especially shoes; nearly 1,000 men were in the field barefoot despite efforts to shod them.

Philadelphia Occupied

On September 25, Howe marched his army 11 miles into Germantown, which was just five miles from Philadelphia. While Washington contemplated his next move, William Howe maneuvered into position to march into Philadelphia unopposed the next day.

Philadelphia was eerily quiet on Friday morning, September 26, 1777. The entire city was at a standstill. The usual throng of people who entered the city from the countryside to sell their produce and wares at Saturday's market day failed to materialize. The wharves were also still and largely vacant. Entire sections of the city were empty of inhabitants who had fled ahead of the British. After a night of rain, the weather had cleared and gradually gave way to sunshine.

Charles Cornwallis received the honor of leading a column of troops into Philadelphia to occupy and garrison the colonial capital. The general selected about 3,000 troops

▼ The Stenton House, used by William Howe as British headquarters during the occupation of Germantown. (Author's collection)

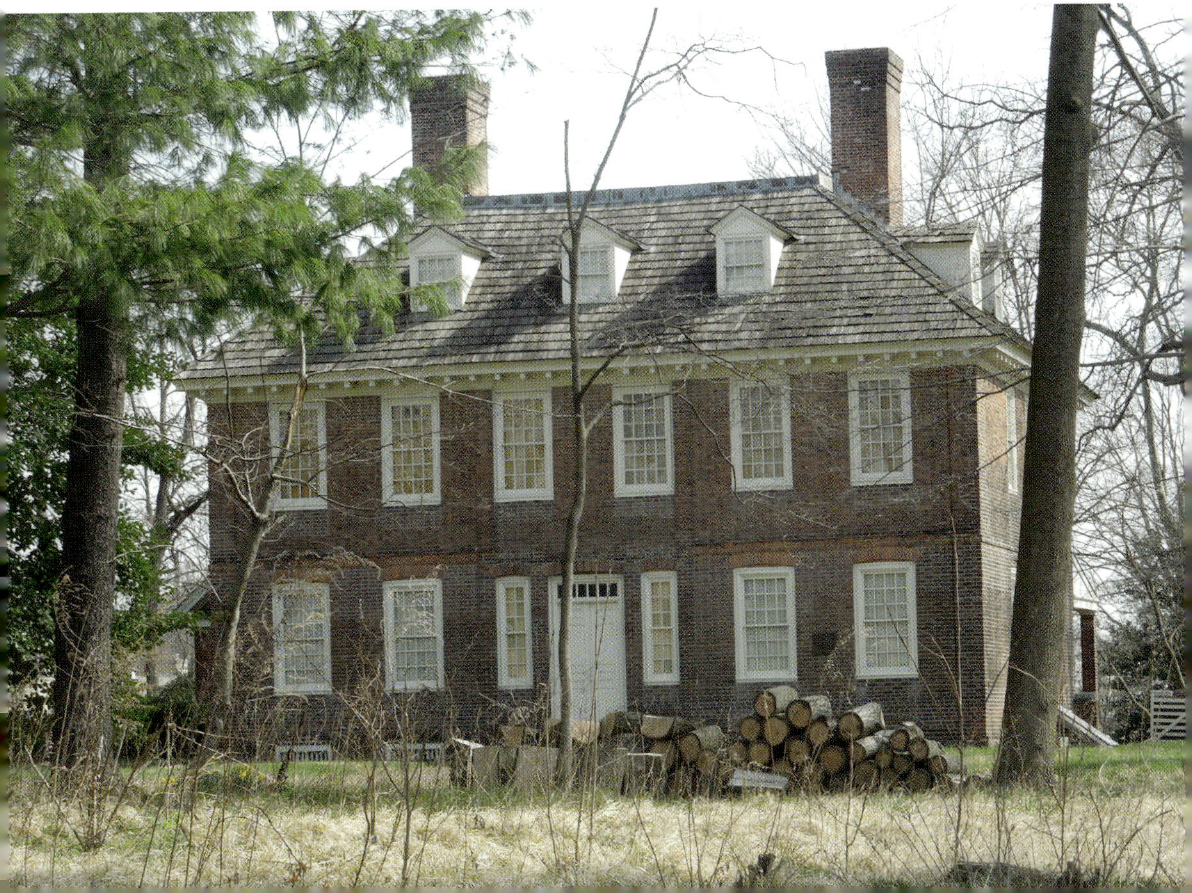

and marched them in from Germantown. Two squadrons of the 16th Light Dragoons under Lt. Col. William Harcourt formed the head of the column. Behind Harcourt was the brigade of British grenadiers and two battalions of Hessian grenadiers. As a further show of force, six medium 12-pounders and four howitzers brought up the rear.

Several notable Loyalists trotted their mounts ahead of the column symbolizing the return of Royal government. One was Andrew Allen, the former attorney general of Pennsylvania and delegate to the Second Continental Congress, and the other his brother, William Allen, Jr., a former officer in the 2nd Pennsylvania Battalion. Both had changed allegiances after the signing of the Declaration of Independence. Their brother John was with them as well. Loyalist Joseph Galloway, a member of the First Continental Congress and former friend of Ben Franklin's, rode with the Allen brothers, returning to the city he had abandoned the previous year. Philadelphia Loyalists Phineas Bond and Enoch Story guided the long column, which comprised a quarter of Howe's effective force. The insertion of the troops into Philadelphia significantly weakened the garrison left behind at Germantown.

Cornwallis had formed his column that morning on the heights just southeast of Germantown. From there, the British could see Philadelphia in the distance about four miles away. The men stepped off down the Germantown Road about mid-morning and tramped past the Rising Sun Tavern at the Old York Road. It was an impressive display of pomp and might. The sun gleamed off the Delaware in the distance, beyond which shimmered the pine forests of New Jersey. Shaping the skyline were the spires of Christ Church and the Pennsylvania State House, known today as Independence Hall. Off to the right meandered the chocolate-colored water of the Schuylkill River, which the army had crossed to organize the celebratory march.

The martial column approached Second Street and the small suburb of Northern Liberties, which spread out for a mile above the city boundary at Vine Street. Behind it a half mile away stood the village of Kensington along the Delaware River. When the head of Cornwallis's column reached Second Street it turned right and crossed the Cohocksink Creek and marched past the large brick French and Indian War-era barracks. A mixed aroma greeted the marchers, including a mixture of reeking tanneries, boiling cabbage, and the malty fumes of breweries and distilleries. Crossing over Pegg's Run, the men ascended a low ridge to Callowhill Street and approached the city limit at Vine

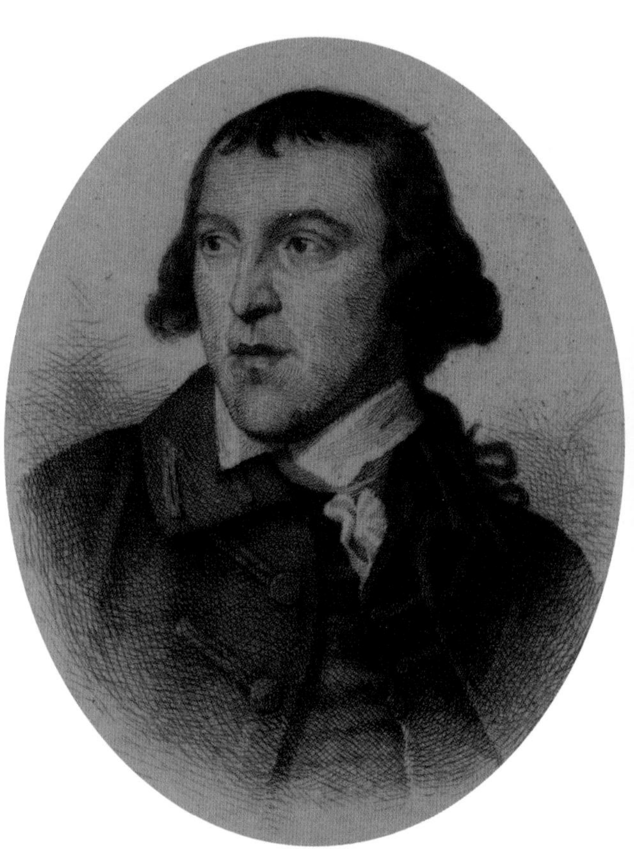

▲ Andrew Allen was the former attorney general for Pennsylvania and a delegate to the Second Continental Congress prior to joining the British cause. (New York Public Library)

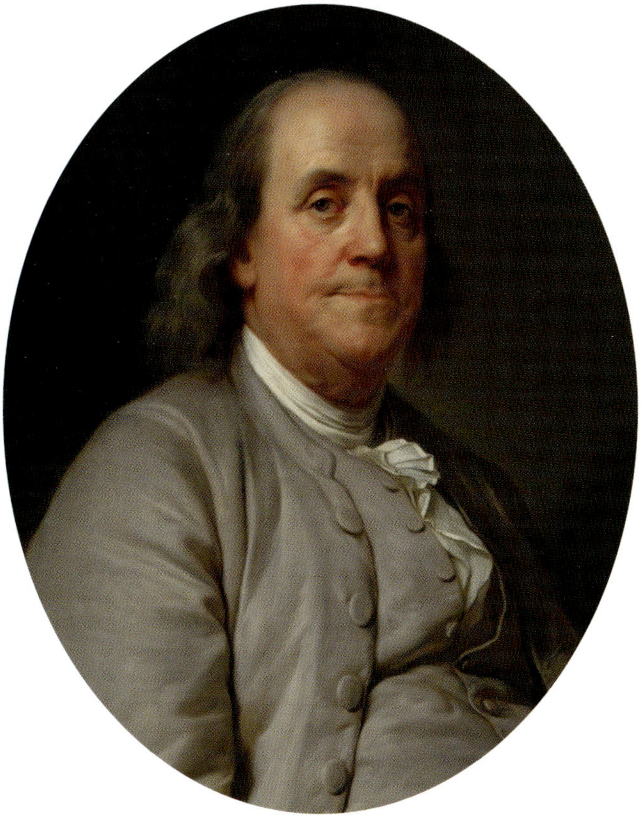

▲ During the Philadelphia Campaign, Benjamin Franklin was in Paris negotiating a Treaty of Alliance with the French. (National Portrait Gallery)

Street, where the muddy road gave way to cobblestone.

One of the men riding with the artillery was Captain-Lieutenant Francis Downman. "[T]he roads and streets were crowded with people who huzzaed and seemed overjoyed to see us," recalled the officer. "Whether they were pleased or not at our entrance, they must have been struck with the appearance of a body of such fine fellows as the British grenadiers."

Continuing down Second Street, the conquerors tramped past Christ Church. Two very different men, Joseph Galloway and Anthony Wayne, had been married inside. Just up the road from Christ Church the troops crossed the 100-foot wide intersection at High Street (modern-day Market Street), where market sheds stretched down the middle of the road for three blocks. They marched past the old Court House, where independence was proclaimed on July 8, 1776, and one block farther turned right on Chestnut Street. As they crossed Third Street, the elegant town houses of men like Benjamin Chew came and went, and, beyond that Carpenter's Hall, where the First Continental Congress had met three years earlier.

So began what would be a nine-month occupation, one month and one day after Howe landed his army in Maryland. His campaign that began back in June had taken nearly three months to complete. He had planned to move quickly, capture Philadelphia, and return with sufficient forces to New York to assist John Burgoyne. That may have been possible two months earlier if he had ascended the Delaware River in July. Instead, he managed to meander both on land and at sea. He fought several engagements along the way, including the major battle along the Brandywine on September 11. The 80-day endeavor isolated and doomed Burgoyne, who would surrender his army at Saratoga in another month.

The Marquis de Lafayette was resting in Bethlehem recovering from a wounded leg suffered at Brandywine when the city fell. The Frenchman rarely hesitated to express his opinion, and he took the opportunity to do so with vigour on this occasion in a letter to his wife: "I must give you your lesson, as the wife of an American general officer. They [Your friends] will say to you, 'They have been beaten:' you must answer—'That is true; but when two armies of equal number meet in the field, old soldiers have naturally the advantage over new ones; they have besides, had the pleasure of killing very many more of the enemy, many more than they have lost.' They will afterwards add: 'All that is very well; but Philadelphia is taken, the capital of America, the rampart of liberty!' You must politely answer, 'You are all great fools! Philadelphia is a poor forlorn town, exposed on every side, whose harbor was already closed; though the residence of congress lent it, I know not why, some degree of celebrity. This is the famous city which, be it added, we will, sooner or later, make them yield back to us.'

Benjamin Franklin heard the news while in France negotiating a treaty of alliance, and offered the same basic opinion held by the Marquis de Lafayette, though in his usual clever manner. "Instead of saying Sir William Howe had taken Philadelphia," he opined, "it would be more proper to say, Philadelphia has taken Sir William Howe."

If the British could gain control of the Delaware River, Philadelphia would remain in the hands of the Crown. If they could not navigate the Delaware at will, they would not have sufficient supplies to remain in place and would almost certainly have to evacuate the colonial capital.

On September 26, Washington and his army crossed Perkiomen Creek from Camp Pottsgrove and arrived at Pennypacker's Mills ten miles closer to Philadelphia but still more than 20 miles outside the captured capital. The Continentals established their new camps thoroughly exhausted, having marched some 140 miles in the past eleven days. While the Virginia commander settled in, news arrived of Burgoyne's defeat in upstate New York. The potential surrender of an entire British army energized the Continentals. Washington used the news of Burgoyne's defeat at Saratoga to raise the morale of his army by ordering artillery salutes

▼ 1897 marker denoting the location of Washington's campsite before and after the Battle of Germantown at Pennypacker Mills. (Author's collection)

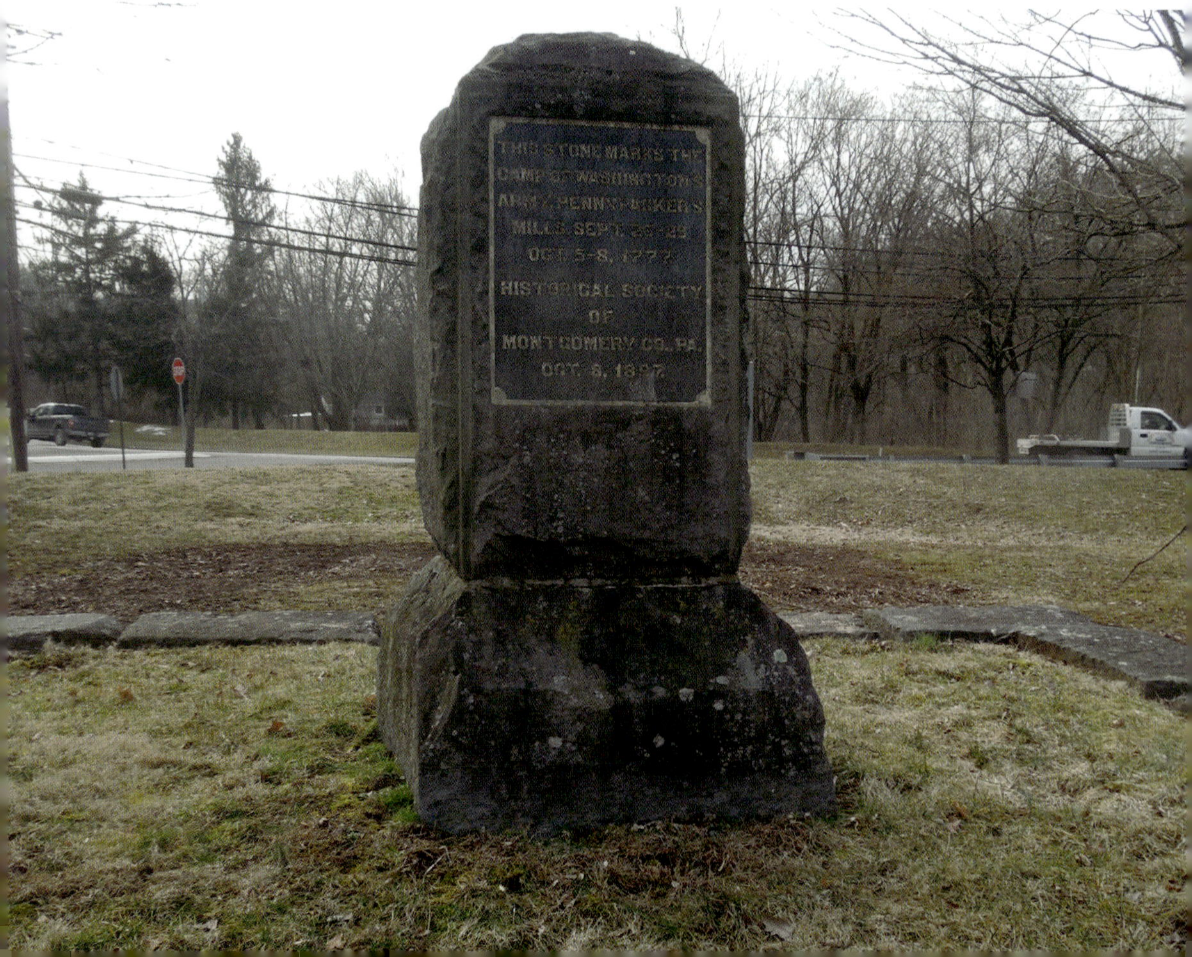

and extra rations of rum. The news only made the naturally aggressive Washington more anxious to match the exploits of the northern army and strike his own decisive blow. The only questions were when and where he would attack.

On September 29, Washington moved closer to the British. The troops marched down Skippack Pike five miles to the village of Skippack, where the army went into camp once more for what turned out to be three days of rest. September 30 found Washington sending out scouting parties to learn about the British at Germantown.

The respective forces closed September 1777 with Howe in Philadelphia and moving to open the Delaware River, the British fleet poised to sail up and supply him, and Washington's Continentals about 20 miles northwest of the city seeking an opportunity to strike. It had been a tough month for the Americans. Despite fighting well at Brandywine on the 11th of the month, poor intelligence and a mishandling of the army had resulted in its defeat and the loss of hundreds of men. The aborted Battle of Clouds five days later risked the army and could well have led to its destruction had the rain not interceded to save it. Wayne's Pennsylvania division had been roughly handled at Paoli. Philadelphia had fallen, and Congress was on the run to York, Pennsylvania.

Despite these and other problems, Washington knew the Continental Army could not afford to sit outside Philadelphia and wait for winter or remain idle and receive an attack on Howe's terms. The initiative had to be seized, and the Virginian was determined to take it.

Washington had the Continental Army moving again on October 2. The march took the men four miles beyond the crossroads in Worcester Township onto Methacton Hill. The high ground provided an excellent viewing platform toward Philadelphia and the army a strong defensive position should one be needed. Washington was now fewer than 20 miles from the city limits and about half that to Germantown. Rumours trickled into British headquarters of the American advance and offensive plans. Howe was isolated from his Loyalist spies in the countryside and could not verify such reports. Washington's dragoons and militia patrols had cut off access to the city by anyone outside the British lines.

Battle of Germantown

Washington estimated that Howe's army had lost between 1,000 and 2,000 men during the entire campaign. With the 23rd Royal Welch Fusiliers now serving elsewhere, some 3,000 grenadiers ensconced in Philadelphia, and 2,000 Scots and Hessians at Wilmington and Chester, Washington and his staff calculated the remaining British forces in Germantown to number perhaps 8,000 men.

It had taken less than two days for Washington to plan his assault on Germantown and gain the full consent of his generals for the undertaking. Surprise was a key element of the plan, which would require a great deal of discipline, coordination, and good luck. Once approved, Washington intended to divide his army into four columns designed to meet on the northern and western edges of Germantown simultaneously at 5:00 a.m. on October 4. The columns would move silently through the darkness for 14 to as many as 20 miles over a series of poorly marked roads. These movements would show whether the army was capable of a nighttime march and a coordinated surprise attack. Washington had learned though hard experience that stand-up fights against the British were a losing proposition; thus, his preferred tactic was to strike isolated enemy detachments, which is precisely what he was attempting to do against the depleted British garrison holding Germantown.

In truth—as Washington well knew—the plan was bold, complicated, and risky for an army like his to attempt. Similar in scope to but much larger in scale than his designs for the attack on Trenton the previous December, Washington hoped to drive into a major village along four different roads, using timing his men would have to pull off in the dark. Coordinating the movements of each column so that they would arrive in Germantown simultaneously was more than ambitious. On paper Washington counted nearly 17,000 men, but the army that marched and fought on October 4 six miles outside Philadelphia was much smaller; it had been bleeding stragglers and deserters throughout the campaign, and some men had to be left behind to protect the encampment and wagons. Most sources put the number who marched to Germantown at about 11,000. Regardless of the actual number, Washington was moving a numerically superior force into the fight. It was the first time during the war that Washington launched his own army in a major attack against the main British force.

To achieve maximum effect and complete surprise, it was imperative that each of the four columns reach its assigned location at the same time—a rather tall order given that each column had to march a different distance in the dark. Coordinating the

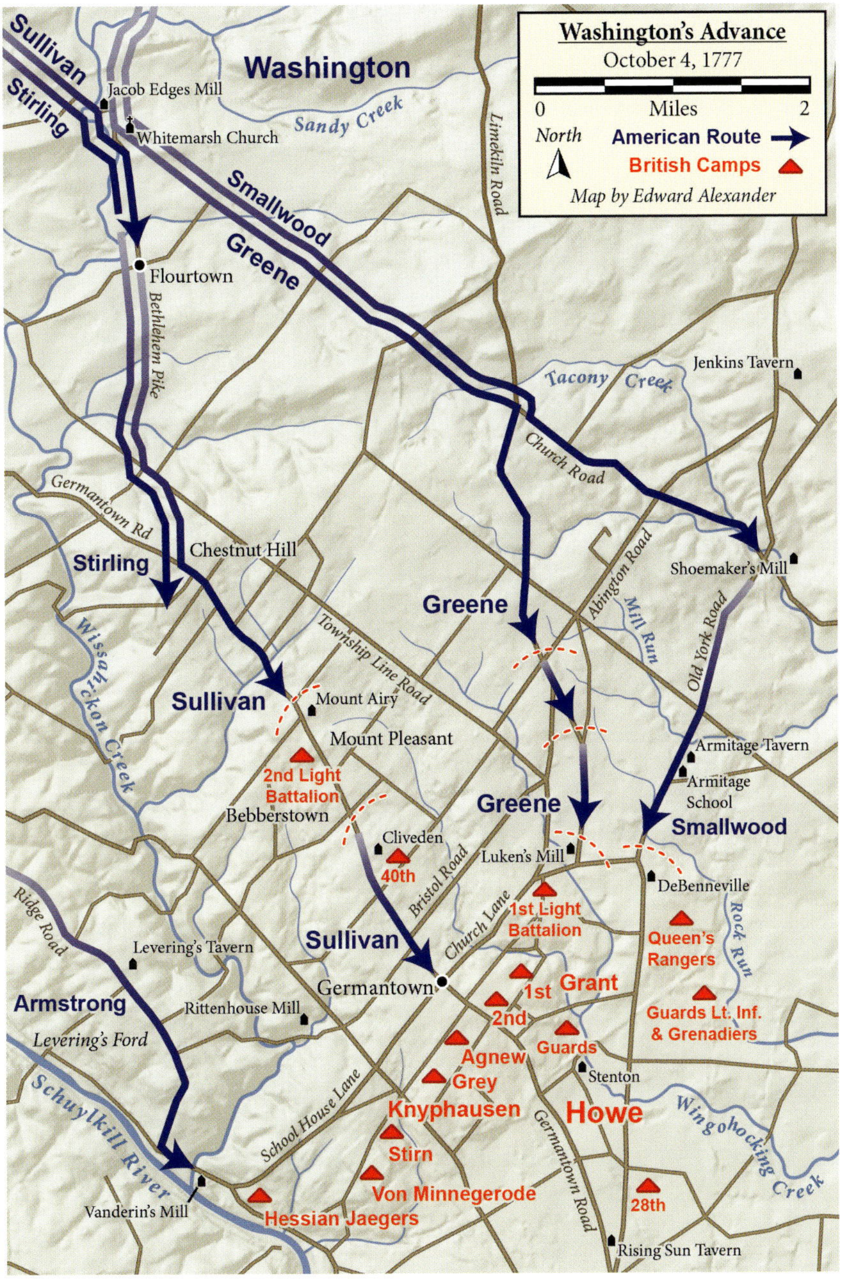

timing of departure was crucial; any such errors could throw the entire attack plan off and result in piecemeal assault, leaving the British to concentrate troops as each attack developed. A final key to the battle plan was destroying Howe's Germantown garrison before any reinforcements could arrive from Philadelphia, six miles away. If all went according to plan, the Americans would have a six-mile semicircle formation with each column separated by broken country and deep ravines.

The British high command was warned of the impending attack and had at least two hours to prepare to receive it. Unfortunately for the men at the front, not all the units at Germantown were warned that the enemy was approaching in the dark, including the outposts that would be hit first. The mental and physical fatigue brought about by months of campaigning had worn down the British leadership by October 4, 1777.

Miraculously, each of Washington's columns arrived at their designated positions outside Germantown within about fifteen minutes of each other. Whatever Washington learned from Trenton, by the time Brandywine was behind him he firmly believed his army could undertake a much more complicated task. His command had spent the months before Germantown rebuilding itself and was semi-professional at best. Much of this army was still composed of mostly raw militia. Perhaps the most surprising achievement that day was that all four columns arrived where they were expected. Despite poor communication and the lackluster performance of Casimir Pulaski's horsemen, who failed to maintain contact between the four columns, they also arrived almost simultaneously.

Just as day was breaking and thick fog blanketed the ground, Washington's divisions attacked. On Washington's right, Pennsylvania militia assaulted the Hessian jaegers near the mouth of Wissahickon Creek. To their left, John Sullivan led five brigades of Continentals directly down Germantown Road to strike to heart of the British camp. Aiding Sullivan's drive, Nathanael Greene commanded another five Continental brigades down Limekiln Pike on Sullivan's left. Rounding out the American formation, Maryland and New Jersey militia struck the British right flank. If and when success was achieved, Washington held Lord Stirling's division in reserve to exploit any breakthrough.

Brigadier General Casimir Pulaski, 1745–1779

Casimir Pulaski was born on March 6, 1745, on a family estate near Warsaw, Poland. In the late 1760s he led a partisan force against the Russian army during a series of revolts in his native land. By 23 he was in command of the military arm of the Confederation of Bar, a patriotic movement that sought to evict the Russians from Poland and restore sovereignty to the country. Pulaski was captured by the Russians but managed to flee Poland. He briefly aided the Turks against Russia, spent time in a French debtors' prison, and immigrated to America. Pulaski landed at Marblehead, Massachusetts, on July 23, 1777, and caught up with Washington's army on August 21.

(New York Public Library)

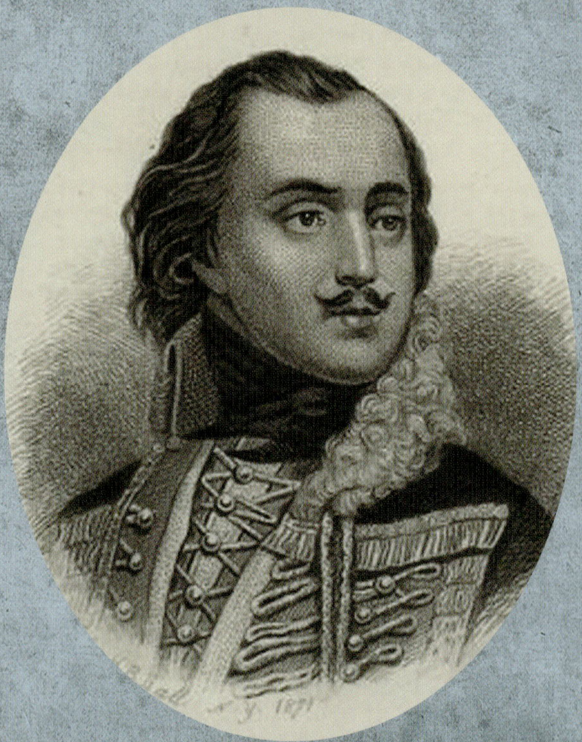

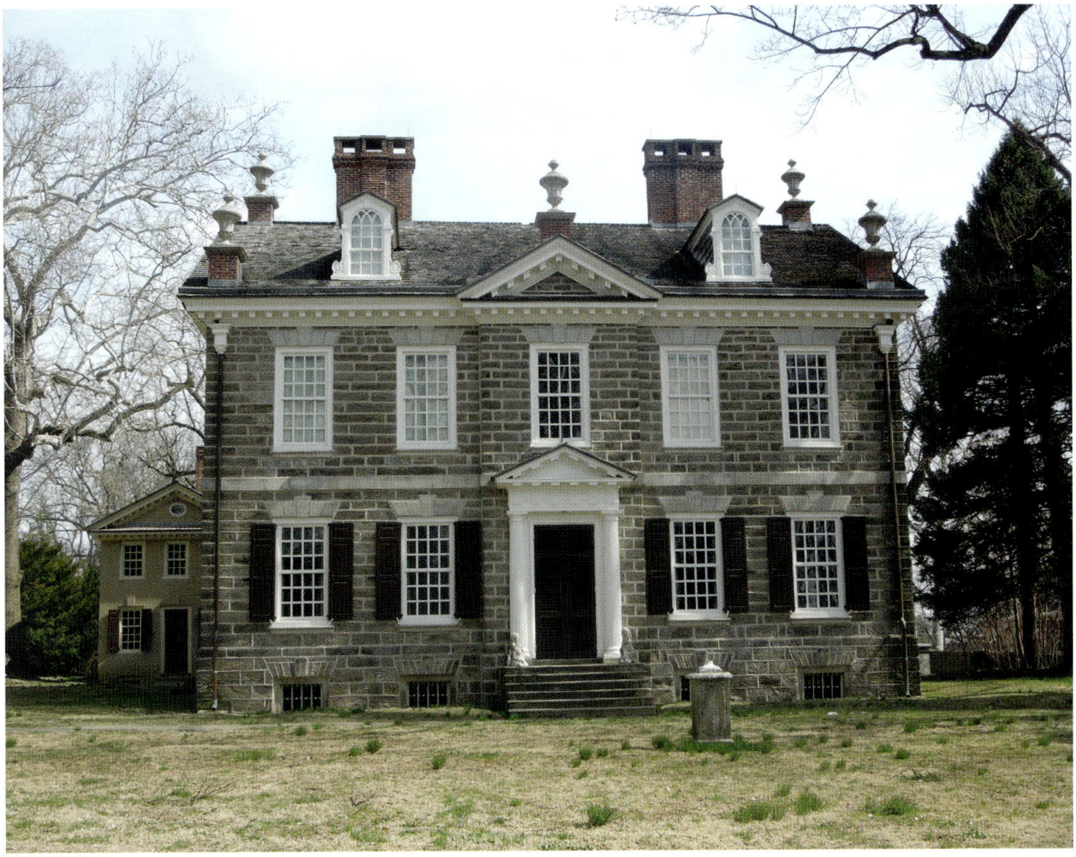

▲ Present-day view of Cliveden. The 40th Regiment of Foot camped in the rear of the house and turned it into a stronghold during the battle. (Author's collection)

▶ Present-day view of the Bensell House, where the argument over assaulting Cliveden took place. (Author's collection)

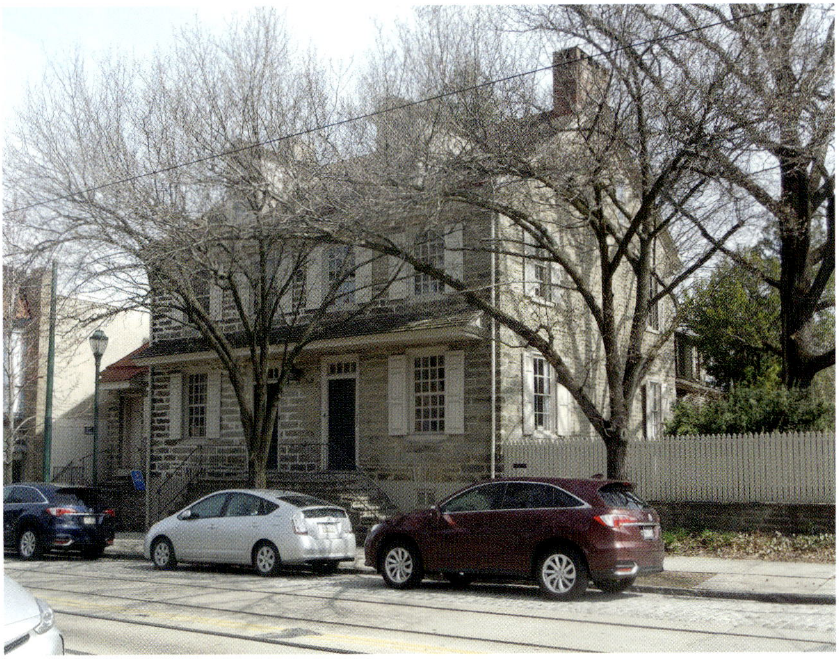

Once the engagement began, the British light infantry experienced a complete breakdown of discipline and were overwhelmed by superior numbers and, at least early in the fighting, better tactical management. Their conduct disgusted Howe, but the superior discipline within the British ranks proved decisive in the end despite the shortcomings of Howe and the tactical surprise achieved by Washington.

At the height of American success, elements of the 40th Regiment of Foot barricaded themselves within Benjamin Chew's substantial stone house. Thomas Musgrave's decision to save his regiment by moving into Cliveden rather than buckle to surrender on the spot or rout with the rest proved fatal to Washington's attack. American indecision and preoccupation at Cliveden allowed the stunned British legions to regroup. Once the rallying began, Generals James Grant, Charles Grey, and James Agnew moved their brigades forward and pushed the Americans out of Germantown.

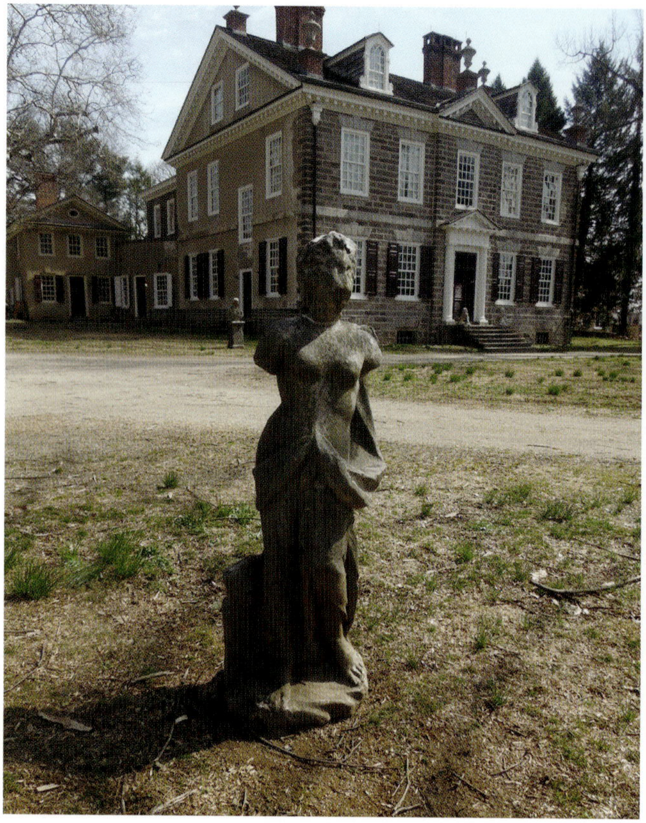

▲ A surviving example of the Cliveden statuary showing battle damage. (Author's collection)

Regardless of the performance and ability of the four columns, the responsibility for the defeat rested with Washington. Once the American columns arrived and the British line was collapsing, the pivot point of the battle rested on the decision made at Cliveden to surround and assault Musgrave's men holed up inside the Chew house. Rather than make his own intuitive decision, Washington held an impromptu council of war on the field. Henry Knox insisted the troops inside the house had to be neutralized before continuing to drive south into Germantown. It was a tactically flawed decision that tied up many hundreds of men and commands that would otherwise have continued the attack and kept the British off balance. Washington's decision turned the initiative over to the enemy. Men like Timothy Pickering argued against the move, but Washington ordered the assault stopped while Lord Stirling's reserve division deployed to eliminate Musgrave's position.

A much better policy would have been to leave an exhausted regiment or two behind to keep Musgrave inside the house while the balance of the available men continued the attack. Stirling's fresh units may well have proven decisive in overwhelming the British camps deeper in Germantown. Instead, the men under Anthony Wayne and Sullivan well to the front heard firing in their rear, believed they had been flanked, and reversed course. During the chaotic withdrawal Americans fired into one another. The time wasted around Cliveden and withdrawal of the two divisions in the middle of the American assault gave the British the time they needed to regroup and push back.

The well-trained veteran British troops pushed back the confused and inexperienced Continentals, regained the lost ground, freeing Musgrave's men from Cliveden, and driving the Americans off the field. The rank-and-file Americans did their duty and performed heroically. Once again, the choices made at the highest levels failed them. Just as poor intelligence had doomed the Americans at Brandywine, poor tactical decisions did the same at Germantown. Ultimately, Washington failed the army; the army did not fail him.

The village of Germantown had hosted the battle without a say in the matter and paid the price for that dubious honor. Destruction was visible as far as the eye could see, in all directions, and the smell of death and ashes filled nostrils. The once-stout fences that had interfered with organized lines of battle had been ripped apart or knocked to the ground. Manicured fields and orchards, churned by thousands

Colonel Timothy Pickering, 1745–1829

Timothy Pickering was the senior staff officer traveling with Washington's Continental Army. Born in Massachusetts in 1745 and graduated from Harvard in 1763, he was employed in Salem in the office of the registrar of deeds until the eve of the war. He rose to the rank of colonel in 1774. Pickering's "Plan of Discipline" was widely used in the army until it adopted Baron von Steuben's manual in 1778. Pickering took part in the Lexington alert in 1775 and in the New York and New Jersey campaigns through early 1777. His service brought the 32-year-old to the attention of Washington, who appointed Pickering to his top staff position, adjutant general, on June 18, 1777.

(Library of Congress)

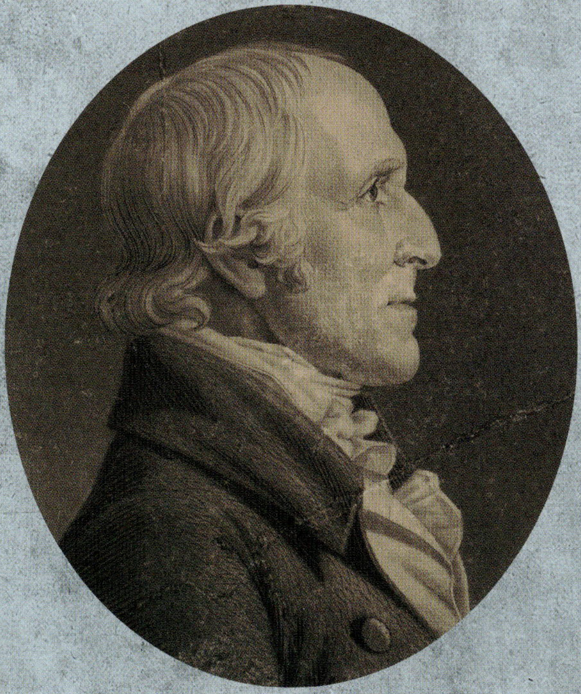

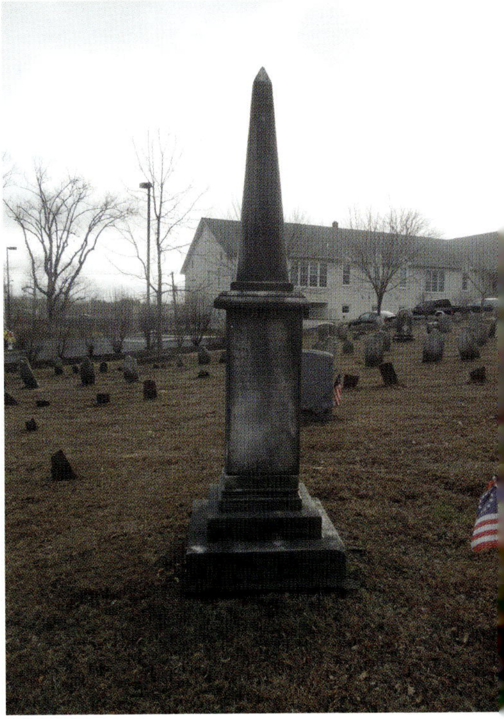

▼ The grave of Brig. Gen. Francis Nash in Towamencin Township, PA. (Author's collection)

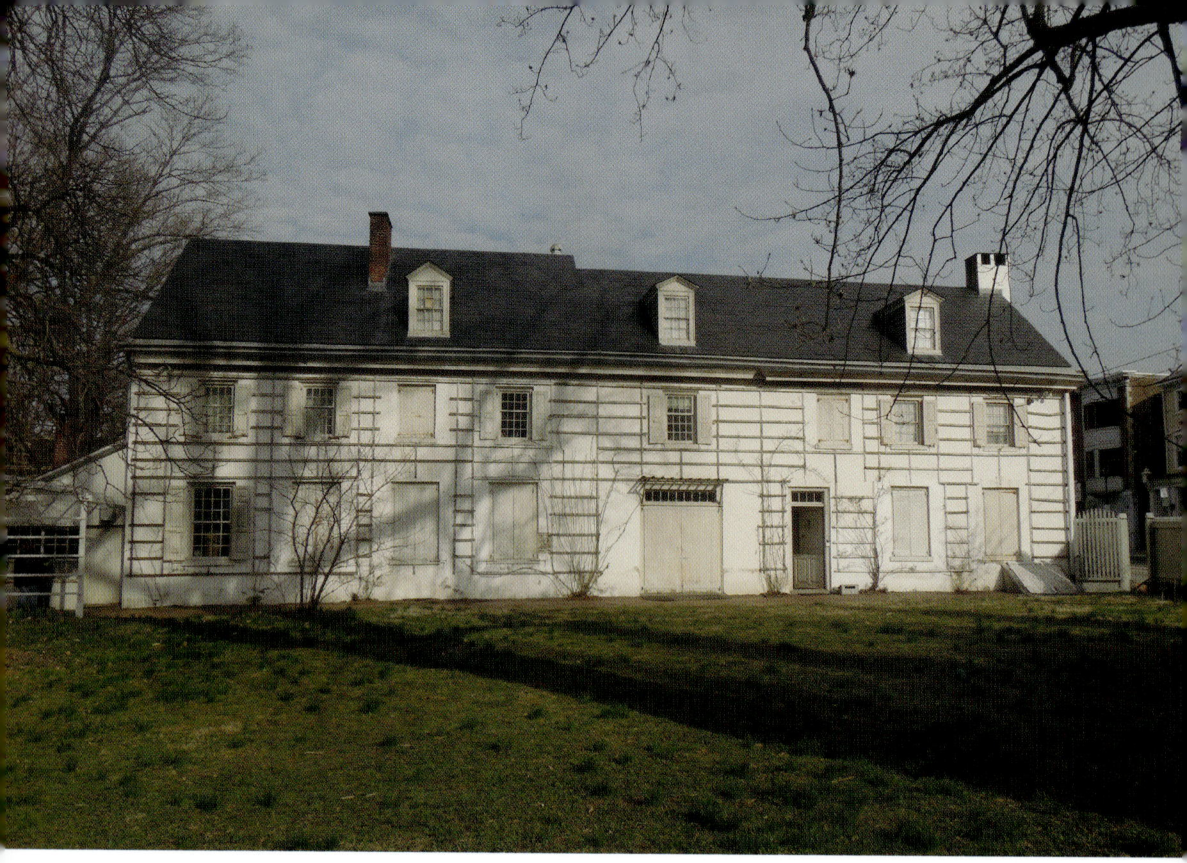

of feet and gouged by musket balls and cannon fire, lay in ruins. The amber buckwheat, where the British light infantry had been surprised and slaughtered had been trampled and ruined. Blood stains were visible on trees, fence posts, rocks, and the sides of houses. Cliveden's grounds were strewn with dead Continentals, and American artillery fire had permanently damaged the house's stone walls.

George Washington reported 152 men killed, 521 wounded, and "upwards" of 400 captured, including 54 officers. Unfortunately, no official casualty reports for individual regiments, brigades, or divisions have been found. On average, each Continental brigade lost just under 100 men; the militia suffered negligible casualties as they were not as heavily engaged.

William Howe's army suffered 80 killed, 426 wounded, and 14 missing among the British troops, and another 24 wounded in the Hessian ranks. Unlike the casualties suffered at Brandywine three weeks earlier, the Germantown losses were incurred within a concentrated area in just four hours of fighting. Howe's casualties at Brandywine had been spread across ten

▲ Present-day view of Wyck. The home would be used as a field hospital following the battle. (Author's collection)

▼ Following the battle, many homes in Germantown were converted into field hospitals for the British casualties. (Author's collection)

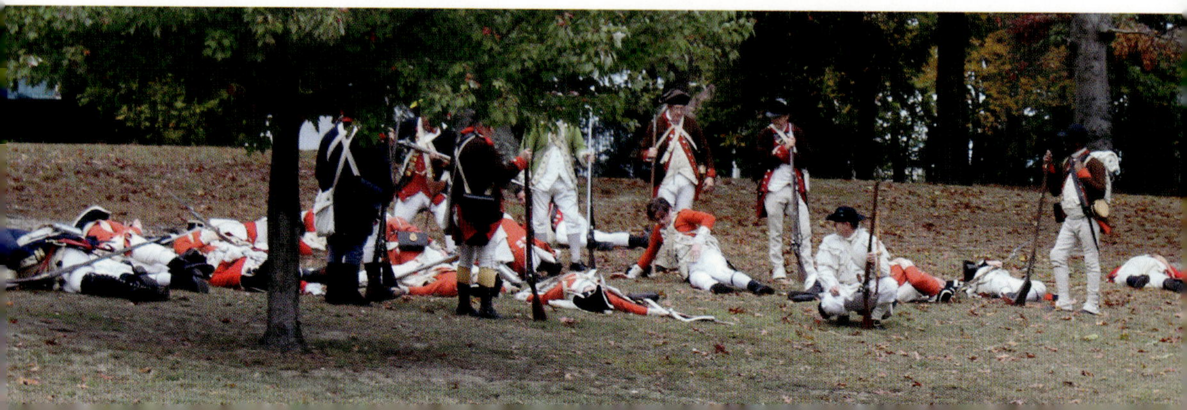

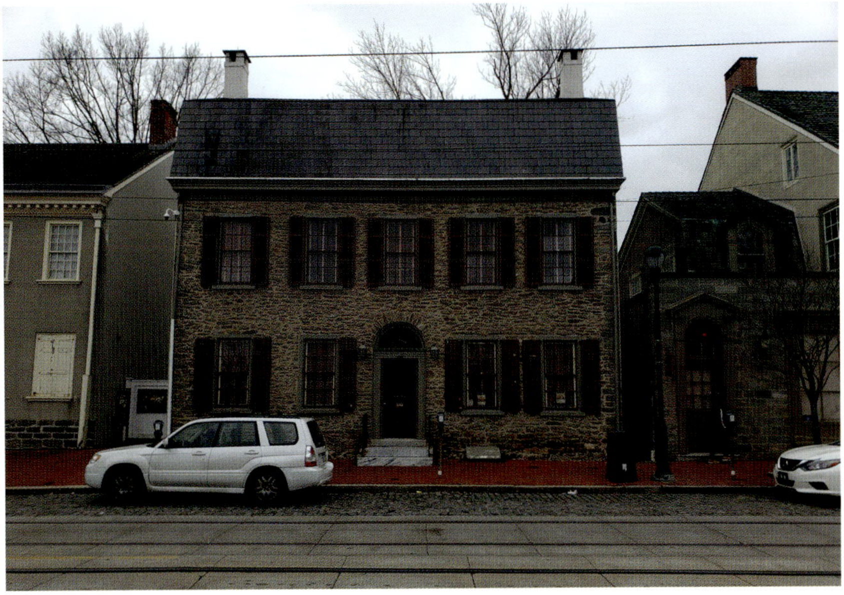

▶ Present-day view of Bringhurst, where Lieut. Col. John Bird died of his wounds. (Author's collection)

square miles and were incurred over the course of one very long day.

The September 11, 1777 Battle of Brandywine was the largest battle of both the Philadelphia Campaign and the Revolutionary War and garners most of the attention from historians and readers. Germantown, however, fought about three weeks later on October 4, stands out in its own right. It was one of the larger engagements of the Revolution and like Brandywine ended in a sharp tactical defeat. Unlike the earlier battle, it was the first time George Washington launched an assault against the main British army in North America. He nearly won.

One of Nathanael Greene's brigade commanders, George Weedon, found reason to be optimistic in the wake of the defeat. "[T]he British Army is by

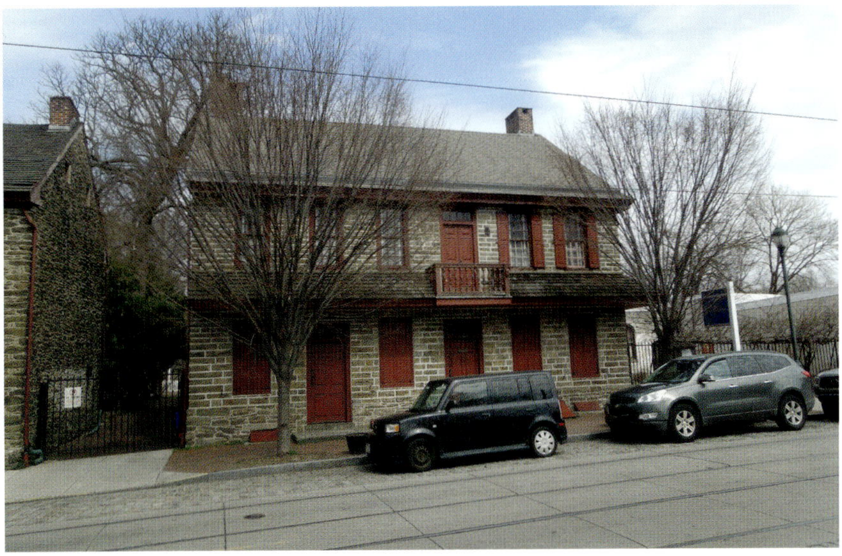

▶ Present-day view of Grumblethorpe, where Brig. Gen. James Agnew died of his wounds (Author's collection)

these Engagements diminishing fast," he observed, "ours are reinforcing . . . we shall be stronger than the first day we opened the Campaign." Weedon turned philosophical about the misfortune. "The chance of war [is] so uncertain, that when victory was in our hands, we had not Grace to keep it, Indeed the misfortunes of that Day was owing to the most horrid Fogg I ever saw," he complained. "That with the smoak together rendered it impossible to Distinguish our men from the Enemy at a greater Distance than sixty yards, and many favourable advantages were lost, from not being certain who were friends & who Foes, And From the Different Divisions and Brigades not being able by that means, to Co-operate with each other." So much had hinged on the battle's outcome, and the rebels were as close to victory as they had ever been. "[T]he Grand cause was in my opinion in one Quarter of an hour of being finally settled that Day, to the eternal honor of America," he asserted. "They [the British] confess themselves had we Continued the attack fifteen minutes longer, a general retreat over the Schulkill would have taken place, to Chester in Delaware where their shipping lay, it was ordered by Genl Howe just as we gave way."

Pennsylvanian Anthony Wayne, who marched in John Sullivan's column, had faced his own difficulties following Paoli but had nothing but praise for Washington. "You are now in my Humble Opinion in as good if not a better Situation than you were before this Action," he explained. "[Y]our Men are convinced that the Enemy may be drove, and Altho' we fell back yet our people have gained Confidence—and have Raised some Doubts in the Minds of the Enemy which will facilitate their total Defeat the Next Tryal ... which I wish to see brought to Issue the soonest Possible. Upon the Whole," he concluded, "it was a Glorious day." Wayne concluded with a word of caution: "I don't yet despair; if our Worthy General will but follow his own good Judgement, without listening too much to some Counsel." Wayne, in his unique way, was warning Washington not to depend upon artilleryman Henry Knox as much as he had before Cliveden at the fatal hour at Germantown.

Light Horse Harry Lee of the light dragoons wrote a significant amount on the battle as his life progressed. Victory, or as he described it, "This precious fruit is only to be plucked by the cooperating skill and courage of the whole body. Unfortunate as was the issue of the battle at Germantown," he elaborated, "it manifested the unsubdued, though broken spirit, of the American army; and taught the enemy to expect renewal of combat, whenever adequacy of force or fitness of opportunity should authorize repetition of battle." The sharp combat at Germantown, he concluded, "gave, too, animation to the country at large, exciting in congress, and in the people, invigorated zeal in the great cause in which they were engaged."

Numerous politicians commented on the battle and campaign. Maryland congressman Charles Carroll remained as optimistic as many of Washington's officers. "Our cause is just, our men are becoming more warlike, the blood already spilt will raise a spirit of obstinacy & revenge which will supply the place in some measure of discipline. We have many resources, if we have sense enough to [use] them; then let us hope we shall make use of them, and that we shall conquer in the end." Connecticut congressman Eliphet Dyer insisted that before the fog—which he labeled "this Unfortunate mistake"—"Snatched [victory] out of our hands the prospect was full, of our Army in a very few hours again entering Philadelphia but once more

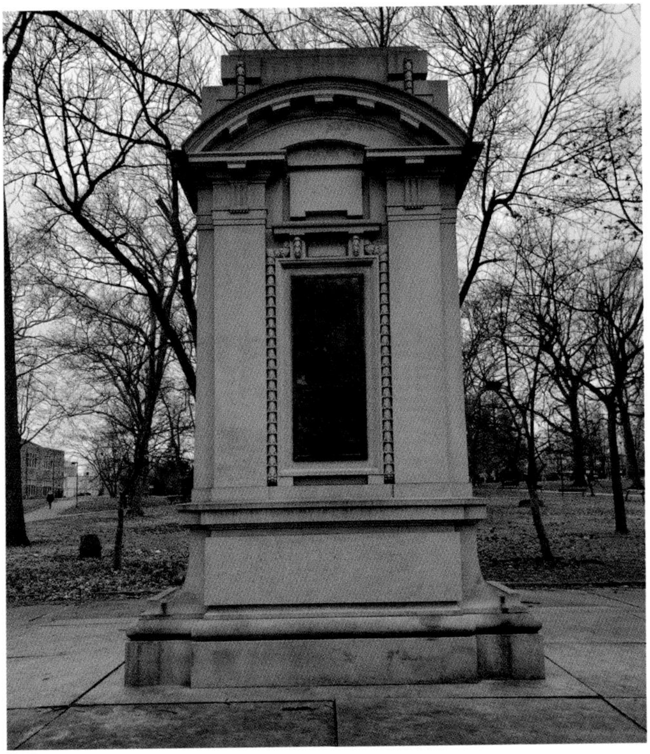

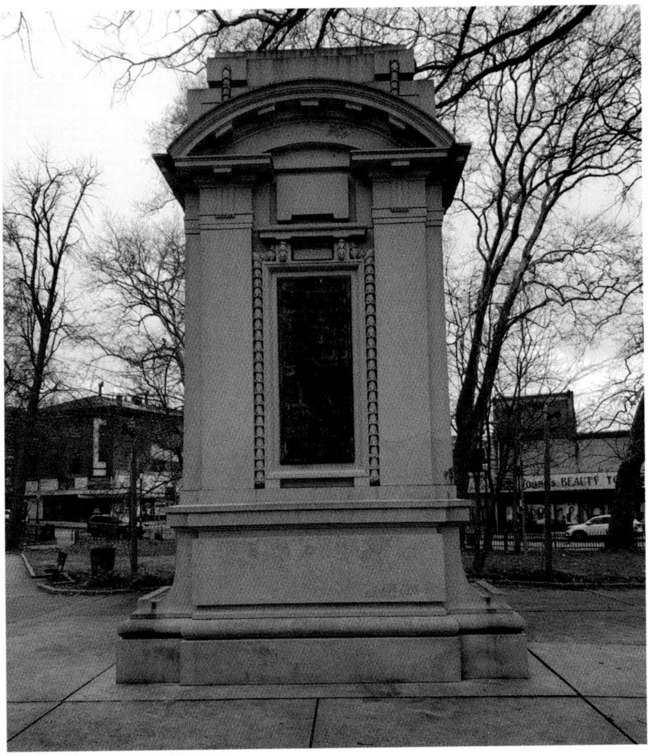

disappointed." John Adams firmly believed that the heavy attack at Germantown helped negotiations with the French and wrote to fellow congressman James Lovell precisely that. "General Gates was the ablest negotiator you ever had in Europe; and next to him, General Washington's attack upon the enemy at Germantown. I do not know, indeed, whether this last affair had not more influence upon the European mind than that of Saratoga," he added. "Although the attempt was unsuccessful, the military gentlemen in Europe considered it as the most decisive proof that America would finally succeed."

There was plenty of blame to go around—even within the victorious army. William Howe made no effort to put his Germantown camp in a defensive posture in the days leading up to the battle. The matter of his deployment interested Parliament, before which he testified on the matter. "I beg leave to inform the Committee, that my first position at German-Town was taken to cover Philadelphia, during the operations carrying on against Mud-Island [Fort Mifflin], and was therefore more extended than it otherwise would have been," he explained. "It is true, however, that I did not expect the enemy would have dared to approach after so recent a defeat as that at Brandywine. In this Idea I did not direct any redoubts to be raised for the security of the camp or out-posts," he continued, "nor did I ever encourage the construction of them at the head of the line when in force, because works of that kind are apt to induce an opinion of inferiority, and my wish was, to support by every means the acknowledged superiority of the King's troops over the enemy, which I considered more peculiarly essential, where strength

◄ Front and rear views of the 1906 Battle of Germantown Monument located in Vernon Park in Germantown. (Author's collection)

was not to be estimated by numbers, since the enemy in that respect, by calling in the force of the country upon any emergence, must have superior." Howe concluded, "I confess also it was for the above reasons I did not change my position, after making the detachments before mentioned, choosing rather to trust to the well-tried vigiliance of the troops, and the activity of the patroles (though I had intimation that an attack might be made) than to give the army unnecessary fatigue, by making more cautionary preparations."

The decision to stop at Cliveden was a gift for Howe. "The enemy was held up a long time by this fortunate decision," confessed Ensign Wilhelm Freyenhagen of the Hessian von Donop Regiment. "This gave the army time to get organized, meet all the attacks and send the necessary reinforcements there. General Washington, in spite of his overwhelming numbers, was beaten back." Captain von Muenchhausen of Howe's staff confirmed that "this maneuver [into the Chew house] by Colonel Musgrave was extremely helpful to our corps..This eased the situation [the collapse of front]."

While many British seemed reluctant to comment openly on the battle, the Hessians had no such apprehension. Howe's aide, Friedrich von Muenchhausen, even voiced as much. "Everyone admits that Washington's attack was very well planned," he confessed. "He knew our exact positions through his very good spies. He was also aware that all regiments stood in one line in our camp, which by now was not quite as large, several detachments having been sent off. He was further aware that we could not send any regiments to places where he might attack without breaking our line." Jaeger officer Lt. Heinrich von Feilitzsch openly praised the American attack. "If the rebels had only moved forward and had not delayed, our oncoming regiments would not have had a chance to ready their arms; the plan of the rebels was very good," he concluded, "but its execution had flaws." The Anspach jaeger criticized the British high command. "At our army, everything was in confusion, a few battalions of Hessians which were located behind the Jagers, did not even take up their weapons, they had been completely forgotten, under these circumstances, a bold enemy could do anything. It was previously known, that the enemy wanted to attack, the army had been informed," he chastised, "and still, those at headquarters were so lax—I don't know what to think of that!"

Captain Johann Ewald, who was critical of British decision-making throughout the war, praised Lt. Col. Thomas Musgrave's defense of Cliveden but bashed Howe's generalship. "This example of a single brave and intelligent man, through whom the entire English army was saved, shows what courage and decision in war can do," asserted the German. "For had the English army been defeated here, enclosed within the angle of two rivers with a large city of rebellious-minded inhabitants in the rear, all honor truly would have been lost, though it would have been destroyed solely through the negligence of the Commanding General."

With the Battle of Germantown behind him, William Howe turned his attention to the Delaware River. It was time to clear the obstacles blocking the Royal Navy from docking at Philadelphia.

The Delaware River War

Thus far in the campaign, the Delaware River defenses played only a minor role in the decision making of both armies. At the end of July when William Howe entered the Delaware Bay with his armada, he made the fateful decision to not land his army somewhere along the Delaware River. Howe chose not to do that and returned to sea and the Chesapeake Bay. Not until after the Battle of Brandywine six weeks later was any serious consideration given to the Delaware River defenses again.

Once Philadelphia fell on September 26, Washington decided to cause as many problems as possible for the British by controlling the Delaware River. If Washington could bar access to Philadelphia by the Royal Navy, he might be

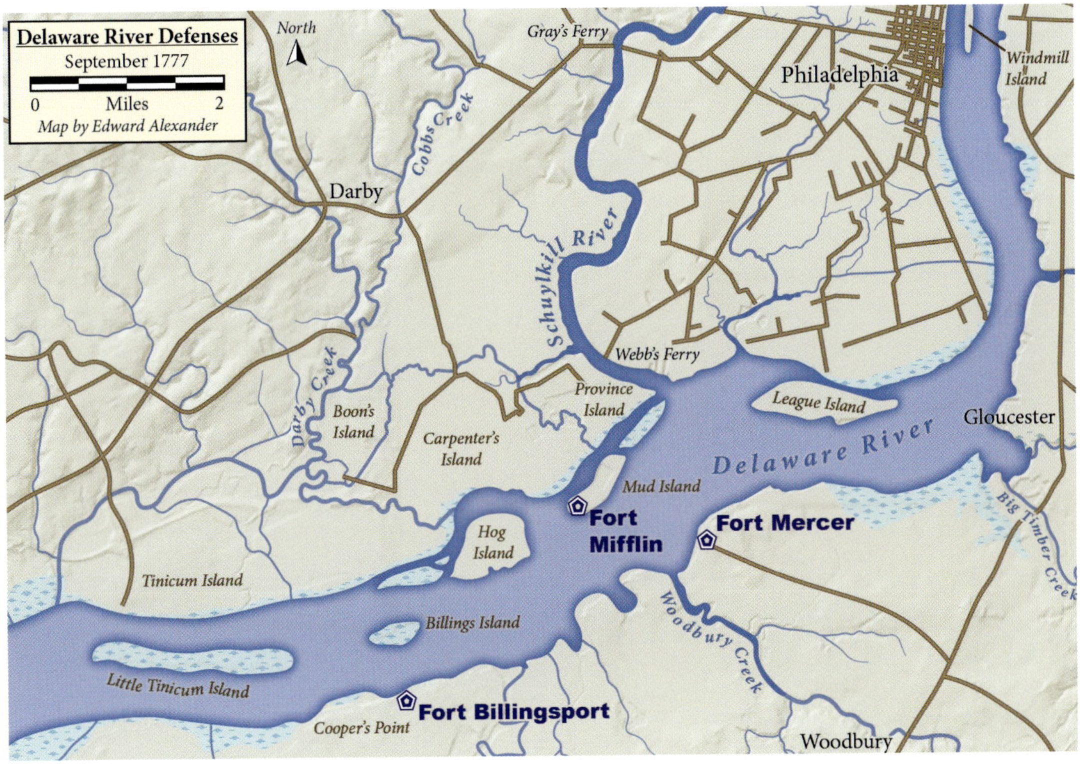

able to starve Howe's army into submission much as he had done at Boston two years previously. Washington remained upbeat about his chances of holding the river and beating Howe. The seat of the American government had fallen, but Congress reestablished itself in the Pennsylvania backcountry. Where it operated was not nearly as important as was the fact that it was still in existence. The army's major supply depot in Reading remained intact, and was still supplying his growing army. If the war had demonstrated anything thus far, it was that occupying a city meant little in a sprawling multi-colony revolution like this one. The British had once occupied Boston but had been forced to leave. New York had been lost, but the war continued apace. It was slowly becoming clear that who held which major city meant much less in this war than it did on the European continent.

The host of problems and decisions Washington had to make included the management of the vitally important American defenses along the Delaware River. This line consisted primarily of three forts: Mercer (on the east bank of the river at Red Bank in New Jersey); Mifflin (directly across from Mercer on a mud island on the Pennsylvania shore); and Billingsport, two miles downstream on the same side of the river as Mercer. Three lines of chevaux de frise blocked the river and were protected by the placement of the forts. All four of these forms of defense were in place by the beginning of October and each depended on the others for success. The Pennsylvania Navy under Commodore John Hazelwood assembled several watercrafts near Fort Mifflin to prevent the approach of the Royal Navy.

With Philadelphia now in hand, Howe needed to keep the Continental Army at bay while his own command, with the assistance of the British fleet, endeavored to open the Delaware River to provide provisions and supplies to his army.

▼ Map showing fortifications and chevaux-de-frise positions erected by Washington's troops along Delaware River, 1777. (Library of Congress)

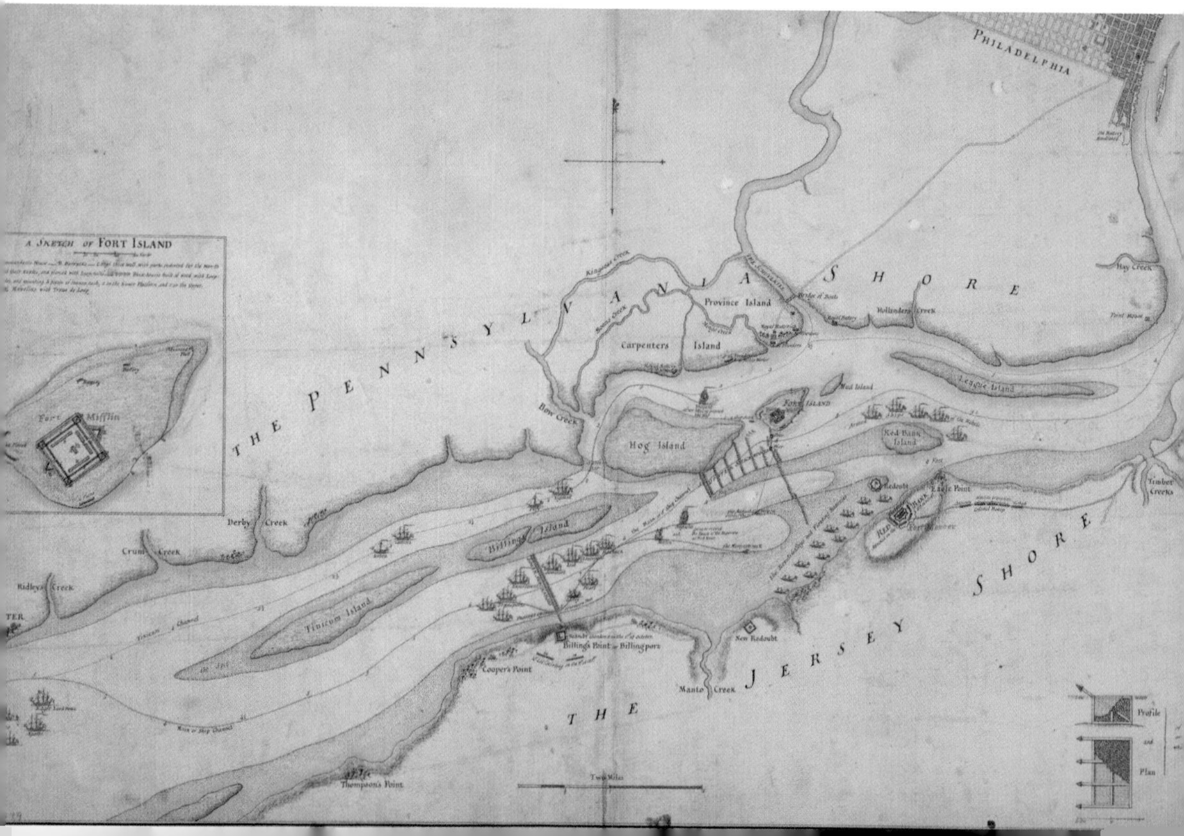

▶ Map showing course of Delaware River around Philadelphia, 1777. It shows several works constructed by British troops following their taking of the city in September 1777. (Library of Congress)

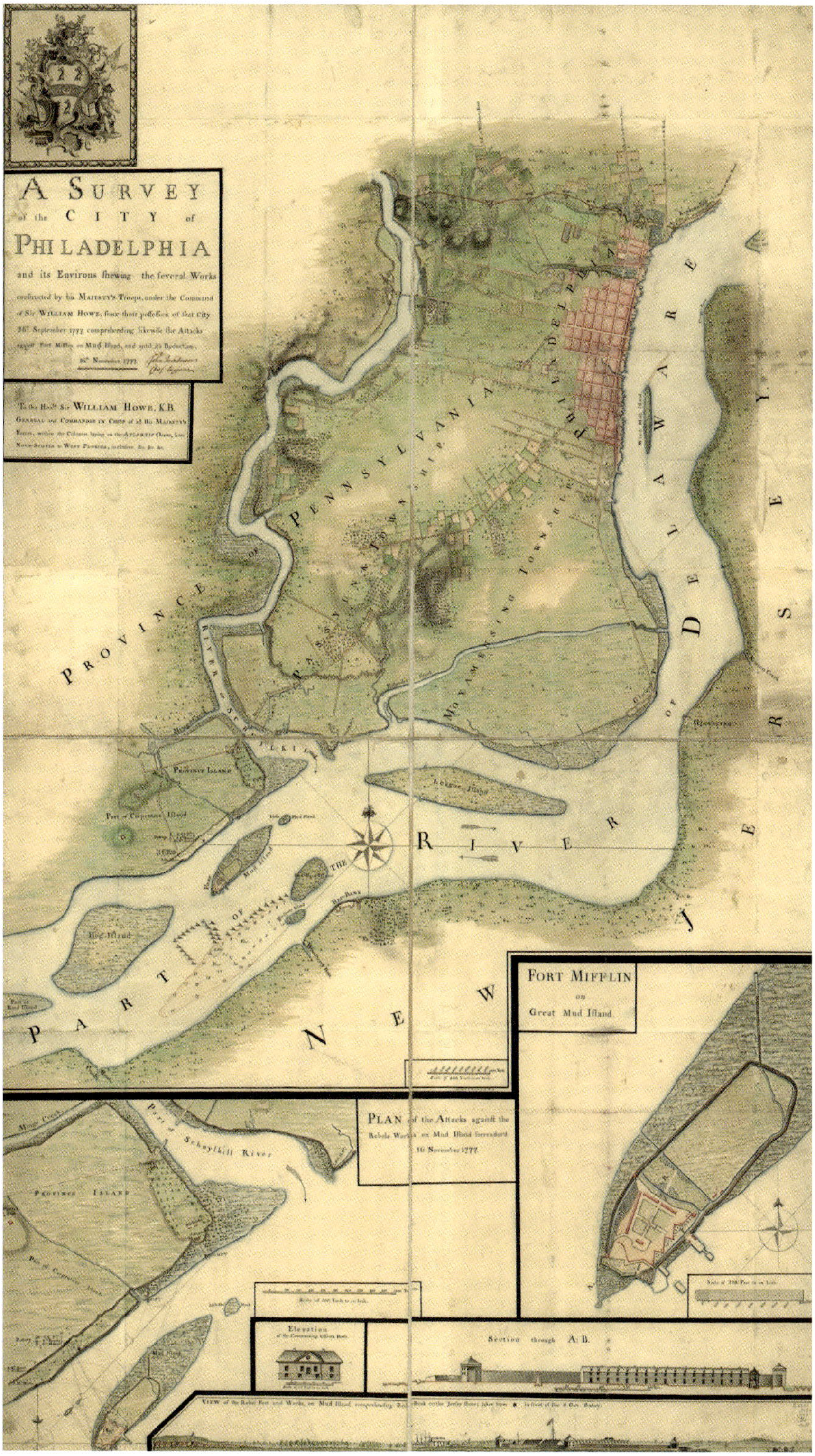

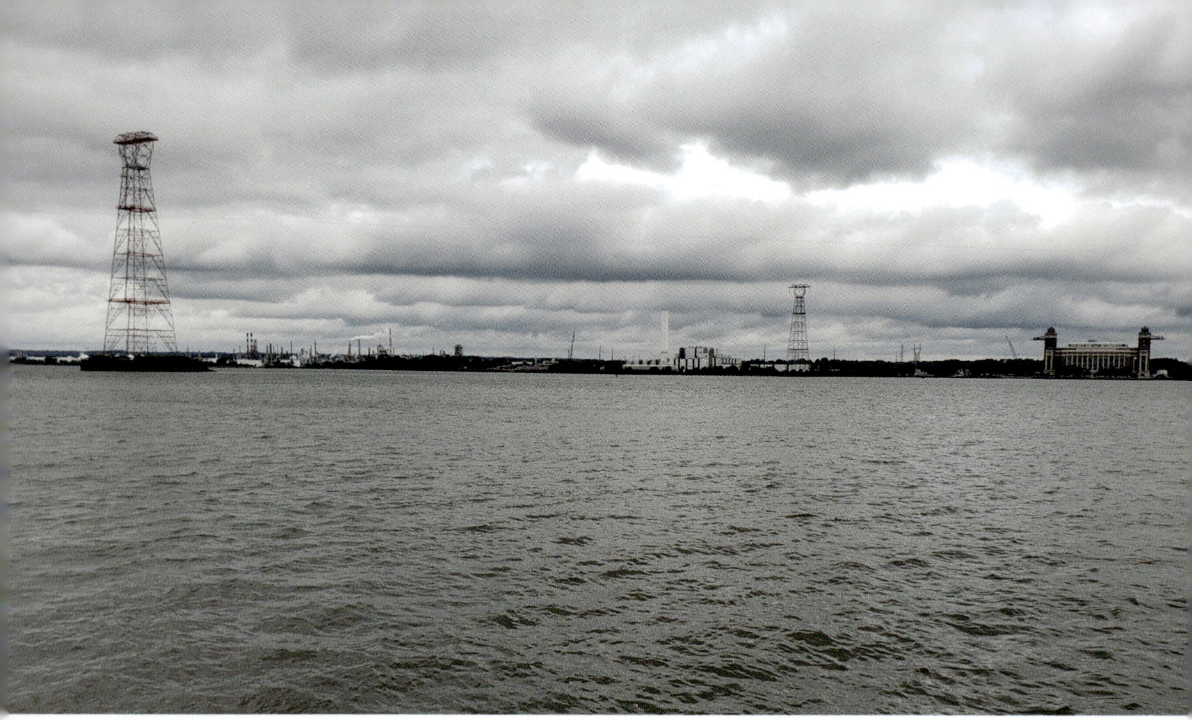

▲ Present-day view of location on Delaware River where the British crossed for the Billingsport operation. (Author's collection)

The Loss of the *Delaware*

The citizens of Philadelphia were greeted with the sound of cannon fire rolling across the waters of the Delaware on the morning of September 27. None of them knew what to make of it.

The combined Continental and state fleet that morning consisted of the 24-gun *Delaware* and her 150-man crew in the lead, together with the 24-gun State guard ship *Montgomery*, Continental 8-gun sloop *Fly*, and five row galleys, each carrying a single gun. When the *Delaware* rounded Gloucester Point, British drummers alerted the garrison and Royal artillerymen and grenadiers of the 1st British Battalion formed up to prepare for whatever was coming their way.

Those aboard the *Delaware* felt anything but secure as British rounds began striking the frigate. Flaming embers flew in every direction and spread small deck fires that threatened to engulf the ship. Confusion mounted on the *Delaware*. Amid the chaos, sailors mismanaged the sails as a British howitzer round crashed through the foredeck near the bow, setting the hull ablaze. The *Delaware* grounded on the lower end of Windmill Island. The crew tried to return fire as best they could but were overwhelmed by the weight of British metal. With the ship stuck fast and portions in flames, the captain had little choice but to strike her colors. By the time he did so, one crewman was dead and six wounded out of his 152-man crew. The British would later float the *Delaware* off the sandbar and repair her for their own use.

This hour-long fight around the shipyards of Philadelphia marked the beginning of

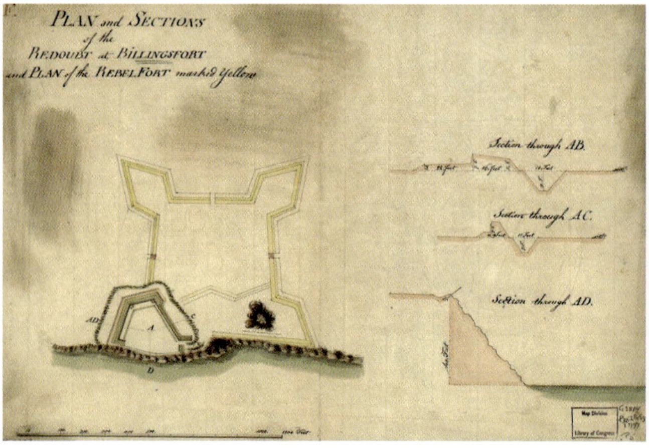

▼ Plan of the redoubt at Billingsport, 1777. (Library of Congress)

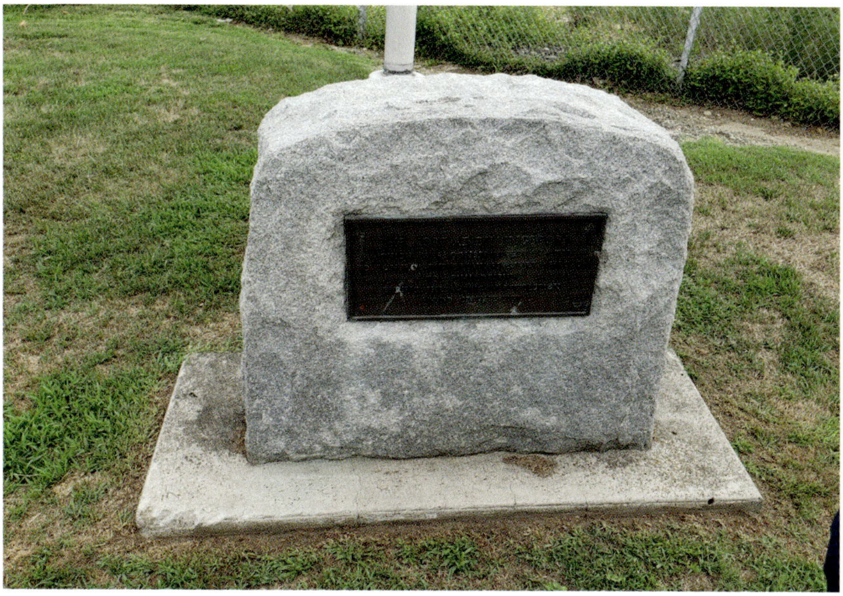

▶ Marker at the site of Fort Billingsport in Paulsboro, New Jersey. (Author's collection)

fighting for control of the Delaware River that would consume the next two months. Despite the capture of the Delaware and ease with which the American fleet had been turned back, the British worried that the river forts and obstructions were likely to cause grave long-term injury to the army. Howe set his eyes on breaking through the American river defenses by assaulting the unfinished American defensive point at Fort Billingsport, New Jersey, about two miles below Fort Mifflin and on the opposite bank of the river.

The Fall of Fort Billingsport

General Howe decided to move first against the southernmost enemy position on the river at Billingsport, New Jersey. He assigned the task on September 28 to the 10th and 42nd Regiments of Foot (nearly 1,000 troops) under Lt. Col. Thomas Stirling, together with a pair of six-pounders. Stirling's column left the encampment at Germantown and arrived that evening (September 28) at the Middle Ferry on the Schuylkill, tramped into Chester on the morning of September 29, and met up there with two battalions of the 71st Highlanders, which had come up from Wilmington, Delaware, to protect the depot being established there. The plan called for Stirling's column to cross the Delaware in long boats, march inland, turn north, and seize the unfinished fort, which would effectively remove the first line of obstructions blocking the river.

October opened with Lt. Col. Thomas Stirling's detachment of the 10th and 42nd Regiments of Foot ferrying across the Delaware for the advance against Fort Billingsport. Once organized, they pushed east from the landing site.

Stirling drove pesky New Jersey militia out of his way and the Pennsylvania militia inside the fort fled by boat from Billingsport. Lieutenant Colonel Stirling's men moved in to occupy the vacant fort while American row galleys shelled the position. Four British warships supporting the operation from downriver arrived and opened on the pesky American vessels, driving them back upriver. The loss of Billingsport meant the loss of the first line of chevaux-de-frise river obstructions. The British Navy began removing the obstructions immediately, but the tedious process would require three weeks to complete.

With the Billingsport threat eliminated and the Battle of Germantown behind him, William Howe was ready to turn his full attention to opening the Delaware River to the Royal Navy. Nearly everything Howe's army needed—including military and medical supplies and food—was stored in the holds of British ships stuck downriver from Philadelphia near Chester, Pennsylvania. The Royal Navy was still unable to navigate the Delaware. Given his precarious position, Howe turned his attention to the war along the river.

Forts Mifflin and Mercer were crucial components of Washington's strategy to tighten the logistical noose around Philadelphia. If the Americans could maintain and protect the chevaux de frise blocking the river between the forts, the British supply ships would never make it to the city. Doing, so, however, required the close cooperation of the army and naval forces, which was a near-impossibility.

On October 7, the same day Burgoyne lost the second battle of Saratoga (Bemis Heights), British engineer Capt. John Montresor scouted Province Island opposite Fort Mifflin. The British needed a foothold on Province Island not only for operations against Fort Mifflin, but also to protect its tenuous supply line along Darby Road south of the city. Despite the importance of the Delaware operations, Washington's subordinates did little to slow the efforts of British engineers intent on taking Fort Mifflin.

Fortifying the position opposite Fort Mifflin became the next item of business for the Americans. Fort Mercer, guarding the Delaware River from the New Jersey shoreline, still needed a garrison. Washington soon ordered Christopher Greene, a 40-year-old colonel and distant cousin of Nathanael Greene, to take command of Fort Mercer with two Rhode Island regiments

Fort Mercer

William Howe decided the time arrived to eliminate Fort Mercer on the New Jersey

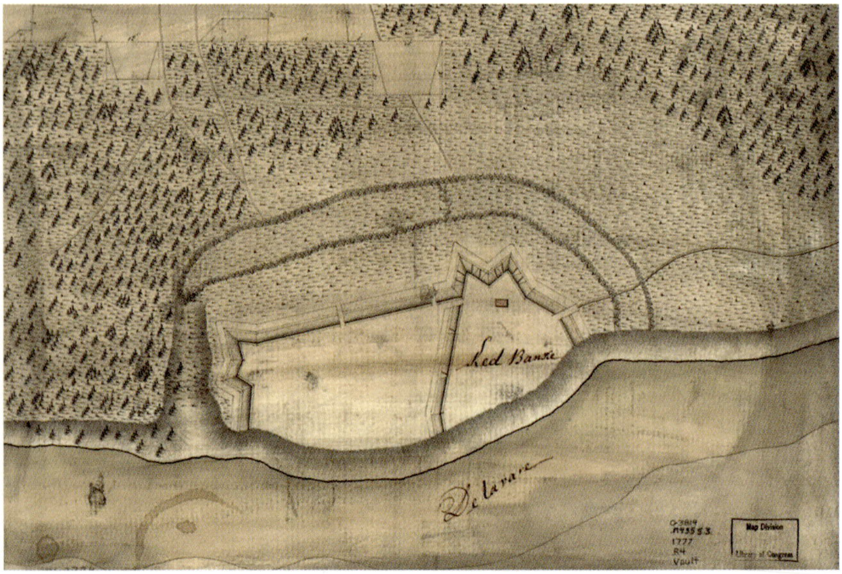

◀ Fort Mercer map, 1777. (Library of Congress)

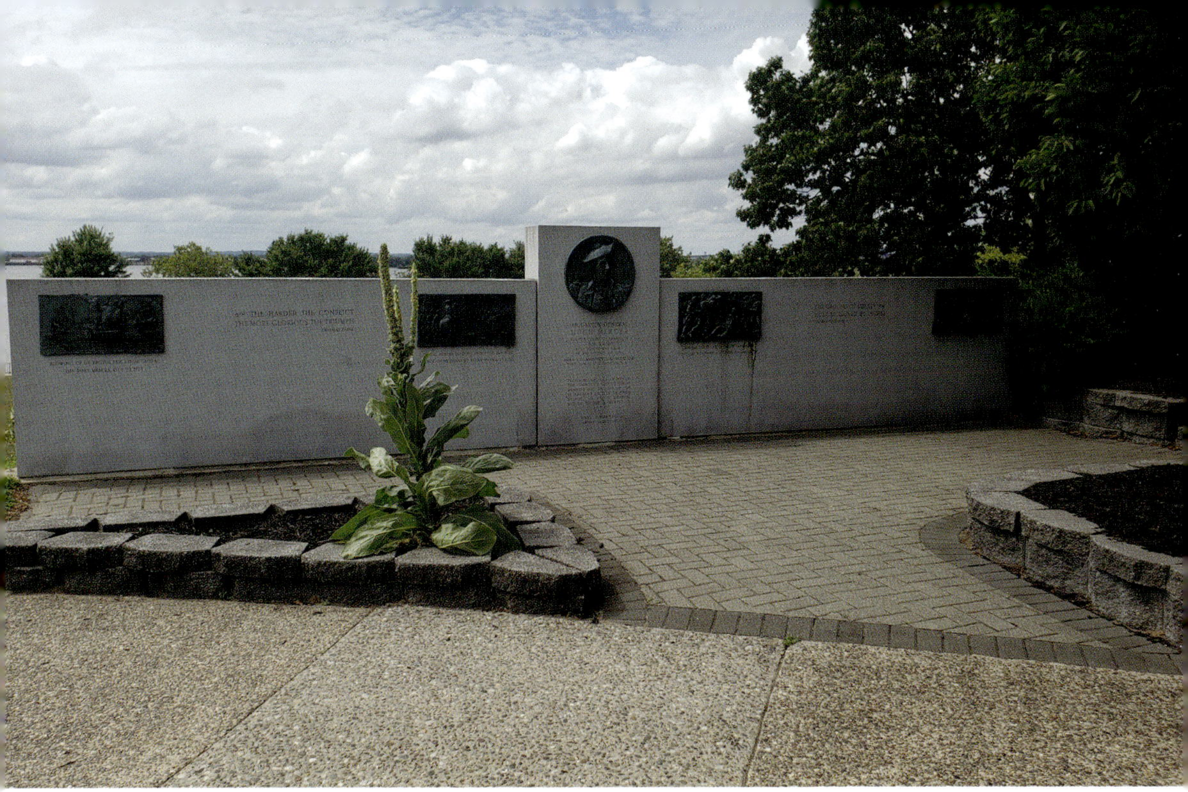

▲ Fort Mercer was named for Brig. Gen. Hugh Mercer who was killed at the Battle of Princeton. (Author's collection)

side of the Delaware River as a threat to his operations. Howe understood Fort Mifflin to be the key to the American river defenses and now realized Fort Mercer represented Fort Mifflin's lifeline. If the British occupied Fort Mercer, they could starve out the Fort Mifflin garrison. The fighting thus far in the campaign bloodied and wore down most of Howe's British regulars. Incapable of independent operations by mid-October, the elite light infantry and grenadiers suffered severely at Brandywine and Germantown. South of Philadelphia protecting Howe's lone supply line, the relatively fresh British Brigade of Guards was unavailable. With

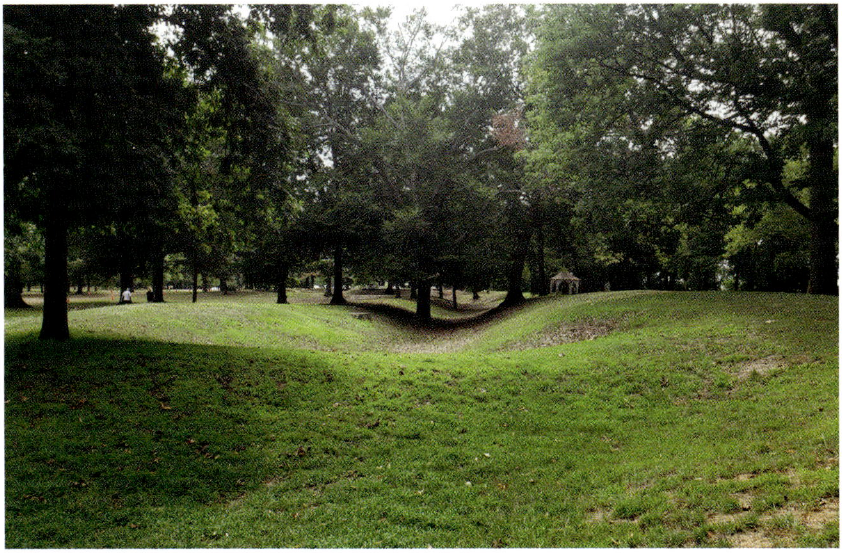

▶ Present-day view of recreated trenches at Fort Mercer. (Author's collection)

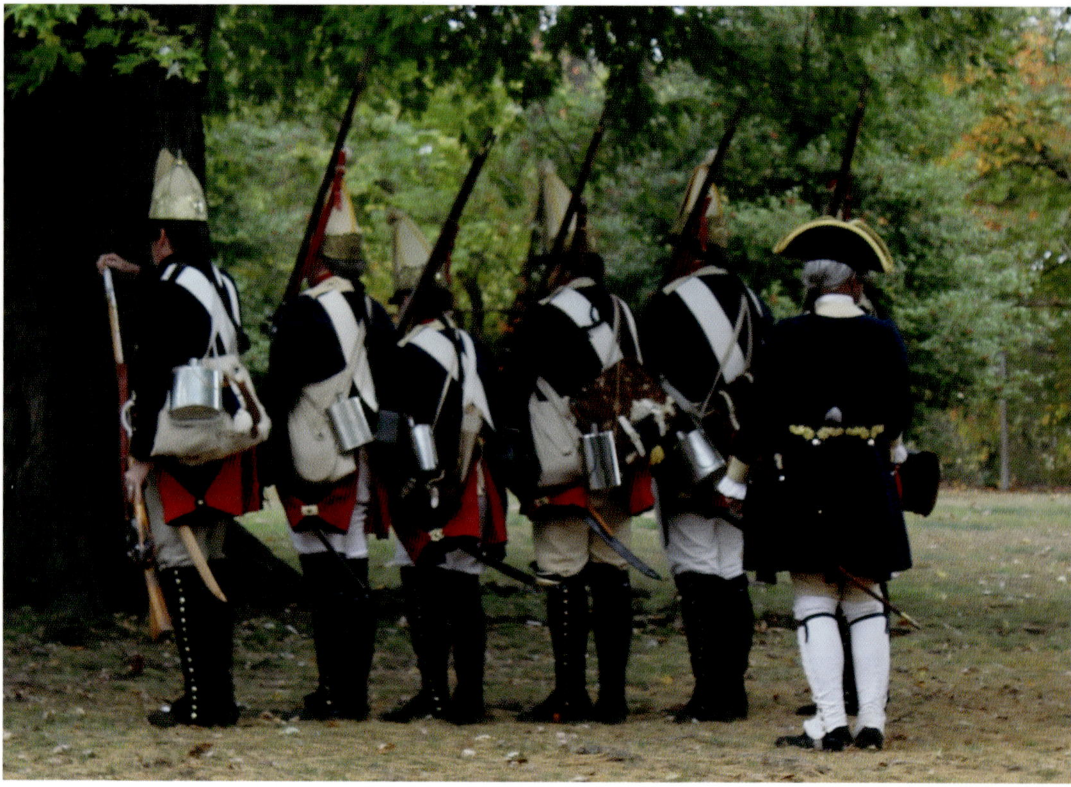

▲ Fort Mercer was assaulted by two regiments of Hessian grenadiers and another regiment of Hessian infantry. (Author's collection)

the exception of the Hessian jaegers that fought well and often in several actions throughout the campaign, the Hessian infantry and grenadiers remained mostly unused and fresh.

Many Hessian officers felt humiliated over the loss at Trenton the previous year and itched for the opportunity to redeem their reputation. The command of the Fort Mercer operation soon went to Col. Karl Emil Count von Donop. Von Donop assembled 2,200 men to complete the task—all three Hessian grenadier battalions and the von Mirbach infantry regiment. Lieutenant Colonel Ludwig von Wurmb's Hessian jaeger battalion joined the grenadiers and infantry. Leaving with the column were the eight Hessian 3-pounders attached to the regiments.

By daybreak on October 21, the Hessian jaegers unloaded at Cooper's Ferry. Militia harassment and the notoriously slow Hessian marching pace slowed the advance to a crawl. Von Donop moved four miles further inland to Haddonfield hoping to deceive the Americans as to his mission.

Von Donop's column approached Fort Mercer the next day after marching seventeen miles over eight hours. The clocked ticked toward 1 p.m. From three sides, the Hessians could assault the fort by land; the Delaware River extended along the entire western side of the works. On the north, east, and to a lesser degree the southeast, the Americans cleared the land for a distance of four hundred yards to permit a field of fire for their artillery. Thick woods lay beyond this clearing. Crawling to the edge of those woods, the moment of decision arrived for Carl von Donop.

Why was Colonel von Donop seemingly so cavalier under the circumstances?

The previous year around New York City the Americans abandoned one fortified position after another. Fort Washington, the one fortification they did not abandon, was stormed and overwhelmed by Hessians in November 1776 where they captured 2,000 Americans. Thus far around Philadelphia, the British repeatedly defeated the Continentals. In the eyes of these Hessian officers, there was little to fear at Fort Mercer.

Colonel Christopher Greene's Fort Mercer garrison consisted of his own 1st Rhode Island regiment and Col. Israel Angell's 2nd Rhode Island. Capt.-Lt. David Cook's Continental artillery company provided the manpower to man the fourteen cannon in the fort. Angell's regiment covered the northern face of the fort and Greene's regiment watched the eastern and southern faces. The total garrison numbered about 550 men including the return of men Greene previously sent to reinforce Fort Mifflin. Colonel von Donop held more than a 4 to 1 advantage. Hessian arrogance influenced decisions that day. If they pushed Greene's garrison with a show of force, the Americans would clearly collapse as they always do.

Von Donop deployed his force to attack from three directions. The von Minnigerode Battalion of grenadiers deployed on the right. In the center, toward the eastern face of the American redoubt, the von Mirbach Regiment prepared. To the left with orders to assault the south face of the redoubt stood the von Linsing Battalion of grenadiers. The jaegers and the von Lengerke Battalion of grenadiers remained in reserve.

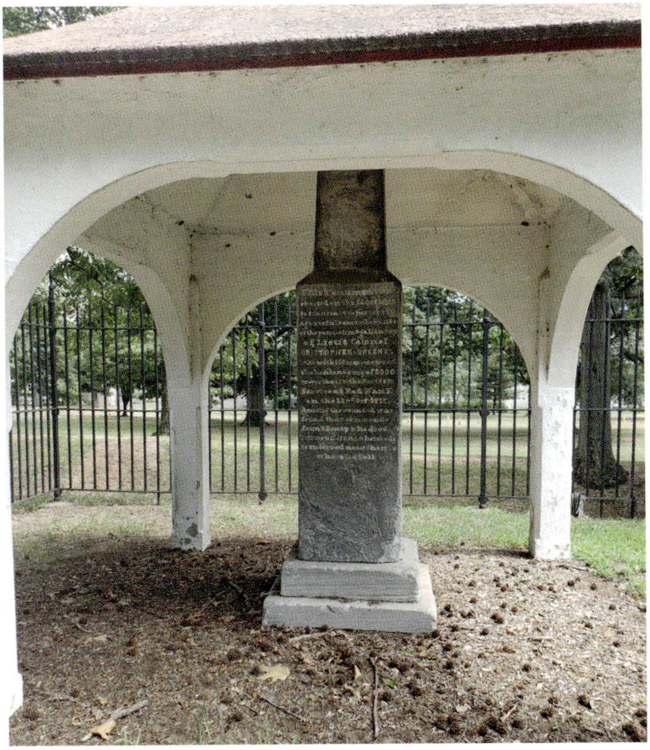

▲ Original Fort Mercer monument. (Author's collection)

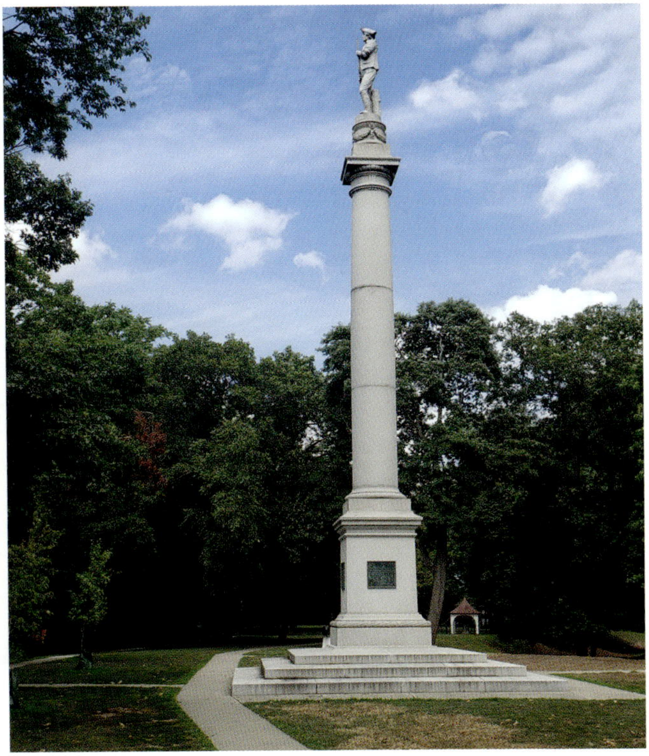

◄ New Fort Mercer monument. (Author's collection)

Hessian artillery fired for just ten minutes providing little time to damage the American works. The Hessian artillery did alert the American naval elements that the attack was coming though. The American gallies unleashed their fire into the woods sheltering the Hessians. As the sun began setting at 4:45 that afternoon, the Hessians emerged from the woods to assault Fort Mercer.

The Americans handily repulsed the American attackers. The Rhode Island defenders suffered 14 killed, 23 wounded, and 1 captured. At a cost of just 7% of his command, Christopher Greene's 500 men repulsed 2,200 Hessian veterans. The victory was shockingly lop-sided and proved to be the only American victory of the Philadelphia Campaign. The Hessians suffered 370 casualties including von Donop—17% of their force. The defeat was devastating and the three assaulting regiments were unfit for some time due to their casualties and officer losses.

Rumors of the defeat quickly spread through Philadelphia. Loyalist Robert Morton felt the British needed to respect the American army. "The great Count, who petitioned for the command in order to signalize himself and his famous Hessians, rec'd a fatal blow of which he shortly died... From this instance we see the important effects of despising the American army, and of Red Bank not being possessed by the British at the time they took Billingsport." An emotional Lt. Col. Ludwig von Wurmb (Hessian jaeger commander) wrote about the disaster four days later. "It is painful to me to lose so many good people, I can't describe it...The tragedy of our poor wounded here in America is not describable without shedding tears and those left behind with the enemy have no aid."

Captain Ewald probably summed up the fruitless attack best: "On the whole, this attack belongs to the quixotic variety, which occurs in war at times. For it was impossible to capture this work without the

▼ Present-day view showing site of the *Augusta*'s explosion. (Author's collection)

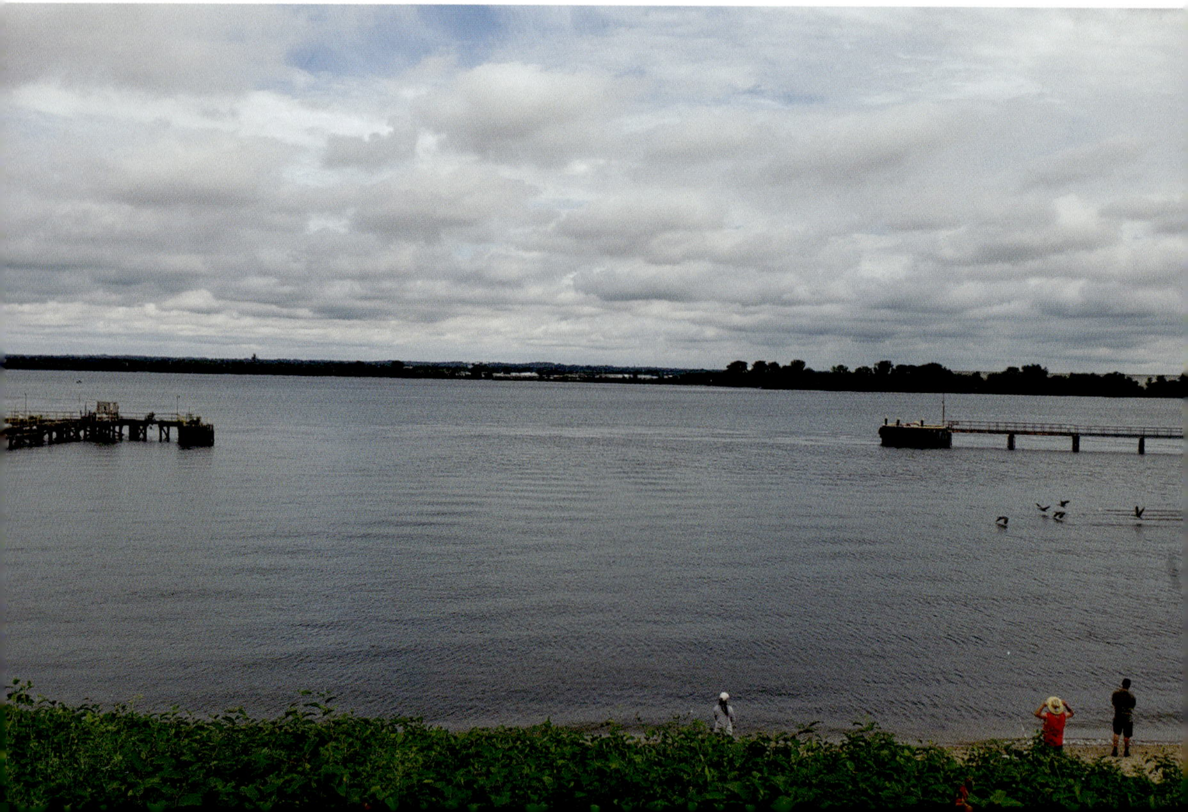

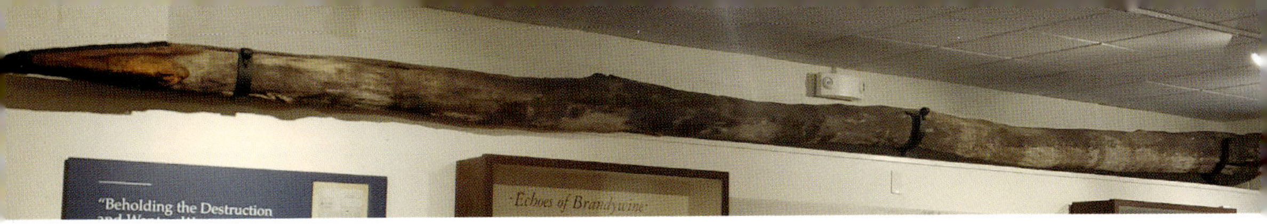

▲ Original 28-foot piece of a chevaux de frise washed up during Superstorm Sandy in 2012. Object is currently owned by the Pennsylvania Historical and Museum Commission and is located at Brandywine Battlefield State Historic Site. (Author's collection)

aid of armed ships, which had to be assigned to drive away the enemy vessels." Ewald continued with, "In a word, Colonel Donop was a man of action. He had compared the siege of Mud Island with those of Bergen op Zoom and Olmutz, and had offered to capture Fort Red Bank with one grenadier battalion, which offended the pride of the English. They led him into danger and he fell, whereby so many men—indeed, so many really brave men—had to bite the dust." Ewald was deeply moved by what he witnessed. "This day was especially sad for me. I lost five of my oldest friends, among whom was a relative, and four of my best friends were severely wounded." Ewald was veteran of numerous fights in Europe and North America. "As long as I have served, I have not yet left a battlefield in such deep sorrow."

The news reached York, Pennsylvania by October 25 where the Continental Congress continued to hold sessions in exile. War conditions appeared on the upturn and an elated John Adams wrote his wife. "I have a seized a Moment, to congratulate you on the great and glorious Success of our Arms at the Northward [Burgoyne's surrender], and in Delaware River. The Forts at Province Island and Red Bank have been defended, with a Magnanimity, which will give our Country a Reputation in Europe."

The *Augusta* and the *Merlin*

During the fighting that swirled around Fort Mercer, several larger British vessels came up to below the chevaux de frise and engaged the American fleet attempting to divert their fire from the Hessians. The ships became tightly bunched in the channel just north of Billingsport. Captain Samuel Reeve with the *Merlin*, to prevent colliding with HMS *Roebuck*, ran aground. Simultaneously, the HMS *Augusta* grounded. As the tide fell the 64-gun HMS *Augusta* and 18-gun frigate *Merlin* sat motionless. Observing confusion in the British squadron, Commodore Hazelwood sent four fire ships downriver which the British deflected. Freeing the two ships consumed the overnight hours.

October 23 dawned with the two ships still fixed to a sand bar. About 9 a.m. several British warships tacked into position to protect and assist the operation. A thunderous roar erupted across the waters of the Delaware River as Fort Mifflin and Fort Mercer arced artillery rounds into the British fleet. The American fleet moved down river and engaged the British shipping as well. The British batteries on Carpenter's and Province Islands then engaged Fort Mifflin. The first large-scale action on the Delaware River in the campaign had begun.

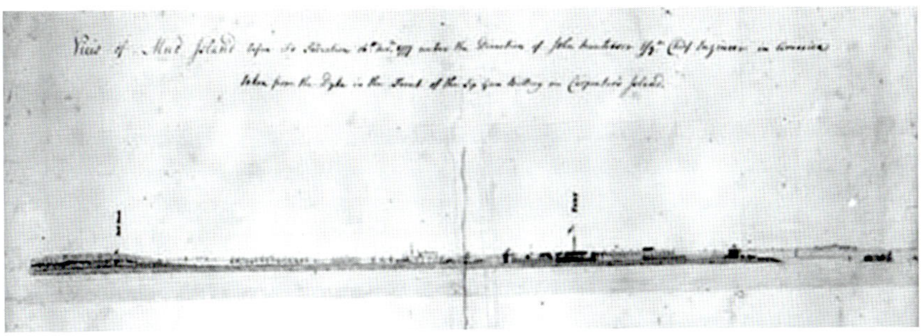

▶ View of Fort Mifflin from Pennsylvania shoreline, 1777. (Library of Congress)

In the midst of the chaos on the river, fire ships launched by the Pennsylvania Navy drifted into the British fleet.

Around 11 a.m., the *Augusta* caught fire—though the accounts disagree how she ignited. The flames spread as the British evacuated the ship. One of the loudest and most powerful explosions of the American Revolution shattered windows in Philadelphia and sent a mushroom cloud hundreds of feet into the air. Soon after the *Augusta* exploded, the crew of aground *Merlin* set her on fire as well. She too soon exploded, but less dramatically than the earlier fire ball. To prevent further destruction and loss, the remaining British ships retired downriver to Hog Island.

Despite defeats at Brandywine, Paoli, and Germantown, George Washington's current strategy was working. American fortifications, obstructions, and naval elements continued to block British naval access to Philadelphia. His now battle-tested army remained full of confidence and was ready to block all the roads leading to the city from the north and west. If the Continentals continued this strategy for another five weeks, the Delaware River would freeze over eliminating any hope of resupply for William Howe. With continued good fortune, George Washington could starve William Howe out of Philadelphia much as he did at Boston two years previously.

As darkness settled over the Delaware Valley on October 23, William Howe's hopes were at low ebb. Despite defeating Washington in every land engagement thus far, a small detachment of Continentals had convincingly repulsed a Hessian column at Fort Mercer and now his supporting naval force had lost two of its ships. Progress in the water and mud to construct the land batteries needed to besiege Fort Mifflin was moving agonizingly slow. The chevaux de frise remained in the Delaware River between Red Bank and Fort Mifflin blocking British shipping. If the situation did not improve soon, his men would begin starving. Philadelphia was under siege.

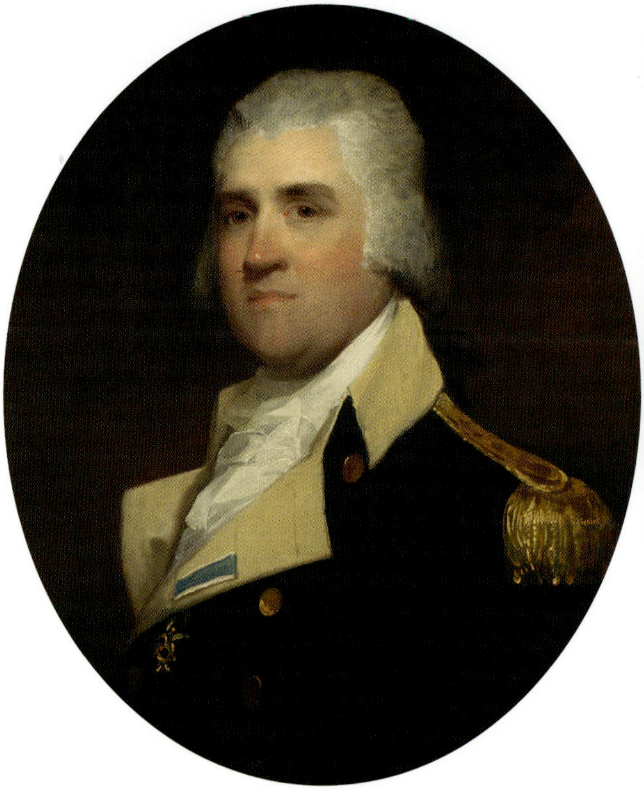

▲ Lieutenant Colonel Samuel Smith who commanded Fort Mifflin for most of the siege. (National Portrait Gallery)

Fort Mifflin

Fort Mifflin remained the key to the American river defense system. The British, who finished erecting four batteries along the dikes of Province and Carpenter's islands, officially opened the siege of Fort Mifflin on October 15. The attenuated British supply line from Chester to Philadelphia limited John Montresor's gunners to only ten rounds a day against Mifflin. These shortcomings served to exacerbate the weakness inherent in the light caliber artillery pieces fitfully discharging toward Fort Mifflin. The balls were too small to inflict serious damage, and what little damage they inflicted was

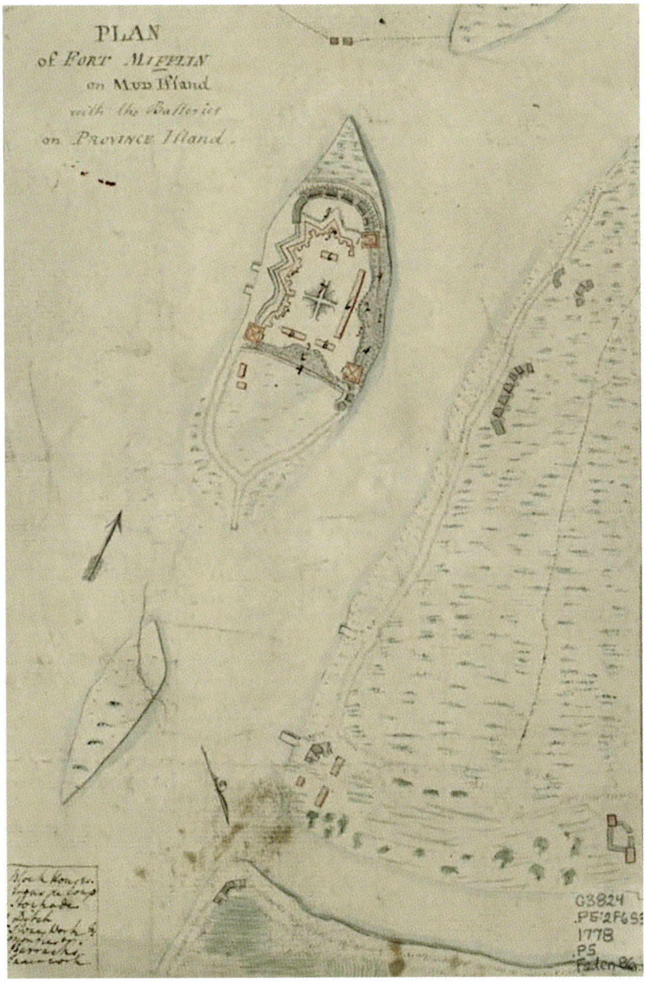

▲ Fort Mifflin map showing positions, 1778. (Library of Congress)

repaired each night. Montresor needed the big 24- and 32-pound pieces from the British fleet if their chances against the American fort were going to improve.

Montresor was not the only one frustrated by the delays. General Howe was losing his patience with the slow progress along the Delaware. Philadelphia needed to be secured and the river opened if his army was going to maintain itself there for the winter. While the Americans celebrated the Saratoga victory, the British tasked with erecting batteries opposite Fort Mifflin struggled against odds as hopeless as those faced by Burgoyne. The men often worked in meadows flooded with water waist deep. With the dikes shot away in places by American artillery, the muddy Delaware waters overflowed the completed gun platforms.

Howe had 18,000 military personnel and 25,000 civilians in need of food and other supplies. If the river remained closed much longer, the population faced the very real prospect of starvation. If William Howe seized the American position on Mud Island, he could start removing the upper rows of chevaux de frise and begin bringing supply ships into Philadelphia's wharves.

By November 9, the Fort Mifflin garrison numbered only 115 men fit for duty and they labored under demoralizing conditions. Lieutenant Colonel Samuel Smith reported to Washington of his original 200 men, only 69 were now fit for service. The 6th Virginia Regiment later brought 120 reinforcements, only 46 of whom were still available.

By this point, the British had built three batteries on Carpenter's Island at a distance of six hundred yards from the fort. There was another battery on Province Island and one at Webb's Ferry as well. The British scheduled the combined land and naval bombardment to begin on November 10 when a full moon would make the tides higher than normal aiding the naval vessels. The British planned to soften the fort's defenses by bombardment over three or four days before a detachment of 300 British Guards would cross.

On the eve of British bombardment, the combined American command lacked cohesion. The commanding officer at Fort Mifflin—Lt. Col. Samuel Smith—despised the naval commander—Commodore John Hazelwood. Fort Mifflin's engineering officer, Maj. François de Fleury, bickered with Smith over responsibility for engineering the fort's defense. James Potter's

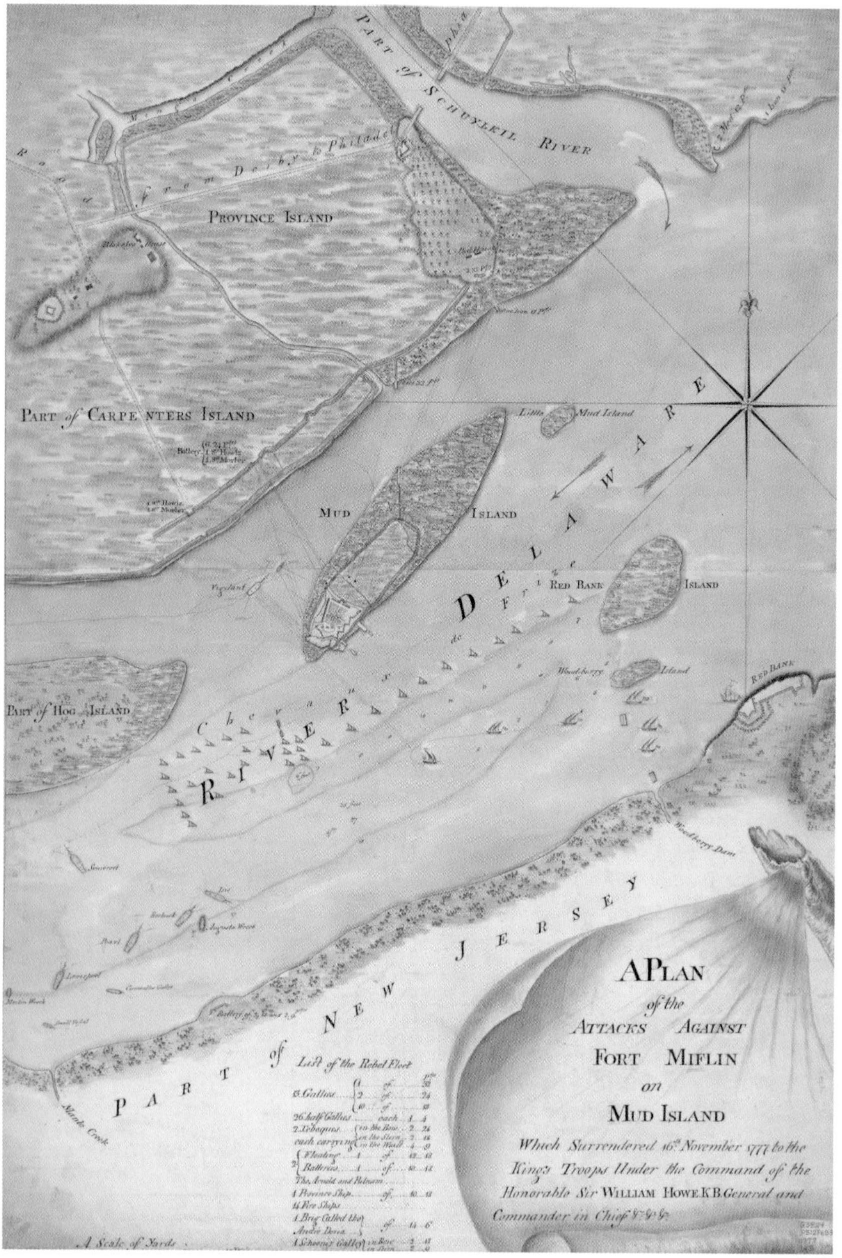

◀ Map showing British plan of attack on Fort Mifflin, 1777. (Library of Congress)

Pennsylvania militia refused to destroy the meadow banks and flood Province and Carpenter's Islands. The New Jersey militia consistently failed to reinforce Fort Mercer. Colonel Christopher Greene seemed to be the only officer uninvolved in all the internal fighting. Brigadier General James Varnum who Washington dispatched to soothe poor feelings and exercise overall command of the river operations, failed to unify the various elements. Under the circumstances, would the Americans hold up when the concerted British attack began the next day?

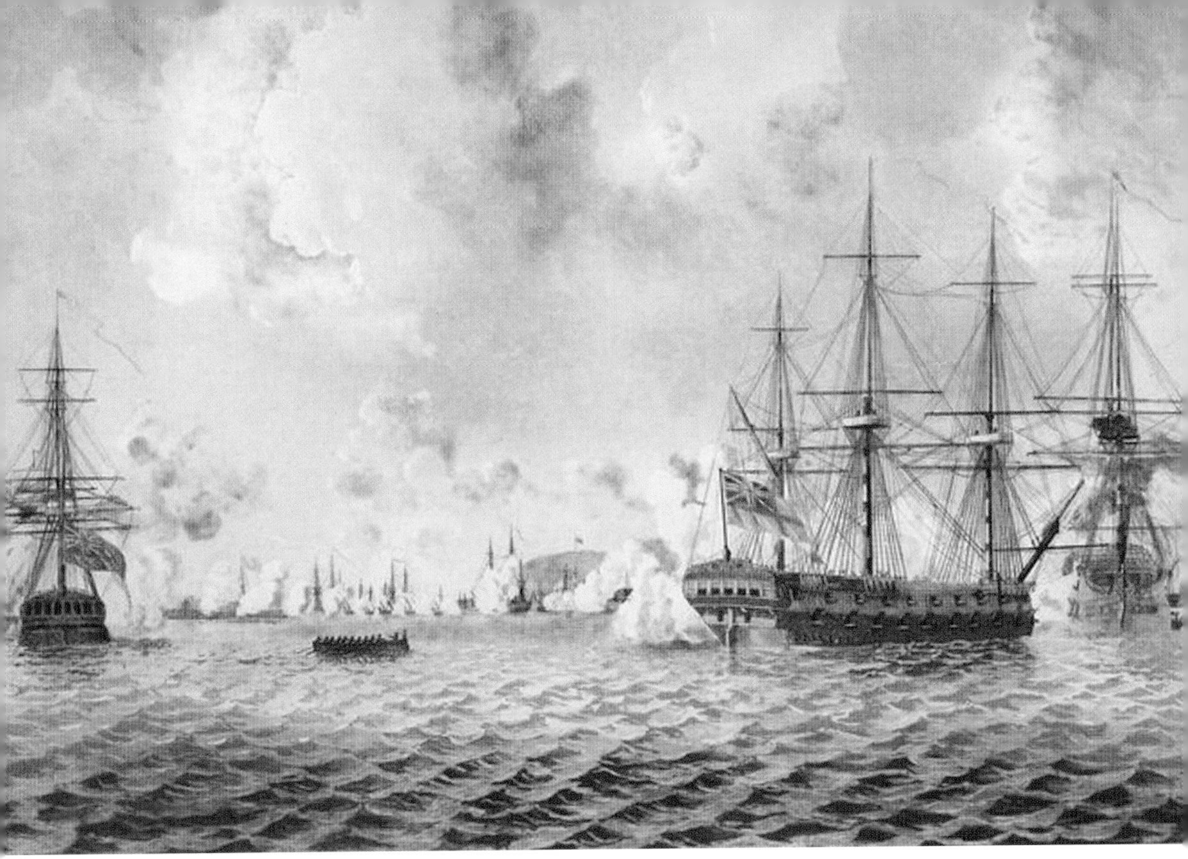

▲ Contemporary images showing naval bombardment of Fort Mifflin. (New York Public Library)

The impressive British array let loose on Fort Mifflin just after dawn on November 10. Amidst heavy dew and poor visibility, the British opened fire at 7:30 a.m. with a bombardment seldom heard in North America. The two sides pounded away at each other at 500 yards and Fort Mifflin took a beating. By noon, the British batteries unloaded 1,020 shot onto Mud Island shattering the American batteries and breaching the palisade wall in numerous places. Amazingly, the Americans suffered no casualties.

November 11 dawned with frigid winds and heavy frost when the British bombardment continued. Within a few hours, Fort Mifflin's commander and artillery chief were down and the fort was in disarray. The seemingly leaderless garrison did not evacuate Fort Mifflin due to the leadership of Capt. François de Fleury. Strong winds throughout the day limited the operations of both fleets. Despite the constant bombardment from the British land batteries, the British men-of-war had yet to significantly add their weight to the contest. All American defenders seemed to ignore the fact eventually the British navy would get involved.

As the American garrison barely hung on in Fort Mifflin over five days against the British land batteries, conditions spiraled downhill when the British navy joined the fight around 8 a.m. on November 15. The *Somerset* and *Isis* tacked into position below the chevaux de frise and opened fire on Fort Mifflin. The largest concentration of firepower in the American Revolution unleashed on Fort Mifflin. Carnage mounted in Fort Mifflin. Fort Mifflin was pulverized beyond recognition. The British batteries and shipping stopped pounding Mud Island about 5 p.m. The American garrison's command structure was shattered, little was left of the fort, and few were able-bodied enough to stand to their post by the night of November 15. Simeon Thayer issued orders after dark to evacuate the fort and destroy anything left behind. Around midnight, the last of the garrison ignited what they could of the materials left in the fort, and boarded boats to row across the river to Red Bank. Over the previous five days, 450 men served on Mud Island at varying intervals—less than 200 left the island unharmed. Less than a dozen British soldiers were killed with numerous others wounded.

As dawn broke on November 16, the torn and tattered garrison flag still flew above Fort Mifflin, but no troops remained within its ruins. The still flying flag symbolized the fort never surrendered. For the first time in over a month, the river fell silent.

The garrison at Fort Mifflin withstood a remarkable onslaught for several weeks, culminating in the largest cannonade in North America prior to the battle of Gettysburg. Looking back on the siege many years later, Joseph Plumb Martin described the defense of the fort: "I was at the siege and capture of Lord Cornwallis, and the hardships of that were no more to be compared with this than the sting of a bee is to the bite of a rattlesnake. But there has been but little notice taken of it, the reason of which is, there was no Washington, Putnam, or Wayne there. Had there been, the affair would have been extolled to the skies. No, it was only a few officers and soldiers who accomplished it in a remote quarter of the army. Such circumstances and such troops generally get but little notice taken of them, do what they will. Great men get great praise; little men, nothing."

Admiral Richard Howe's private secretary, Ambrose Serle, thought the Americans "defended it [Fort Mifflin] with a Spirit, they have shewn no where else to an equal Degree during the War. I went on shore to survey this celebrated Place. Nothing surely was ever so torn & riven by Cannon-Balls. A more dismal Picture of Ruin can scare be conceived." Captain James Murray of the 57th of Foot believed "Mud Island was a most unfortunate obstacle, and cost us two of the most precious months of the war. If the Rebels had taken every advantage of their situation, it is not certain that we should have been able to have cleared the passage at least this campaign."

Thomas Paine, author of *Common Sense*, addressed an essay to William Howe on March 21, 1778: "For several weeks did that little unfinished fortress stand out against all attempts of Admiral and General Howe. It was the fable of Bender realized on the Delaware. Scheme after scheme, and force upon force were tried and defeated. The garrison, with scarce anything to cover them but their bravery, survived in the midst of mud, shot, and shells, and were at last obliged to give it up more to the powers of time and gunpowder than to the military superiority of the besiegers." Paine encouraged Howe to give up the ghost. "Go home, sir, and endeavor to save the remains of your ruined country, by a just representation of the madness of her measures…You are fighting for what you can never obtain, and we are defending what we never mean to part with…Let England mind her own business and we will mind ours."

The meager Fort Mifflin garrison immortalized themselves in the eyes of several American congressmen. New York delegate James Duane noted in a letter to Philip Schuyler on November 19 "The Garrison have already immortalized themselves by uncommon Valour and Perseverance." Cornelius Hartnett of North Carolina wrote to William Wilkinson the same day, "Our Little fleet & forts on the Delaware have behaved nobly." Richard

Henry Lee informed Samuel Adams on November 23 "we have lost fort Mifflin, which our brave garrison was obliged to abandon after a most gallant defence, in which all their guns were dismounted but two, and all the works beaten away about a rod and a half." Elbridge Gerry wrote to Joseph Trumbull on November 27 "The Enemy have obtained possession of Delaware River, from the Delay of the Army to support Fort Mifflin & Red Bank; I think that an Enquiry into this affair…will necessarily take place."

Aftermath of the River War

While Howe now controlled Mud Island, the cheveaux-de-frise river obstructions remained and the guns at Fort Mercer continued to protect them. Seizing Fort Mifflin was a necessary step toward full control of the Delaware River, but William Howe now needed to eliminate the threat at Red Bank. If the American position at Fort Mercer was taken, the pesky American navy would be no more than a nuisance to future operations.

Howe ordered Lord Charles Cornwallis to Chester with a large force of 3,000 to cross over the river and seize Fort Mercer on November 18. Cornwallis was joined by 4,000 reinforcements from New York City under Maj. Gen. Thomas Wilson. On November 20, Cornwallis crossed Mantua Creek. Fort Mercer was abandoned that night and the works destroyed by a detachment that was left behind. During the overnight hours, the Pennsylvania Navy fleet was burned and the crews escaped to Bordentown, New Jersey. Those ships not burned, were withdrawn to near Bristol, Pennsylvania including all the galleys and a number of guard boats and service ships.

Washington finally sent a force to reinforce the New Jersey detachment. Unaware of the abandonment of Fort Mercer, Nathanael Greene's division arrived in Burlington on November 21 but could move no further. Washington hoped Greene's force would attack the rear of the British force besieging Fort Mercer. Daniel Morgan's Rifle Corps, which returned to the main army, went along with Greene as did Lafayette. Lafayette recovered enough from his Brandywine wound to return to the saddle. Around noon on November 21 Cornwallis occupied the remnants of Fort Mercer.

Gloucester Engagement

With Fort Mercer destroyed and the American fleet destroyed or escaped upriver, Cornwallis no longer needed to be in New Jersey. Rather than move toward Cooper's Ferry exposing his right flank to the Americans, Cornwallis swing left toward Gloucester on November 24 for his return to Philadelphia.

With only two wharves at Gloucester, Cornwallis was looking at a two day operation to get across to Philadelphia. Foraged cattle, army horses, baggage, and artillery needed to be ferried over in addition to the troops he had with him. Cornwallis placed strong outposts on his perimeter to protect the operation, including pairs of artillery pieces east and south of the village.

While all this was happening, Lafayette with his aides, a few New Jersey militia, and some of Morgan's riflemen swung north and west to scout Gloucester from the north on November 25. Working their way west, the party arrived just north of the mouth of Newton Creek and observed the British operation to move back across the river. They then returned to Haddonfield.

Lafayette, convinced of the vulnerability of the British operation, convinced Col. Joseph Ellis of the New Jersey militia to help him attack the picket posts. About 150 militiamen joined about the same number of Morgan's riflemen and they began marching about 3 p.m. from Haddonfield. The British crossing was being covered by some Jaegers when firing erupted. After marching two miles, Morgan's riflemen engaged a picket post around 4 p.m. As the sun set, Lafayette commanded an attack by about three hundred Americans consisting mostly of riflemen.

The Jaegers Lafayette's detachment encountered were two companies of reinforcements from Hesse which "consisted of very old men or young lads." The jaegers tried to rally themselves, but the New Jersey militia moved forward with bayonets which the Hessian recruits could not withstand. With sunset at 4:41, it was all over by 5 p.m. Lafayette ordered a withdrawal. Some British and Hessians attempted a pursuit, but were quickly discouraged of that effort by some of Morgan's riflemen. The Jaegers lost nine men killed, twenty-one wounded, and two missing. Lafayette also claimed he captured fourteen men. The Hessians suffered another embarrassment not just in the campaign, but in the war. The Americans lost two officers killed and five privates wounded.

Lafayette reported to Washington the next day. "I take the greatest pleasure to let you know that the conduct of our soldiers is above all praises. I never saw men so merry, so spirited, so desirous to go on to the enemy." Lafayette found the riflemen "above even theyr reputation and the militia above all expectations."

The next morning, Greene scouted Cornwallis's position but did not attack. After holding a council of war, Greene learned his subordinates were against the attack despite Lafayette's success. Greene reported to Washington "I am sorry our march will prove a fruitless one—the enemy have drawn themselves down upon the peninsula at Gloucester—the ships are drawn up to cover the troops, and this country is so intersected with creeks, that approaches are rendered extremely difficult, and retreats very dangerous."

With the river finally opened, British supplies and luxury goods began to flow into the city for the first time in years (due to the non-importation act). British sloops and small vessels began docking in Philadelphia on November 23. Admiral Richard Howe docked at the Philadelphia wharves with his flagship HMS *Eagle* signifying the end of the fighting for the Delaware River.

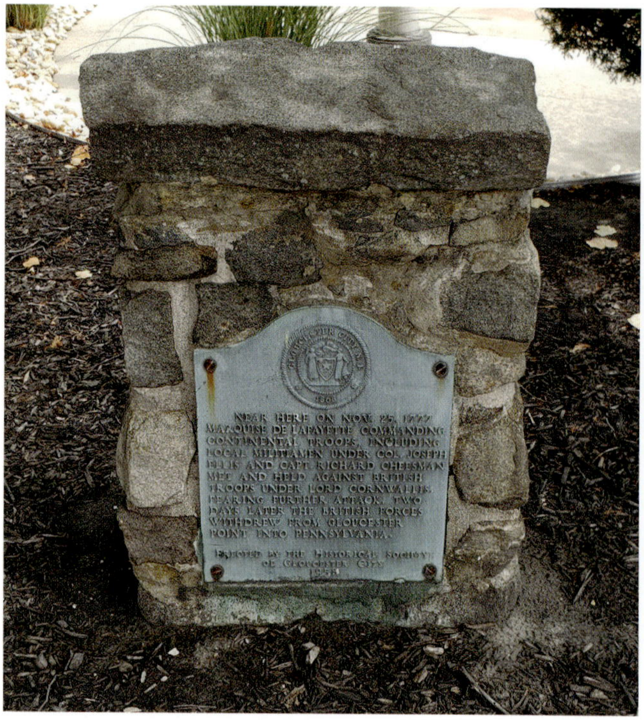

▲ 1955 marker denoting the location of the skirmish at Gloucester. (Author's collection)

Roads to Valley Forge

Having completed operations along the Delaware River, William Howe hoped to engage George Washington's Continental Army one more time before winter ended active operations. While minor fighting would take place around Whitemarsh, Washington soon moved his army to Valley Forge.

Whitemarsh

While the river war raged, on November 2, Washington's army moved forward to Whitemarsh and encamped in an early morning fog with frost on the ground. The army positioned itself on a series of hills fourteen miles north of Philadelphia. To the northeast, a large, steep ridge (Camp Hill) rose above Sandy Run commanding the Whitemarsh Valley, with a clear view over to Chestnut Hill three miles away. In the center, a smaller hill (Fort Hill) rose above Bethlehem Pike. Across the Wissahickon Creek to the southwest, another long ridge (Militia Hill) ran toward Barren Hill, about five miles away. The new American front

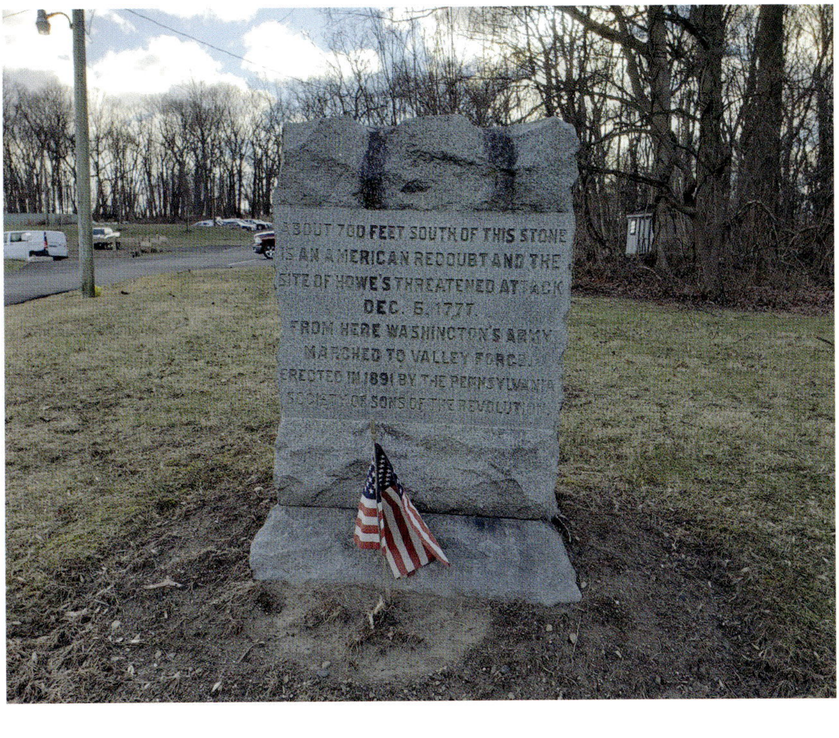

▶ 1891 monument marking the site of the Continental Army's camp at Whitemarsh. (Author's collection)

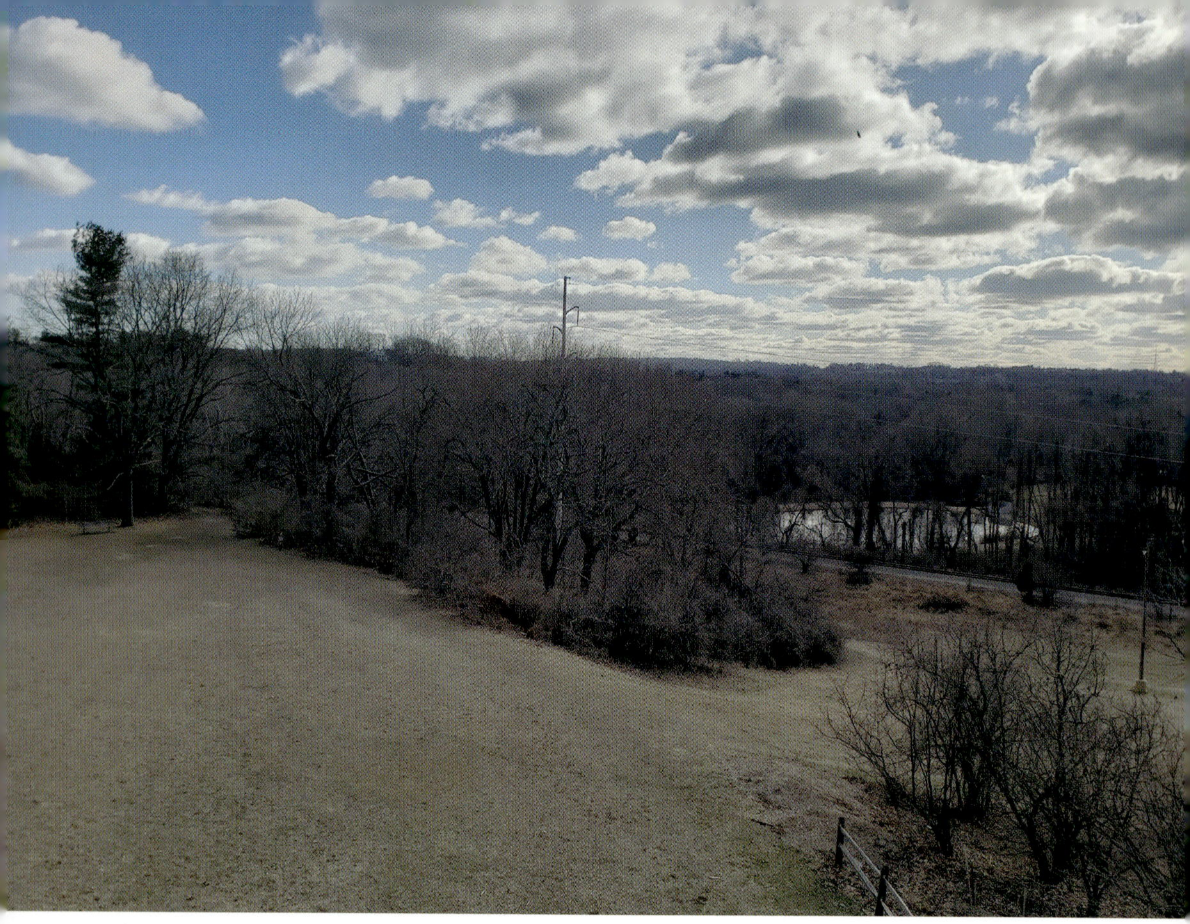

▲ Present-day view looking east from the American position in the Whitemarsh hills. (Author's collection)

stretched five miles over these hills. For the next month, the armies settled into a lull northwest of Philadelphia that included a constant string of guerilla engagements in the no man's land. The armies constantly nipped at each other between Whitemarsh and the Northern Liberties of Philadelphia. The partisan war from early in the campaign in northern New Jersey resumed while the fighting along the Delaware played out.

Following the loss of the river forts, rumors circulated through the army that William Howe was gearing up to attack Washington. Washington actually wanted the British to attack his strong position at Whitemarsh. Such a defensive win might quell the rumblings against him.

At midnight on December 5, Howe led ten thousand troops in two columns out from Philadelphia to Chestnut Hill arriving at 3 a.m. One column took the Germantown Road and the other took Ridge Road. Howe's column was harassed by American light troops and militia during their advance. Washington dispatched Pennsylvania militia and the 2nd Connecticut Regiment from the hills at Whitemarsh to probe the British position. Firing soon erupted at Chestnut Hill and the British pushed back the American probe. During this process, Brigadier General Irvine of the Pennsylvania Militia had three fingers shot off and was captured.

Having driven the Americans back, William Howe rode forward and saw for the first time the strong position afforded by the hills at Whitemarsh. Howe determined that attacking the American position on its series of hills would not prove advantageous. Rather, he opted on a flanking movement toward Cheltenham Township and Jenkintown.

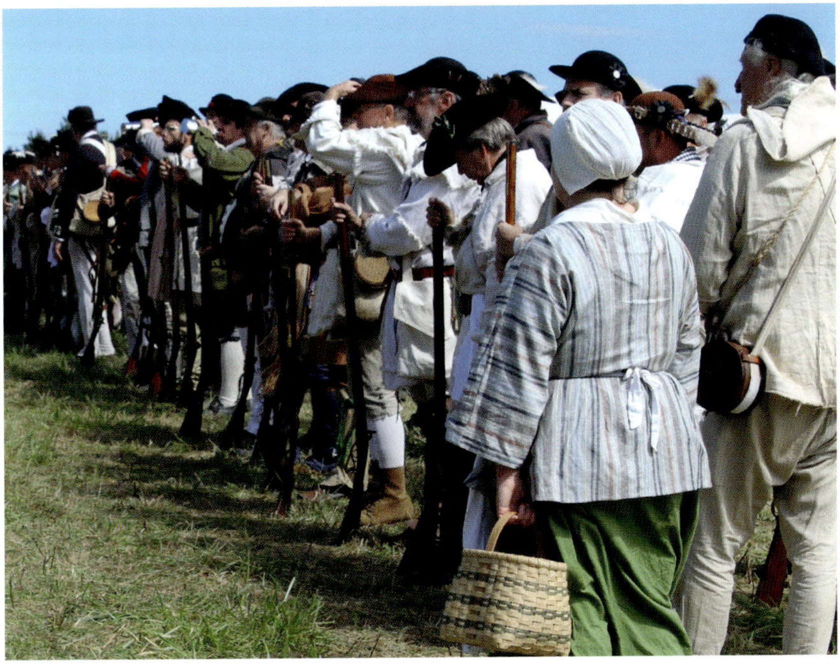

▶ Daniel Morgan's American riflemen were primarily engaged on Edge Hill during the fighting around Whitemarsh. (Author's collection)

The march was conducted during the night of December 6 and they moved to a position near Edge Hill. Edge Hill was a long, steep ridge that ran parallel to the main American position but about a mile in front of it. To cover this flank, Washington had placed Daniel Morgan's Rifle Corps of about 300 men here along with the Maryland Militia commanded by Col. Mordecai Gist. To the right of these troops was James Potter's Brigade of Pennsylvania Militia and the 2nd Connecticut Regiment.

On the morning of December 7, 1777, Howe's offensive marched to the top of Edge Hill. General Charles Grey with the Queen's Rangers, Hessian Jaegers, and the Light Company of the Brigade of Guards was waiting for the main British column when he became impatient. He decided to launch the attack himself. The American militia broke under the assault. The 2nd Connecticut, left alone, was forced to run a gauntlet between the enclosing British troops. Despite the disgrace that was the Pennsylvania militia, the Maryland militia fought well on the American left. The Marylanders and Morgan's men became engaged with Howe's main column. Morgan was eventually pushed back though to the main American line.

After pushing the American militia and riflemen back, Howe halted and looked across the valley to the main American line on the Whitemarsh Hills. The line appeared well entrenched, fortified, with 50 artillery pieces looking down at him. Washington showed no signs of coming down off the hills. Having failed to draw Washington out from his encampment, Howe returned to Philadelphia the next day. Shocked by the British withdrawal, the Americans were overjoyed. The British troops, on the other hand, did not understand the retreat and morale plummeted. Washington did learn a lesson from the fighting around Whitemarsh. His army was too close to Philadelphia and both flanks were vulnerable. In addition, supplies were dwindling and the men were becoming more and more destitute.

The Roads to Valley Forge

Following the fighting around Whitemarsh, Washington needed to move his army. After spending over five weeks on those hills, the Continental Army exhausted the resources of the region. The Virginian needed to find new ground for his winter encampment.

First, Washington sent out militia to scout new ground. On December 10, General James Potter crossed the Schuylkill River with 1,000 Pennsylvania Militia and encamped on the grounds of a plantation called Harriton in the vicinity of Gulph Mills. The same day, Howe organized a massive foraging party under Cornwallis. When this column stepped off the next morning, they easily pushed aside Potter's militia in what became known as the skirmish of Matson's Ford. Potter estimated his casualties as 5 killed, 20 wounded, and 20 captured.

Potter retreated north of the Schuylkill at Matson's Ford. Already positioned at the ford, was the head of a column representing Washington's main army moving toward the Schuylkill from the Whitemarsh camp. A floating bridge had been laid across the river and the army was preparing to cross. Cornwallis's column pushed on to Haverford Township while Washington's army moved upriver toward Swede's Ford and camped in Plymouth Township. Just as Cornwallis's column was returning to Philadelphia on December 13, Washington's army crossed over the Schuylkill at Swede's Ford and established a camp in Upper Merion Township.

▼ Throughout the campaign, the Americans were no match for the professional British infantry. (Author's collection)

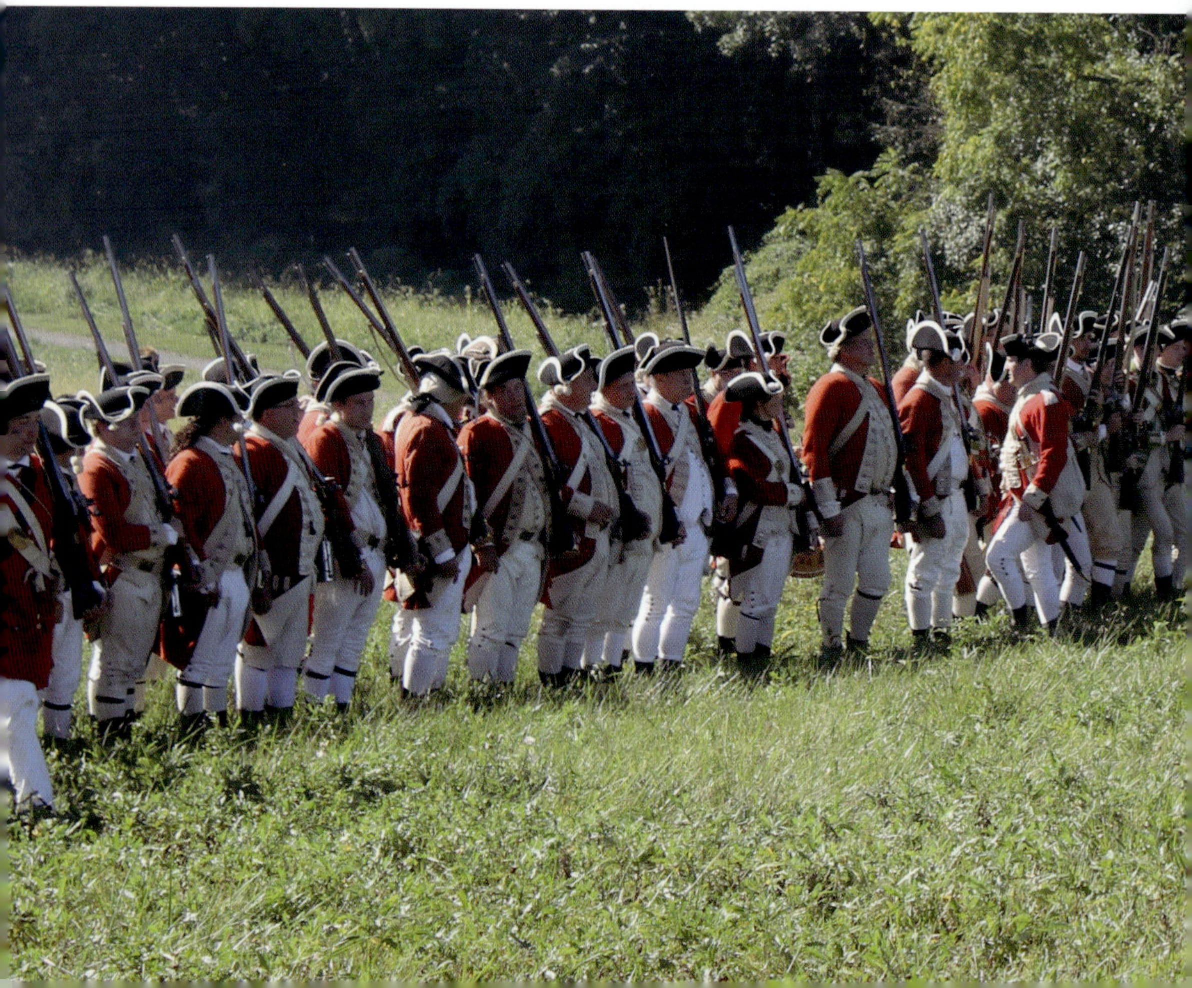

By mid-December, however, campaigning was quickly coming to a close. On December 16, Lord Cornwallis boarded a ship and headed for home with several other officers. Across the Atlantic Ocean on December 17, France decided to recognize American independence.

A serious discussion occurred between Washington and several of his officers to determine the location of a winter encampment. Wilmington, Lancaster, and Reading were suggested. Others favored moving west of the Susquehanna River to recruit and rest the army, especially since the Philadelphia area had been picked clean by both armies. However, moving farther away from the British army would open more of the region to depredations and increase local support for the British. Staying close to Philadelphia to deter Howe, but far enough away to avoid surprises, was a more probable political and military solution. The army was currently a day's march from the Crown forces. However, the hills in the area were steep and rose sharply above narrow valleys. The army could easily be driven into a confined area.

Another consideration for Washington was the fact that several villages in the area were being used not only as supply depots, but also as prisoner of war camps. Clearly, these needed to be protected. Easton was becoming over-crowded with prisoners. The jails and other buildings used to hold them were over-flowing. Many of those captured were sick or wounded, but food and fuel were scarce and many died in confinement. When Congress fled

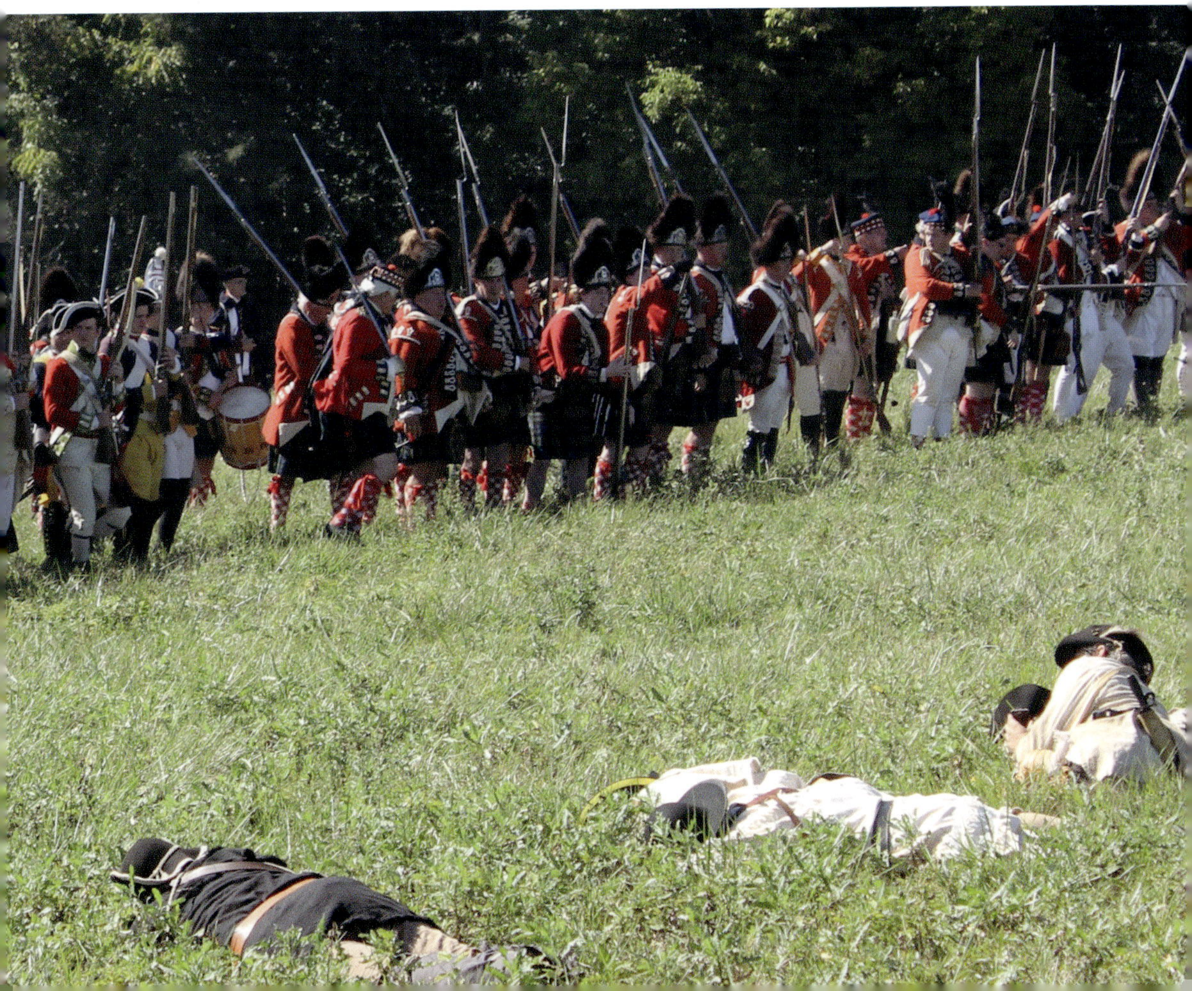

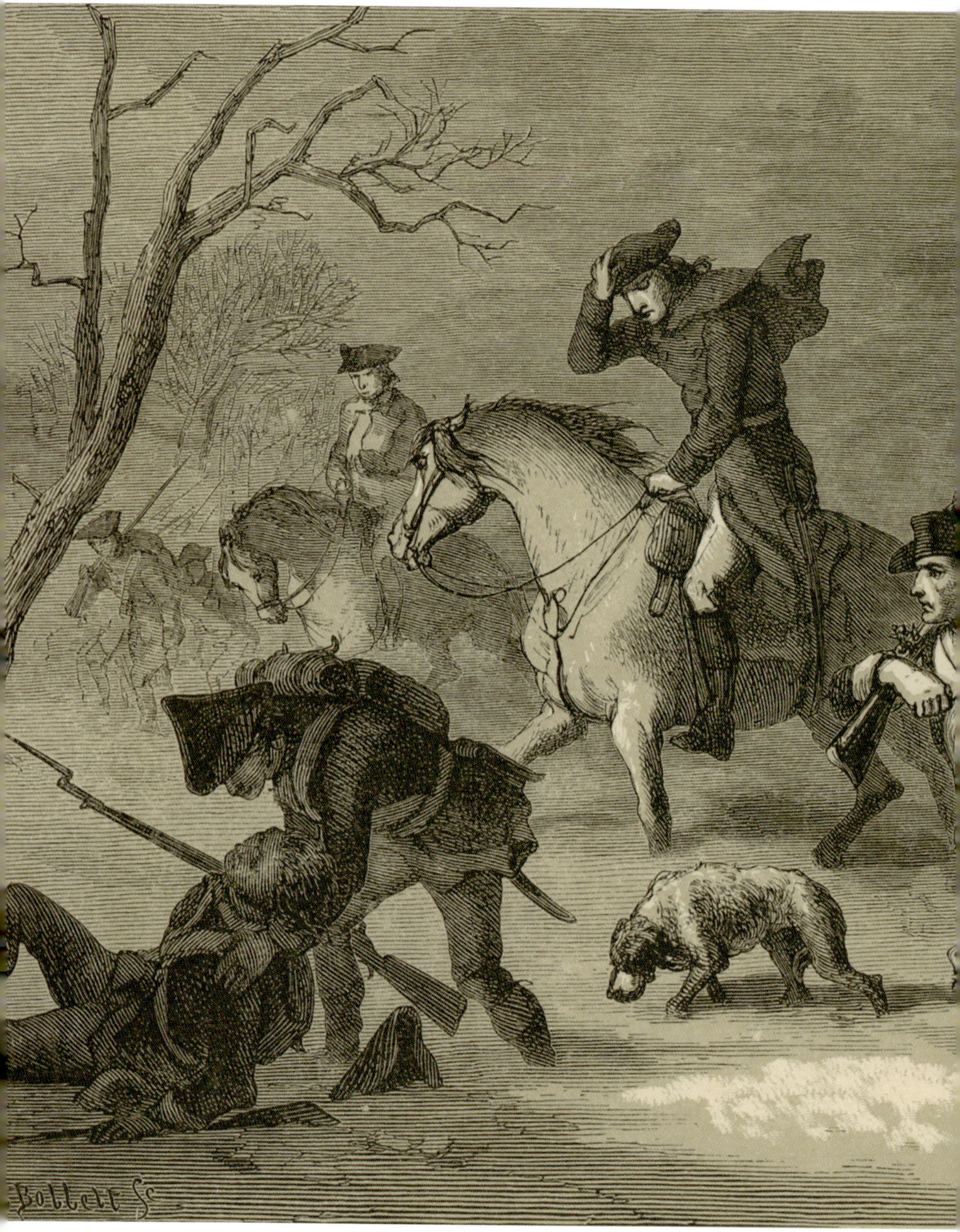

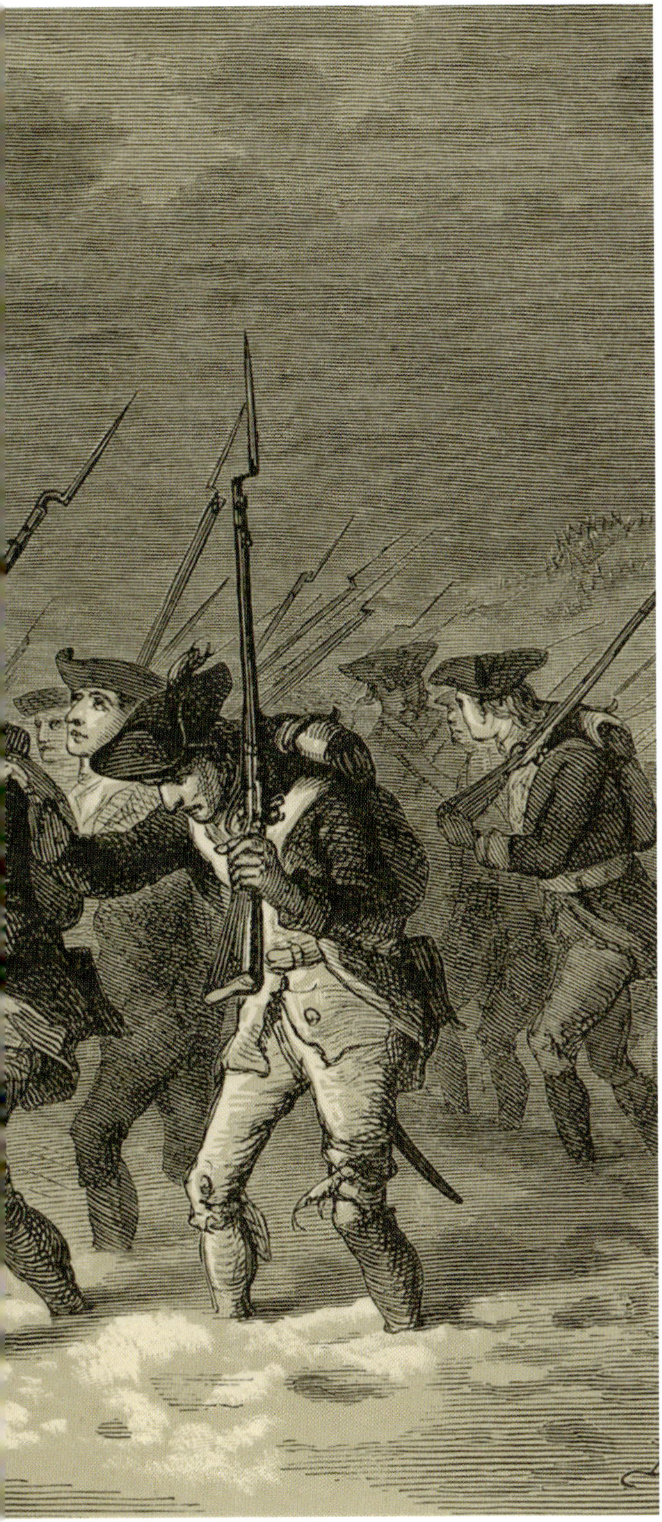

Philadelphia earlier in the year, the official papers, documents, and public funds were temporarily stored in Easton. Bethlehem also was used as an overflow area for prisoners, though its chief function was as a hospital facility.

On the morning of December 19, Washington's army marched seven miles west from Gulph Mills on the Gulph Road to a cone-shaped hill called Mount Joy which rose above the sky line. As the army marched into their Valley Forge encampment, they were eighteen miles from Philadelphia. The region consisted of cleared valleys and hills timbered in hardwood. Valley Creek flowed along the base of Mount Joy and emptied into the Schuylkill River. Near the mouth of the creek stood the burned-out ruins of the ironworks destroyed by the British in September.

◀ The march to Valley Forge (New York Public Library

Afterword

The combined British efforts in 1777 that resulted in the battles at Saratoga and around Philadelphia can arguably be considered the turning point of the American Revolution.

While John Burgoyne became bogged down and eventually captured at Saratoga, New York, George Washington valiantly fought William Howe's army around Philadelphia, Pennsylvania. While William Howe did capture the colonial capital in September 1777, Washington's Continental Army repeatedly showed it could stand up to British and Hessian regulars at places like Brandywine, Germantown, Fort Mercer, and Whitemarsh.

William Howe's decision to go by sea to Philadelphia rather than march overland severely delayed his efforts around Philadelphia. Additionally, the choice to ascend the Chesapeake Bay rather than sail up the Delaware River at the end of July ultimately doomed John Burgoyne. Once the fighting started in southeastern Pennsylvania, Howe's inability to follow-up victories at Brandywine and Germantown allowed Washington to regroup and remain defiant in the face of British might.

Having witnessed the bloodshed caused by a frontal assault at Bunker Hill, William Howe avoided such devastating attacks throughout the Philadelphia Campaign. He utilized a flanking maneuver at Brandywine and attempted to do so again at Whitemarsh. Howe was caught off guard at Germantown and only the tenacity of his regulars and some of his subordinates saved the day for his army.

There was a great deal of disgust among the British officers for not having crushed the American army. Richard Fitzpatrick

▼ Despite repeated defeats, Washington never allowed his army to fall apart prior to marching into Valley Forge. (Author's collection)

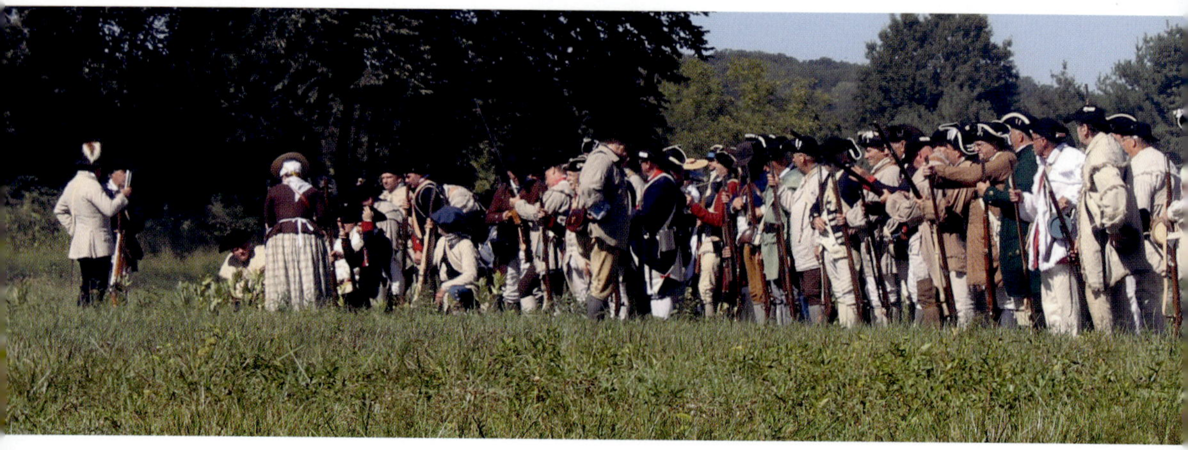

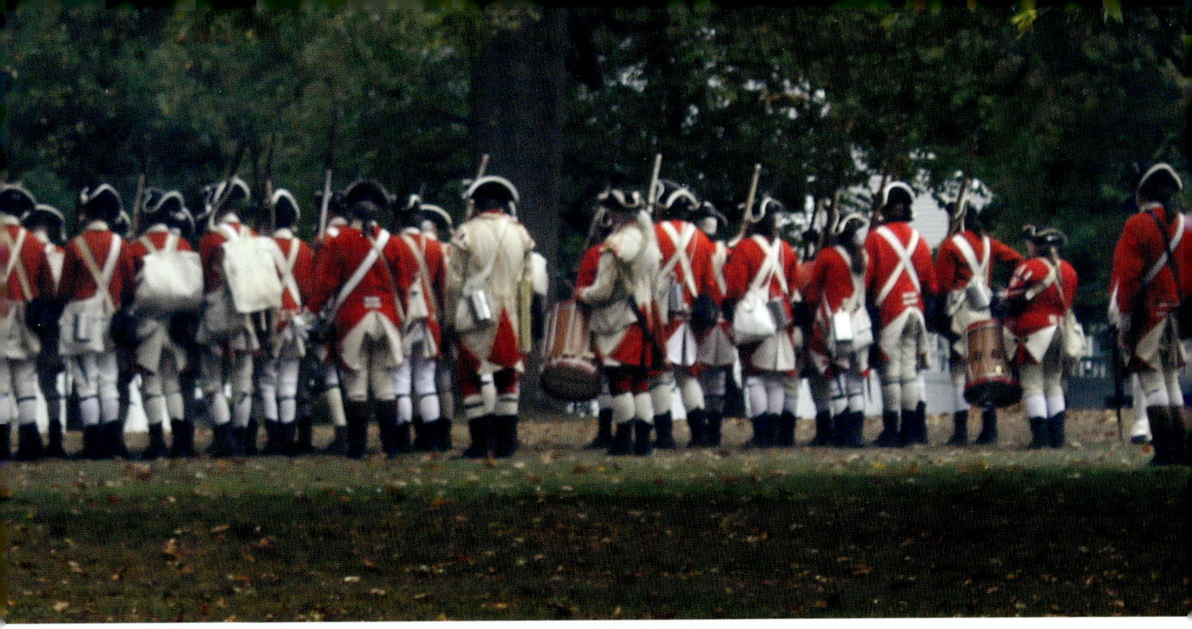

▲ The British and Hessian regiments would spend their winter in Philadelphia. (Author's collection)

would write to his brother, "There is a greatness and dignity in all the proceedings of this people that makes us contemptible indeed. I am well convinced they will be the first and greatest people there ever was an example of in the history of mankind.... Our only Consolation, as Patriots, must be that they are of English origin."

George Washington fought his own demons during the 1777 campaign. Horatio Gates's victory against Burgoyne caused some officers and members of Congress to question Washington's ability to lead the Continental Army. A real effort emerged to replace the Virginian during the late fall of 1777. Despite losing at Brandywine and Germantown, Washington survived these efforts and wisely defended the British efforts at Whitemarsh in early December. What Washington's detractors failed to realize was that, for the Americans, it was more important for the army to remain intact, than to risk it in deadly attacks against British regulars. Washington understood this and never launched a frontal attack against the main British army. Brandywine and Whitemarsh were defensive battles. The Battle of the Clouds was unexpected and unplanned by either army. While Washington did launch attack at Germantown, it was surprise attack at dawn against unprepared positions.

Other American officers emerged from the Philadelphia Campaign with black marks as well. Anthony Wayne's performance at Paoli marred him until his successful attack at Stony Point later in the war. Division commander Adam Stephen was cashiered for drunkenness following the fighting at Germantown.

An underappreciated aspect of the 1777 campaign is the fighting that raged along the Delaware River in October and November. Less than 1,000 Continental soldiers and militia managed to block the British fleet from Philadelphia for almost two months. Two Rhode Island regiments repulsed the combined assault of three veteran Hessian regiments at Fort Mercer. A stalwart band of Continentals withstood the combined land and naval bombardment of Fort Mifflin for nearly a month before abandoning the fort. The Marquis de Lafayette having recovered from Brandywine would lead a daring attack against a Hessian outpost and rose in stature amongst the army's high command.

Washington's tenacity combined with American success against Burgoyne, led to the French alliance that winter and the resignation of William Howe. With French

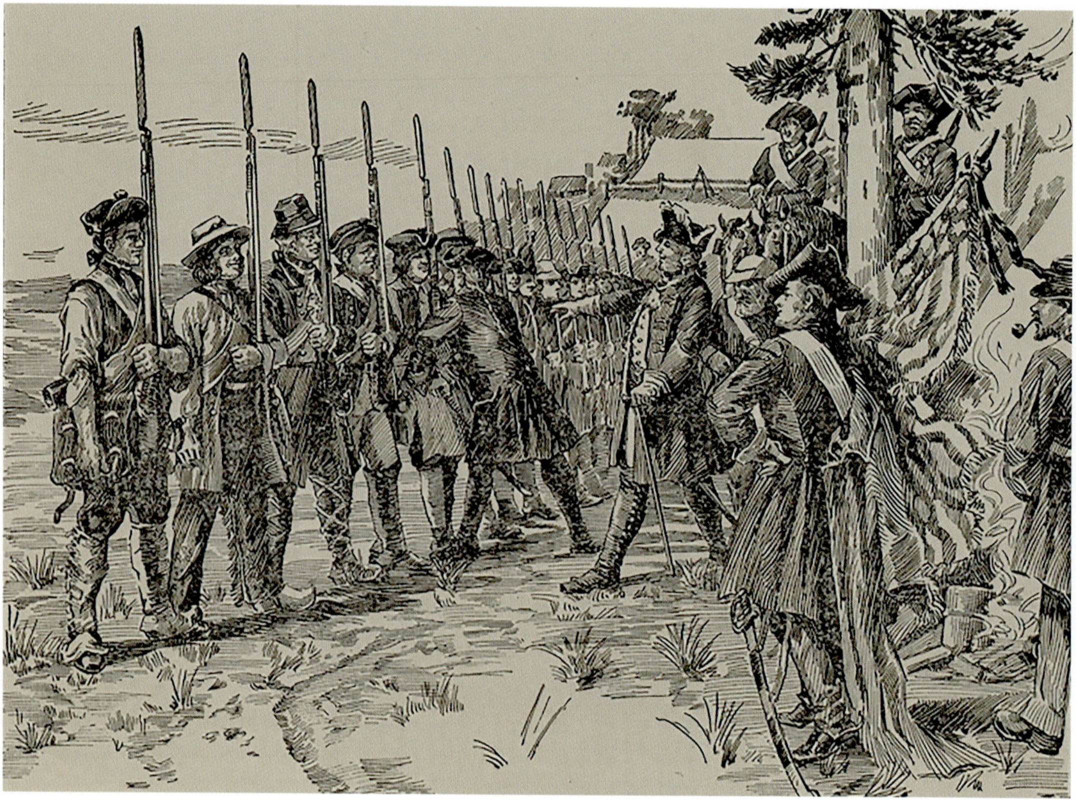

▲ Baron Steuben instructing the officers and men of Washington's army. (New York Public Library)

entry into the war, British war efforts would switch to the southern colonies and the Caribbean. Come spring, the British would abandon Philadelphia after so much blood and treasure was spent in the effort to return to New York City.

If one could look into the future, he would see the transformation of the Continental Army at the hands of Baron von Steuben. The army that would march out of Valley Forge the following spring would go on to fight competently at Monmouth and ultimately force the surrender of another British Army at Yorktown in 1781.

Further Reading

While much writing for the year 1777 has focused on the Saratoga Campaign, the operations around Philadelphia have received greater attention in recent years. Thomas J. McGuire's two volume history on the Philadelphia Campaign and John F. Reed's *Campaign to Valley Forge* are excellent starting points. Samuel Smith's rare *The Battle of Brandywine* is a valuable study of that large battle. For those wanting a more detailed history of the opening months of the campaign and September battle, consult Michael C. Harris's *Brandywine: A Military History of the Battle that Lost Philadelphia but Saved America, September 11, 1777*. The best single volume on the Battle of Paoli is Thomas J. McGuire's *Battle of Paoli*. A fine early effort at studying Germantown is found in Donald Grey Brownlow's *A Documentary History of the Battle of Germantown*. For more details of the period following Brandywine through Germantown see Michael C. Harris's *Germantown: A Military History of the Battle for Philadelphia, October 4, 1777*.

For those interested in the operations along the Delaware River, consult John W. Jackson's *The Pennsylvania Navy, 1775-1781: The Defense of the Delaware*, Samuel Smith's *Fight for the Delaware 1777*, and James McIntyre's *A Most Gallant Resistance: The Delaware River Campaign September-November 1777*.

The thoughts and writings of American generals are highlighted by *The Papers of George Washington: Revolutionary War Series* (volumes 10–12). Division commander Nathanael Greene's writings are found in *The Papers of General Nathanael Greene*, volume 2. Those of John Sullivan can be found in *Letters and Papers of Major-General John Sullivan*, volume 1. Lower ranking, but valuable accounts by Americans are found in *The Revolutionary War Memoirs of General Henry Lee*, and Joseph Plumb Martin's *Private Yankee Doodle*.

Valuable British accounts include *The American Journal of Ambrose Serle*, *John Peebles' American War: The Diary of a Scottish Grenadier, 1776–1782*, *From Redcoat to Rebel: The Thomas Sullivan Journal*, and *Major Andre's Journal: Operations of the British Army Under Lieutenant Generals Sir William Howe and Sir Henry Clinton*. The Hessian perspective can be found in *Enemy Views: The American Revolutionary War as Recorded by the Hessian Participants* and Johann Ewald's *Diary of the American War*.

For those interested in more technical aspects of army operations see Edward Curtis's *The British Army in the American Revolution*, Matthew Spring's *With Zeal and with Bayonets Only: The British Army on Campaign in North America, 1775–1783*, R. Arthur Bowler's *Logistics and the Failure of the British Army in America*, Mary Gillett's *The Army Medical Department 1775–1818*, Robert Wright's *The Continental Army*, and Erna Risch's *Supplying Washington's Army*.

Unpublished, yet valuable manuscripts can be found in repositories throughout the United States and Great Britain.

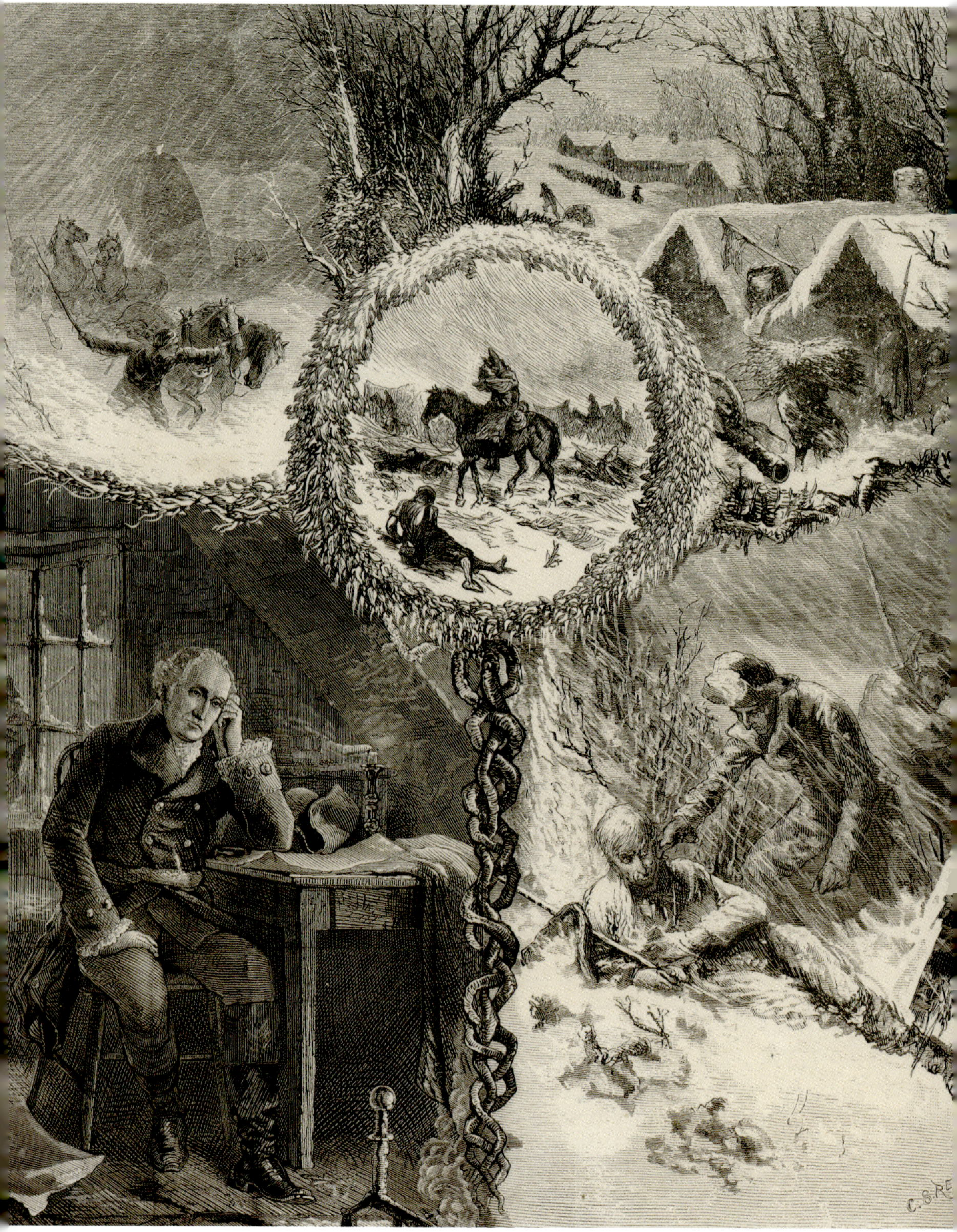

British, American, and civilian accounts can be found at the American Philosophical Society and the Historical Society of Pennsylvania in Philadelphia, Pennsylvania. General George Weedon's letters are located at the Chicago Historical Society, while more British sources are located at the William Clements Library at the University of Michigan and the British National Archives in Kew. Valuable American sources are located at the Library of Congress and the National Archives in Washington, D.C., the Massachusetts Historical Society in Boston, and the New York Historical Society. General James Grant's papers can be read at the National Archives of Scotland in Edinburgh and valuable Hessian accounts can be accessed at Morristown National Historical Park in Morristown, New Jersey.

◀ Washington at Valley Forge – Winter of 1777–78. (New York Public Library)

Index